Bartholomew **Road Atlas Britain** 1973 edition

Motorways with Junction and Service Area	Track, Path
Motorways under construction or projected	Church
Dual Carriageways	(F) Car Ferries
A 46 Trunk Roads	Other Ferries and Sea Routes
A 142 Min. of Transport 'A' Roads	Principal Civil Airports
B 1438 Min. of Transport 'B' Roads	Railways (Passenger)
A 134 B 113 Single Track Roads with Passing Places	Canals
Other Serviceable Roads	County Boundaries
Distances in Miles between circled points	▲ 2450 ·187 Heights in Feet
	75 Page Continuations

1:300 000

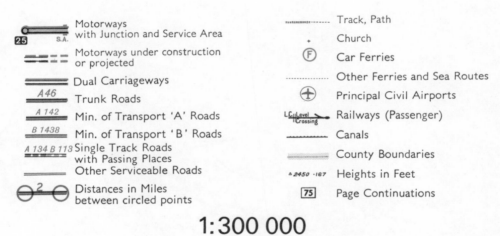

STATUTE MILES
1 0 1 2 3 4 5 — 10
10 miles to 2.1 inches

KILOMETRES
1 0 1 2 3 4 5 — 10 — 15
3 kilometres to 10 millimetres

CONTOUR COLOURING

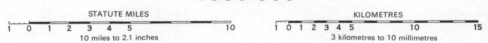

Feet · Sea Level · 100 · 500 · 1000 · 2000 · 3000 · Feet

Printed and Published in Great Britain

© **JOHN BARTHOLOMEW & SON LTD.**

12 Duncan Street, Edinburgh

ISBN 0 85152 813 9

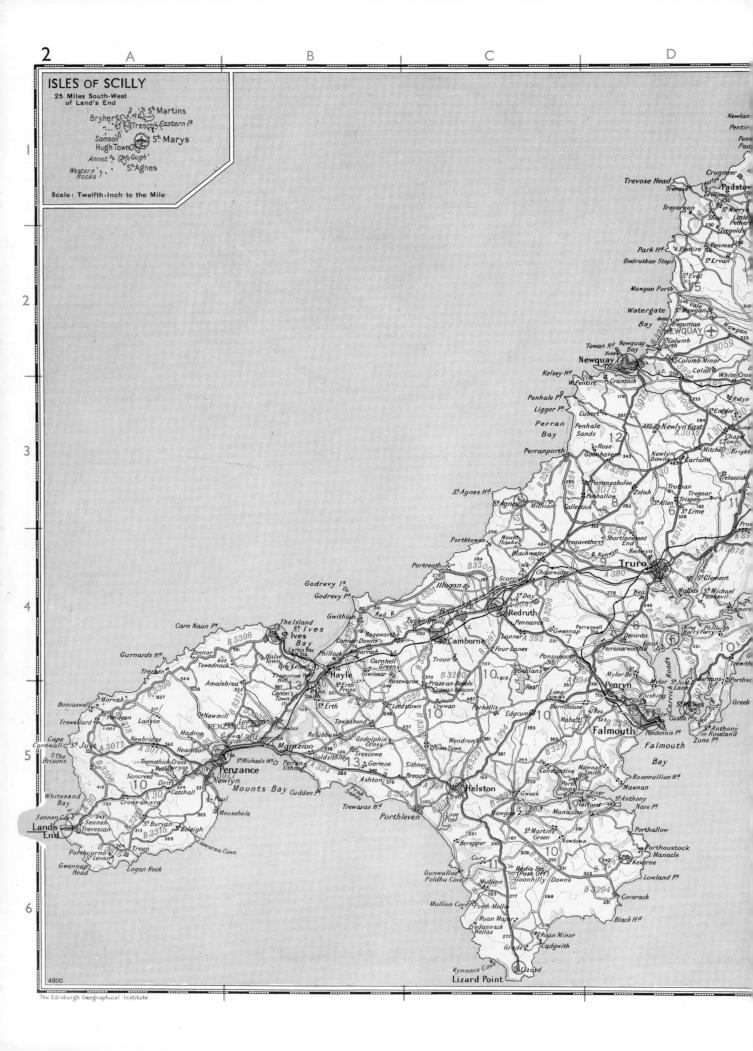

Delabole   Newpark
Camelford
Lower Moor
Lanteglos
Trewalder
Advent
Rough Tor
Brown Willy

The Mouls
Port Isaac
Port Isaac Bay
Portquin
Portquin Bay
Trelights
St Endellion
St Teath
Michaelstow

Polzeath
Trebetherick
St Minver
Pityme
Rock
Stoptide
Chapel Amble
St Kew Highway
Weens
St Tudy
Row

Bodmin Moor

Bolventor
Dozmary Pool
Browngelly Downs
Temple

River Camel
St Issey
St Breock
Wadebridge
Egloshayle
Washaway
Lane end
Blisland

Lewannick
S. Petherwin
Trebullett
Lezant
Dunterton

Five Lanes
Altarnun

Polyphant
Lawhitton
Kelly
Chillaton

Tavistock
Tavistock Hamlets
Gunnislake

North Hill
Coad's Green
Tregoiffe
Treburley

Linkinhorne
South Hill
Upton Cross
Minions
Pensilva
Middlehill

Stoke Climsland
Luckett
Downgate
Kit Hill
St Anns Chapel
Hingston Down
Harewood
Calstock
St Dominick

Callington
Ashton
Newbridge
St Mellion

CORNWALL

Bodmin
Lanivet
Cardinham
Mount
St Neot
Coldwind
Dobwalls
Liskeard

Merrymeet
Pengover Green
Quethiock
Pillaton
Blunts
Botusfleming

St Ive
Menheniot
Clennick
Tideford
Landrake
Trematon
Saltash
St Budeaux

Lostwithiel
Lanlivery
Luxulyan
Bugle
Bridgend
Couchsmill
Lerryn
Lanreath Inn
Tredinnick
Sandplace
Morval

PLYMOUTH

St Blazey
Tywardreath Highway
Par
St Sampson
Tywardreath
Treesmill
Gelant
St Veep
Pelynt
Trenewan
Talland
Seaton
Downderry
Sheviock
Crafthole
Antony
Devonport
Stonehouse

St Austell
Mount Charles
Holmbush
Carlyon Bay
Charlestown
St Austell Bay
Porthpean Bay
Pentewan
Black Hd
Gribbin Hd
Fowey
Polruan
Lantivet Bay
Polperro
Hare Stone
St George's I.
W. Looe
E. Looe
Millbrook
Cremyll
Drake's I.
Kingsand
Cawsand
Cawsand Bay
R. Rame
Penlee Pt
Rame Hd

Whitsand Bay

Mevagissey
Penare Pt
Mevagissey Bay
Chapel Pt
St Ewe
Gorran Haven
Maenease Pt
Boswinger

Veryan Bay
Portloe
Nare Hd
Dodman Pt

Tregony
Creed
Grampound
Hewas Water
Sticker
St Mewan
St Michael Caerhays
Garrah

Southampton 103 m.

Alderney
Braye
Burhou
St Anne

C. de la Hague

CHERBOURG

GUERNSEY
L'Islet
St Sampson
King's Mills
Jethou
Herm
St Martin
St Peter Port
Torteval
St Martin's Pt

FRANCE

Diélette

les Pieux

Sark

28 miles

Carteret

Ecrehos

Grosnez Pt
St Mary
St John
JERSEY
Trinity
Rozel
St Ouen's B.
St Peter
St Martin
Gorey
St Aubin
St Helier
Corbière
St Aubin's B.

CHANNEL ISLANDS
Scale : Twelfth-Inch to the Mile

0   4   8   12 Miles

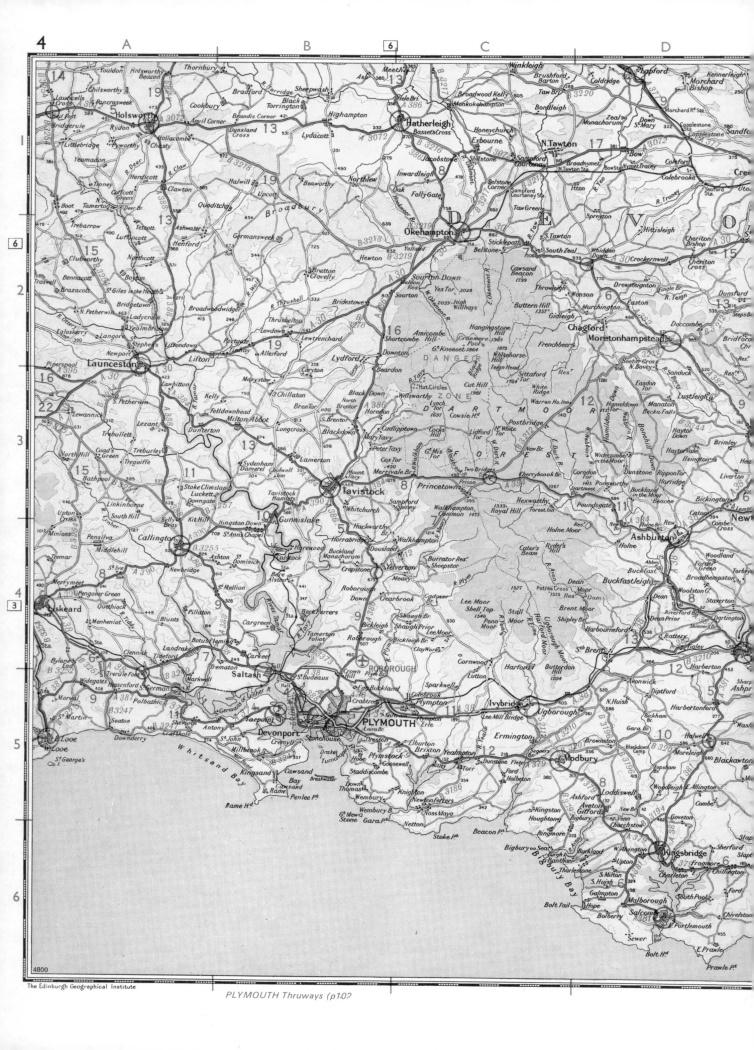

EXETER Thruways (p94)

© — John Bartholomew & Son Ltd.

0 1 2 3 4 5 Miles

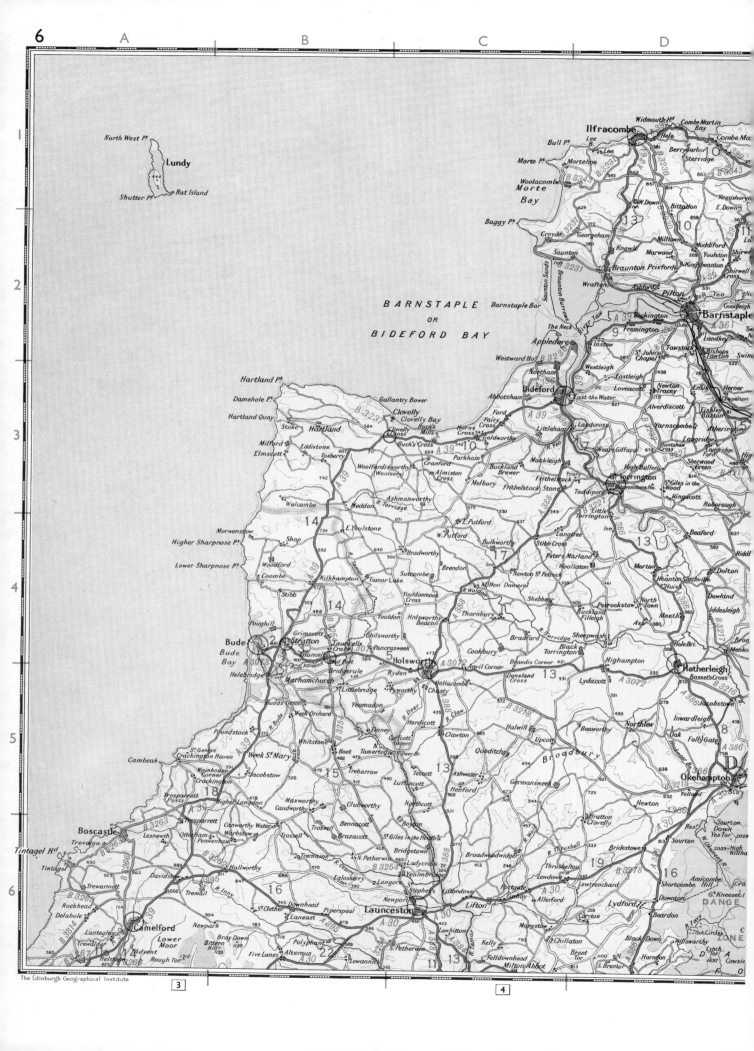

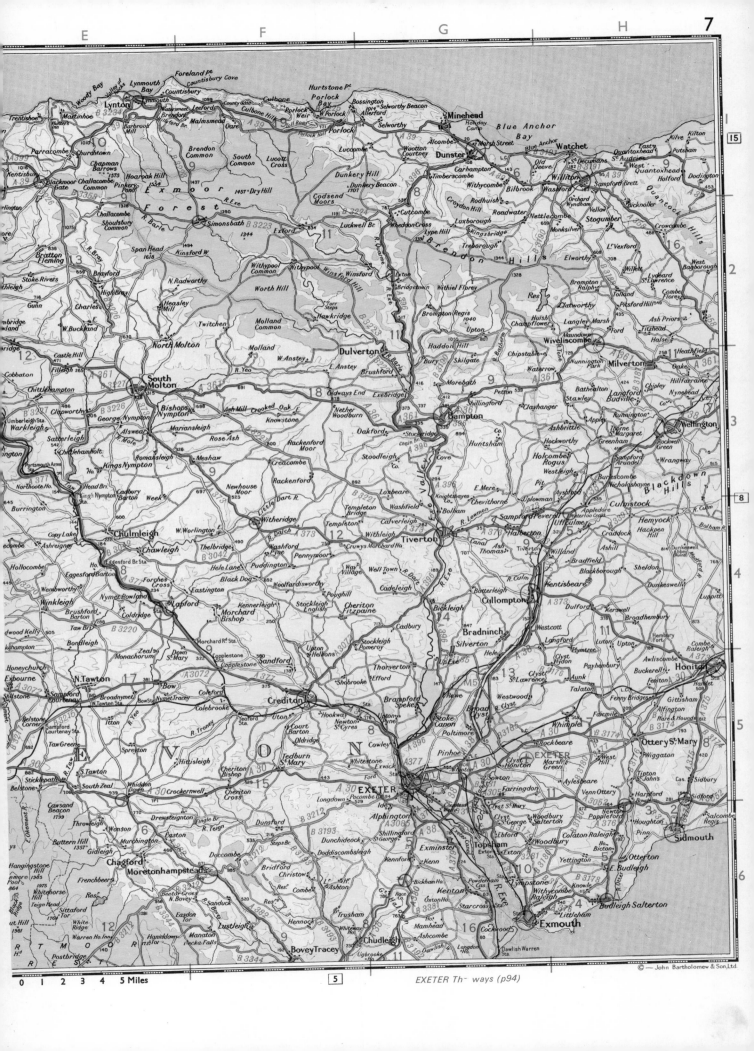

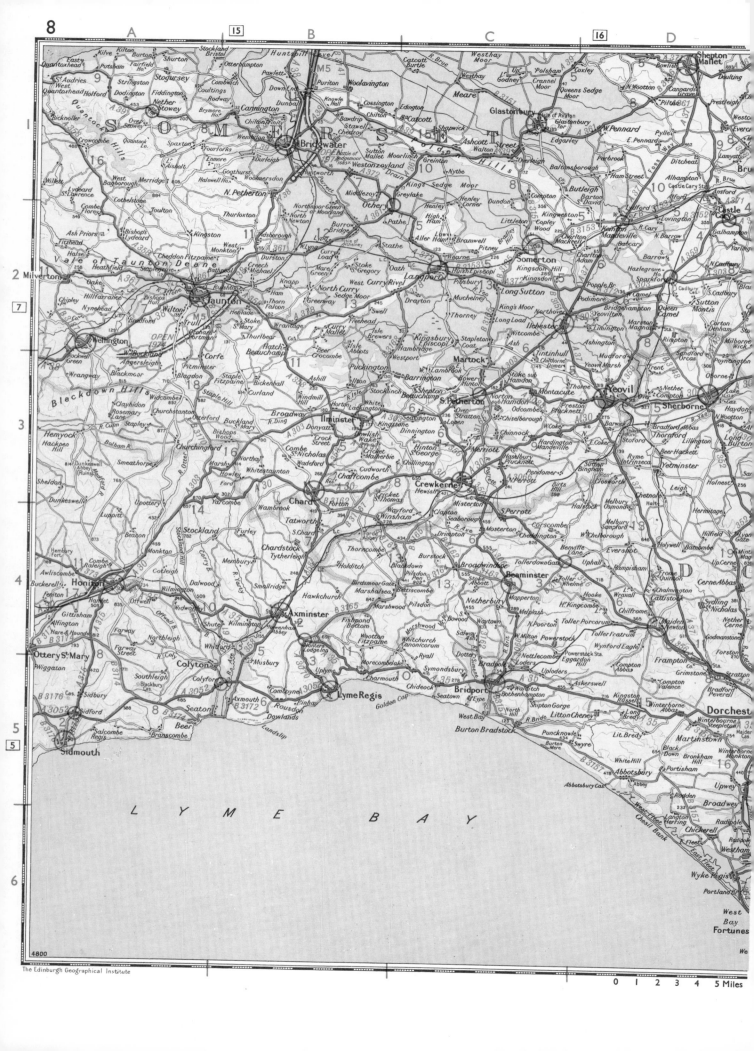

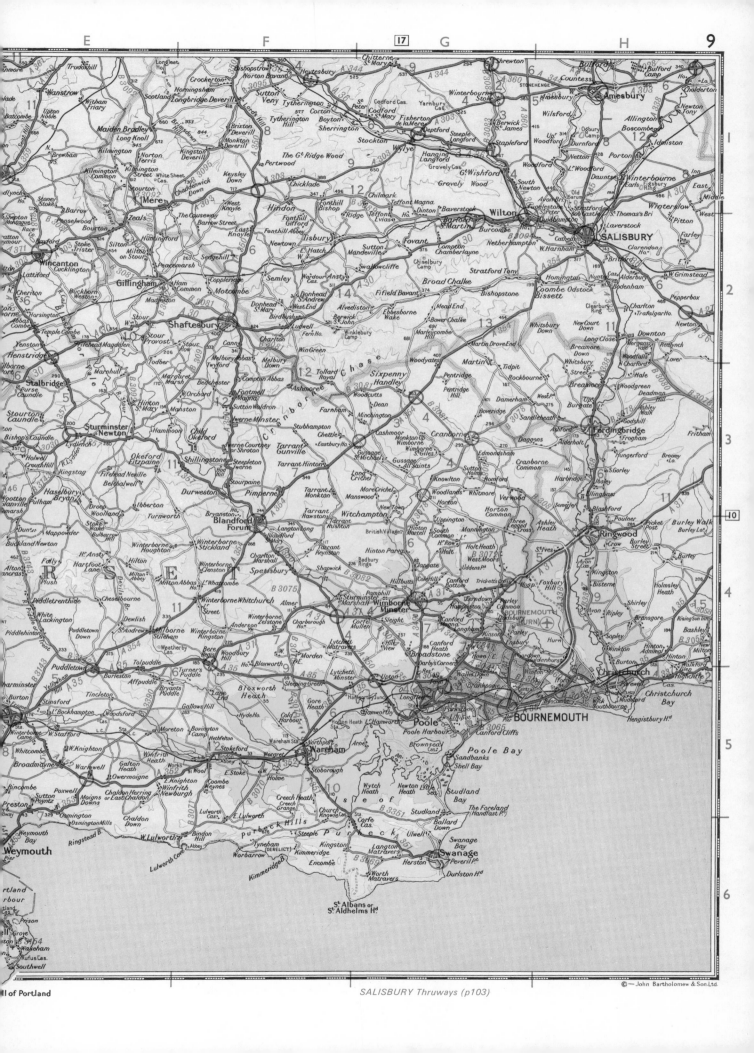

© — John Bartholomew & Son Ltd.

ll of Portland

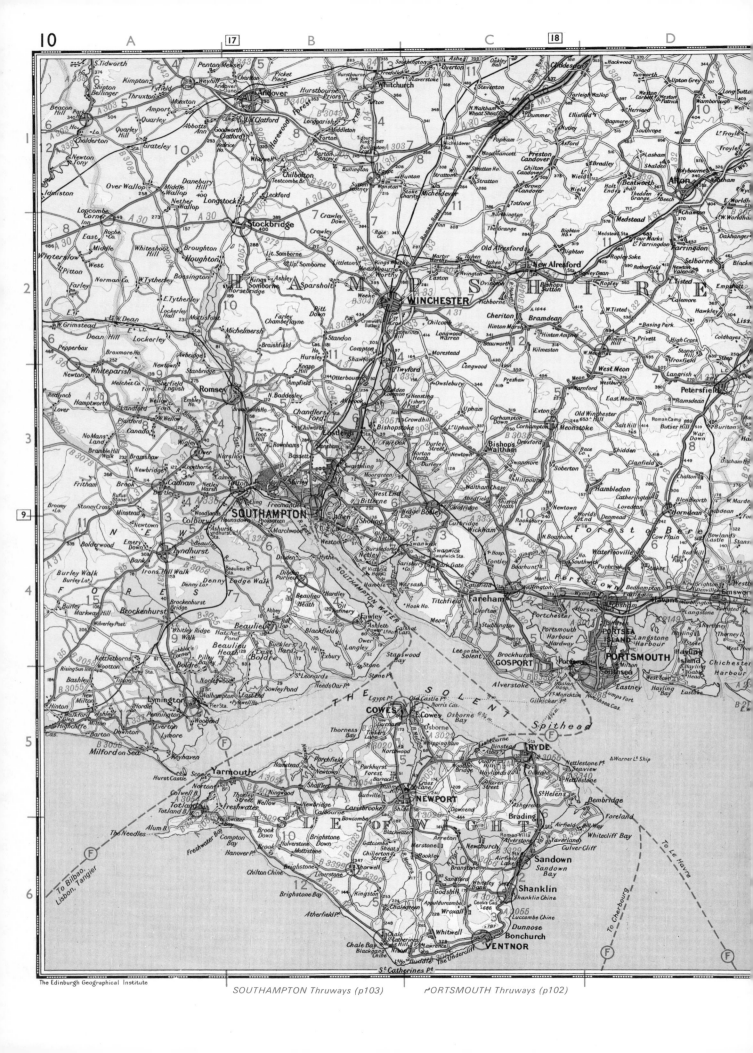

SOUTHAMPTON Thruways (p103)   PORTSMOUTH Thruways (p102)

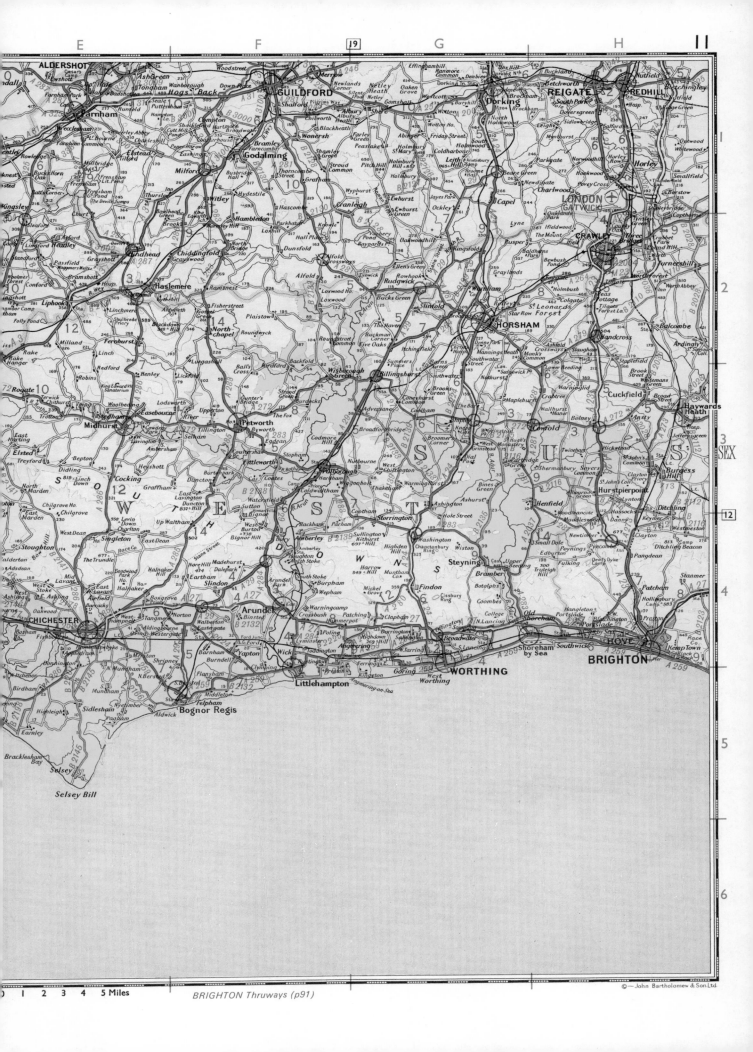

BRIGHTON Thruways (p91)

© — John Bartholomew & Son.Ltd.

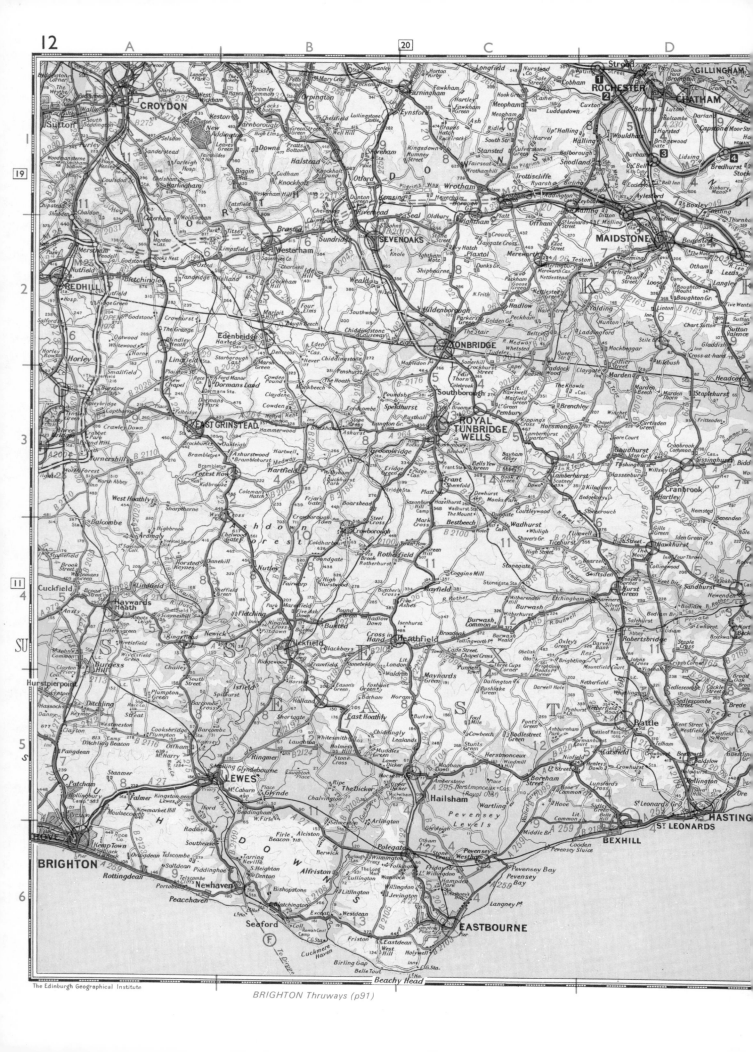

SHEPPEY
Elmley I.
Eastchurch Marshes
Isle of Harty
The Swale

Sittingbourne
Milton
Murston
Bapchild
Lynsted

FAVERSHAM
Whitstable
WHITSTABLE
Whitstable B.
HERNE BAY
Hampton
Herne

Charing
Chilham
CANTERBURY

Wye
Kennington

ASHFORD

MARGATE
Westgate on Sea
ISLE OF THANET
Broadstairs
RAMSGATE
Manston
Minster
Sandwich Bay

SANDWICH
Worth
Eastry

DEAL
Walmer
Ringwould

NORTH DOWNS

DOVER
To Zeebrugge Ostende 68 m.
To Dunkerque
Dover to Calais 22 m.

St Margaret's Bay
South Foreland

FOLKESTONE
Sandgate
Hythe

Lyminge
Elham
Cheriton

STRAIT OF DOVER

Folkestone to Boulogne 26 m.
To Boulogne

ROMNEY MARSH
New Romney
Littlestone on Sea
Dymchurch
St Mary's Bay
Greatstone-on-Sea

ISLE OF OXNEY
WALLAND MARSH
Lydd
Lydd-on-Sea

Rye
Winchelsea
Rye Bay
Camber

WEST ROAD
Dungeness
Varne Light

Cliff End
Fairlight Cove

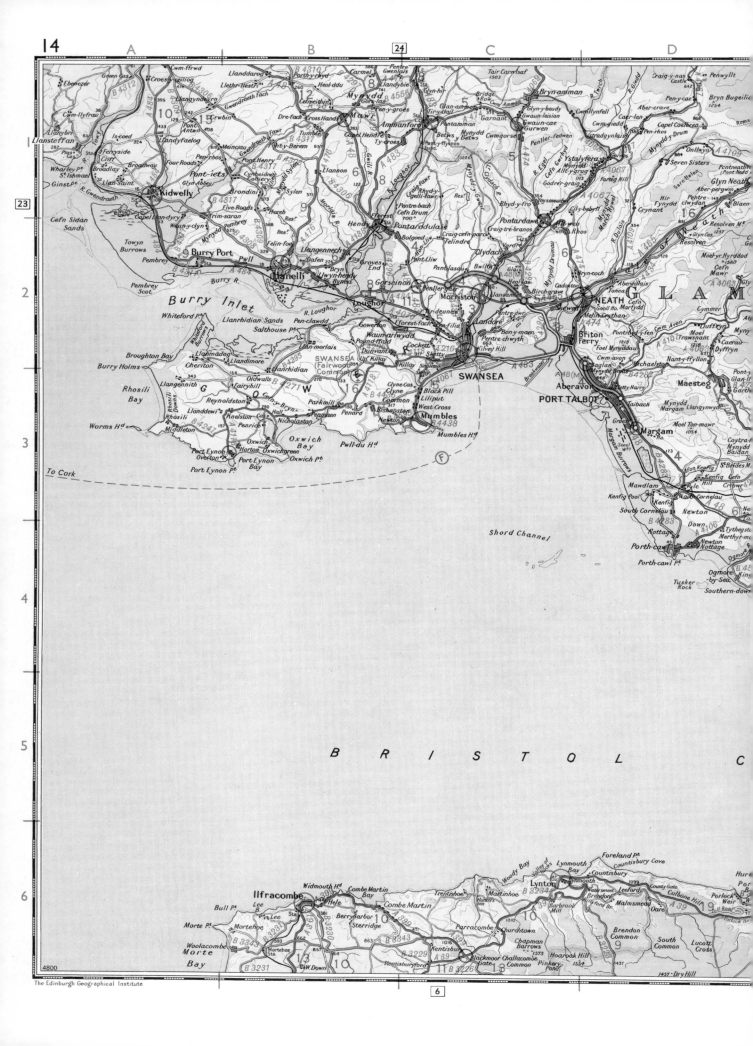

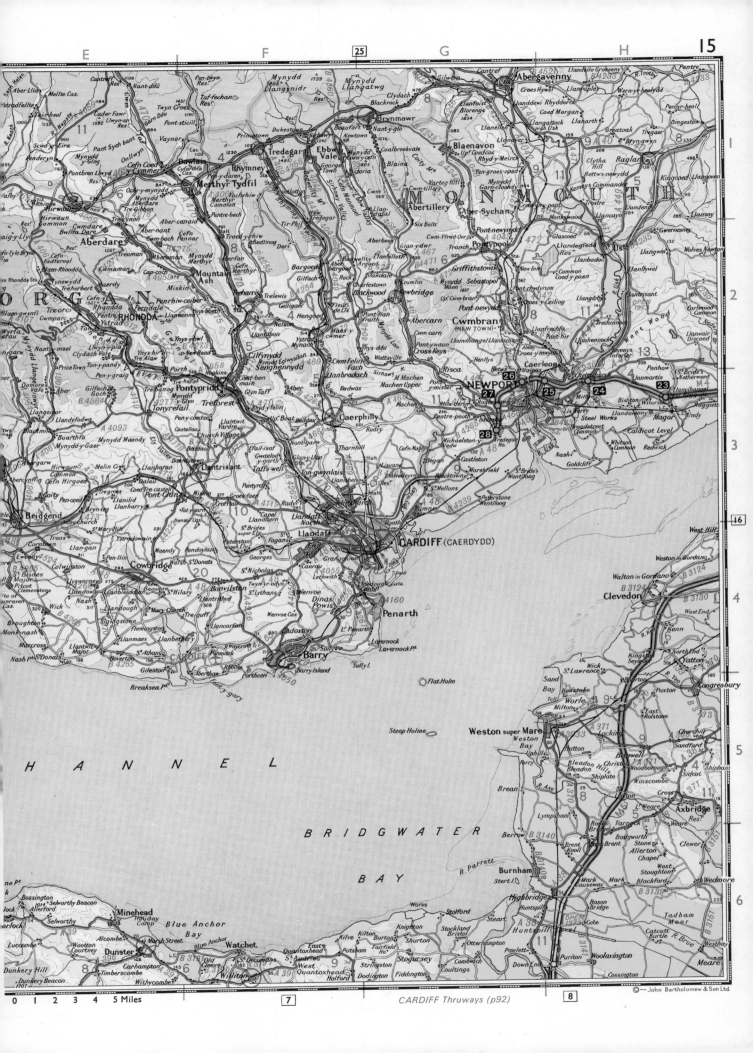

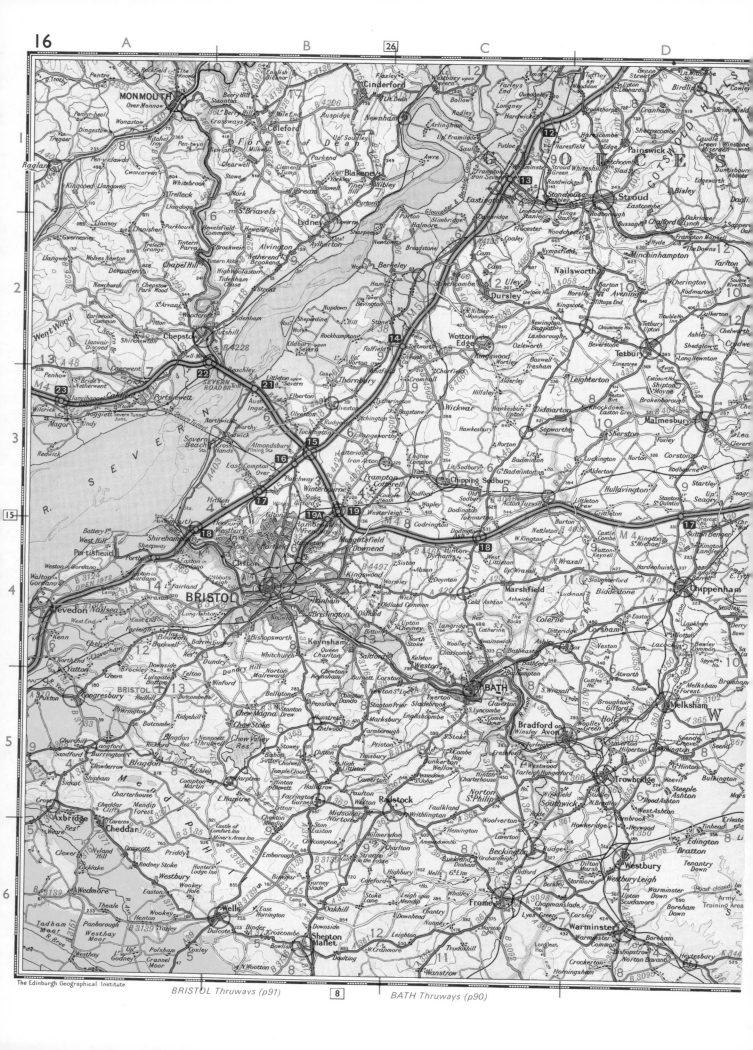

16

A   B   26   C   D

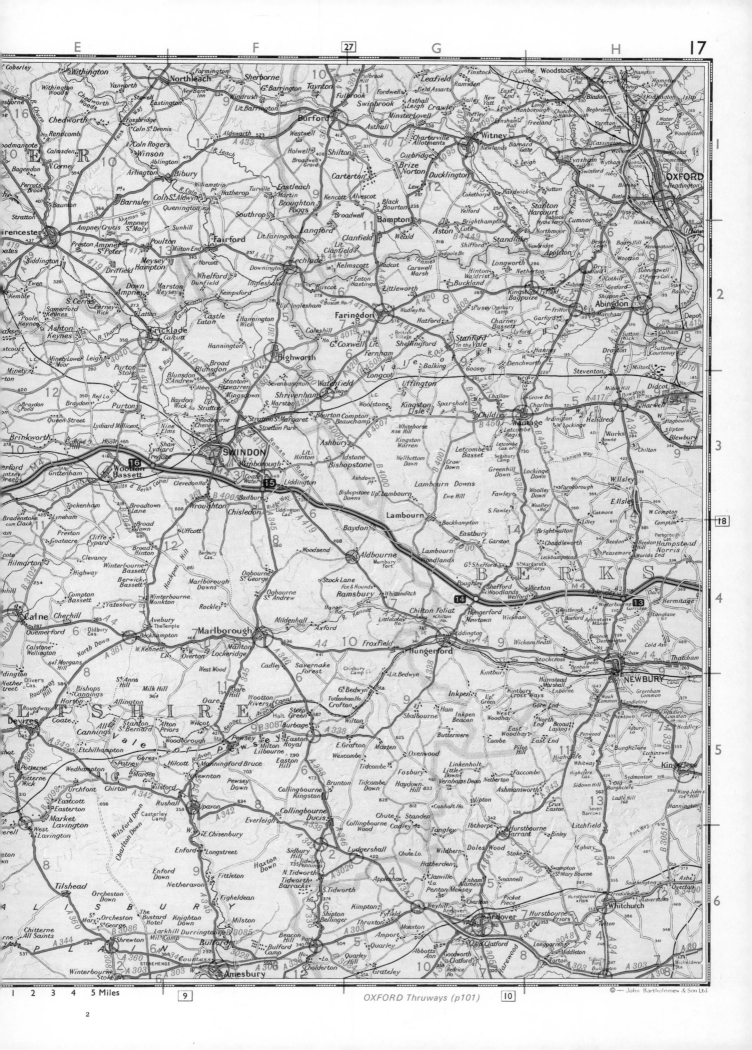

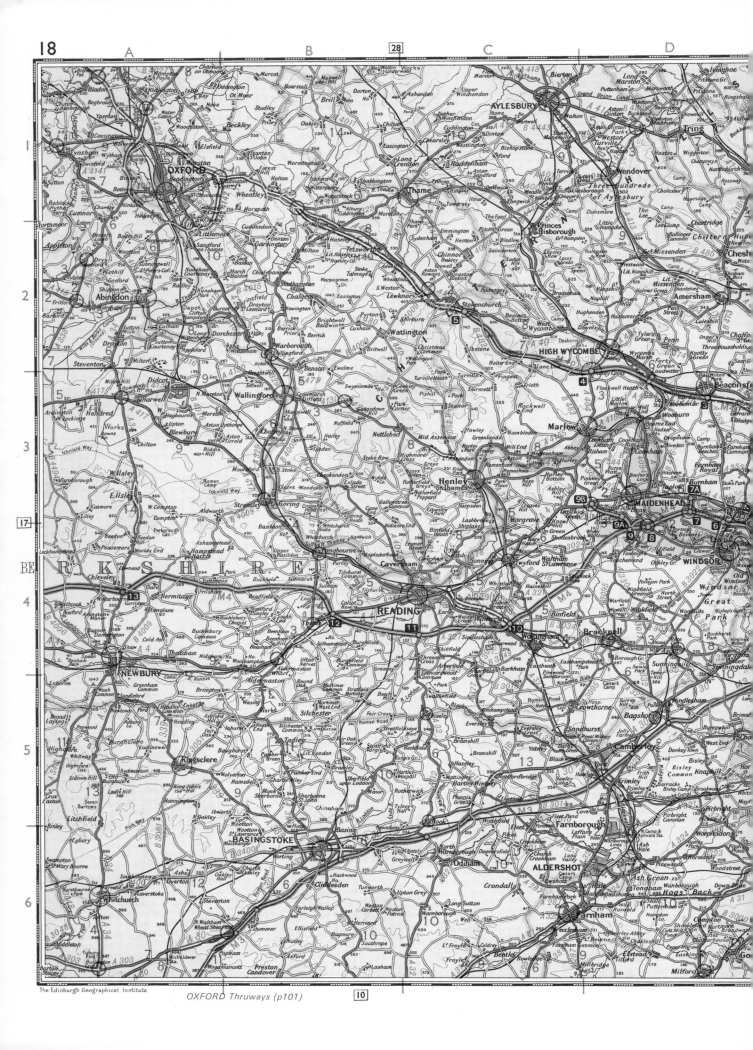

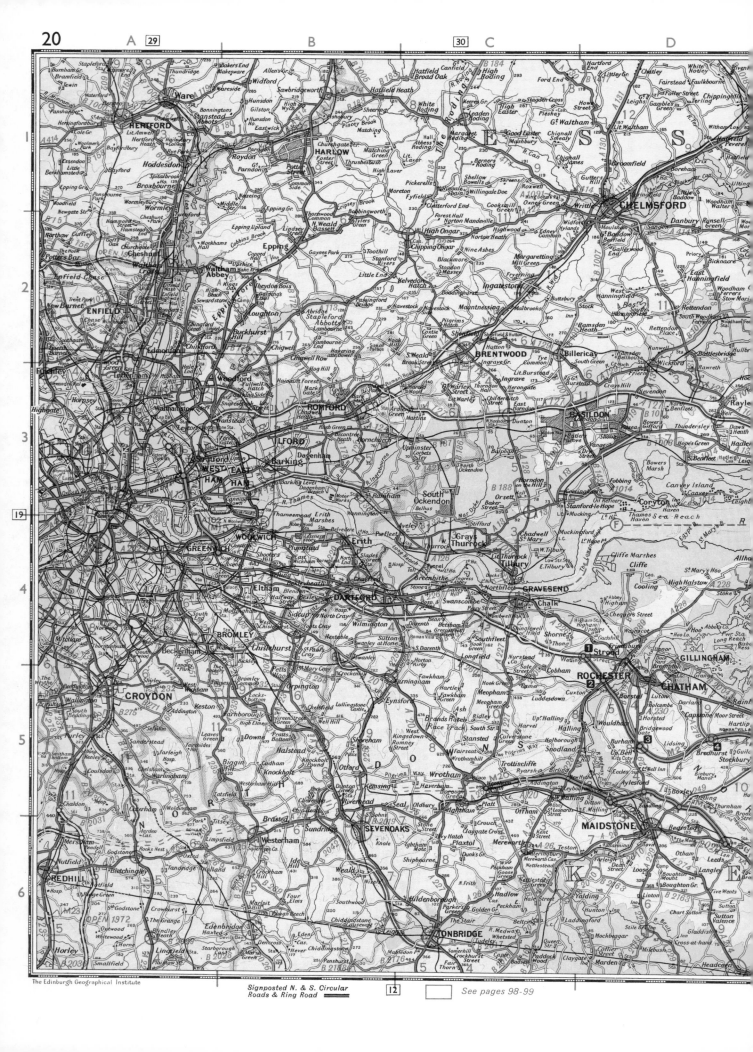

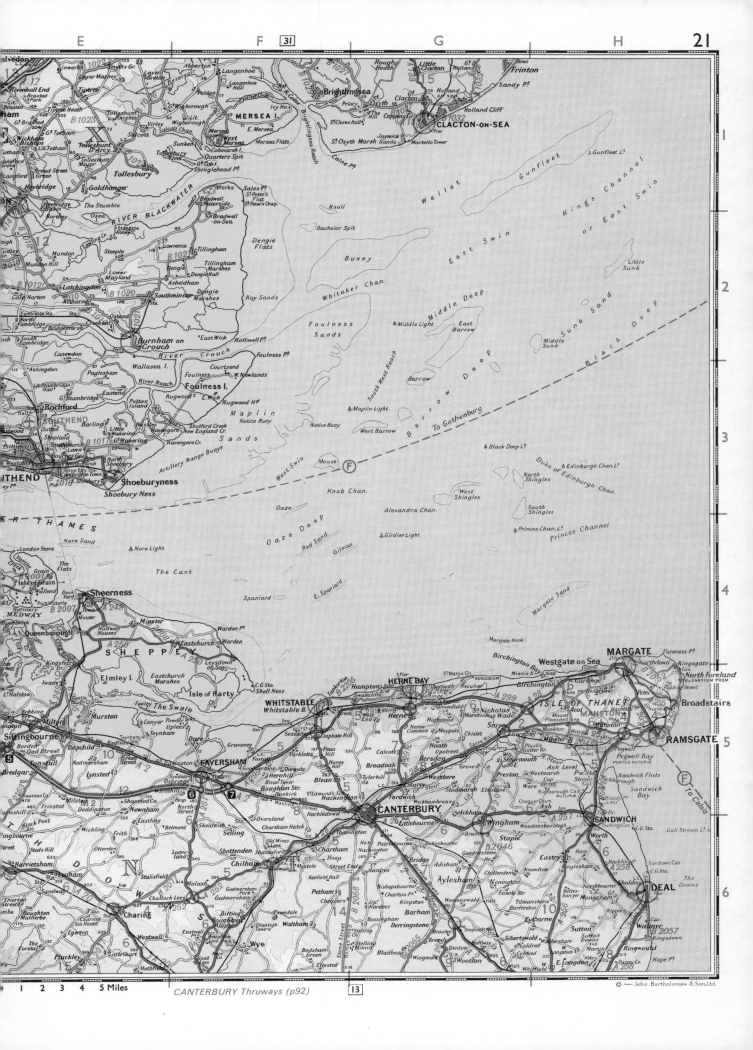

E · 31 · F · G · H

1

2

3

4

5

6

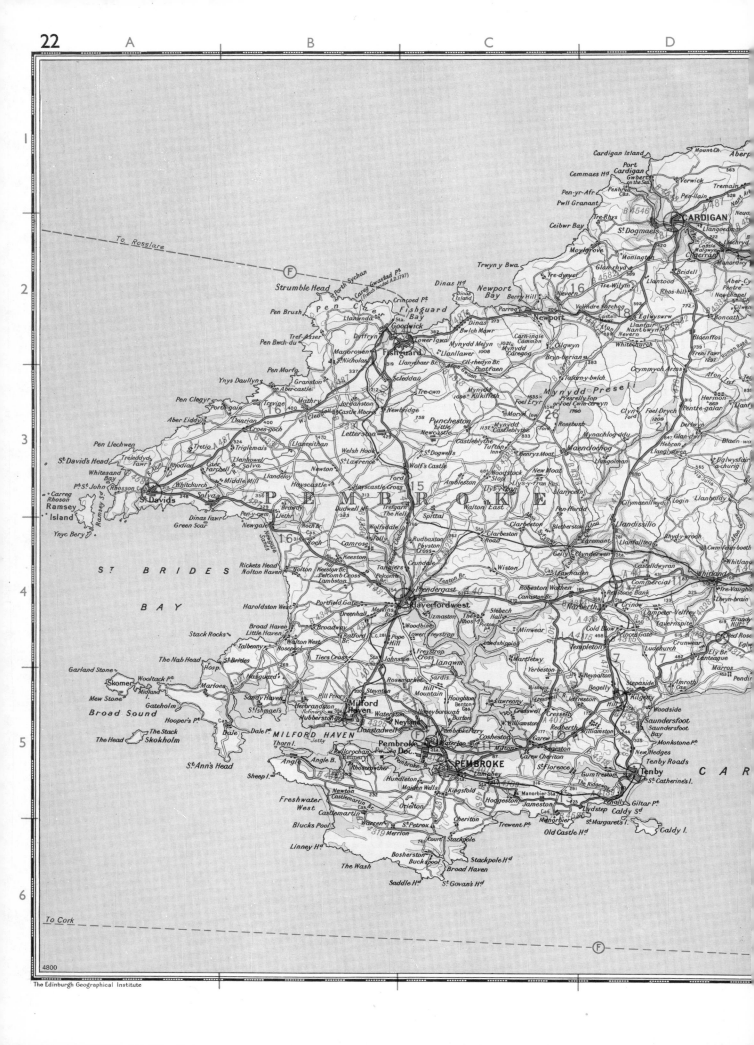

A   B   C   D

1

2

To Rosslare

Strumble Head

Carreg Gwastad Pt
(French landed A.D.1797)

Porth Sychan

Pen Brush
Pen Bwch-du
Tref-Asser
Pen Morfa

Ynys Dauillyn
Pen Clegyr
Porth-gain
Aber Eiddy
Pen Llechwen
Treleddyd fawr
St David's Head
Whitesand Bay
Pt St John
Carreg Rhoson
Ramsey Island
Ynys Bery

Crincoed Pt

Pen Cae

Fishguard Bay

Goodwick
Lower Town
Fishguard
Dyffryn
Manorowen
St Nicholas
Llanwnda
Llanllawer
Llanychaer Br

Dinas Hd
Dinas Island

Newport Bay
Dinas
Bwlch Mawr
Mynydd Melyn
Mynydd Caregog
Parrog
Newport
Berry Hill
Carn-ingle Common

Cardigan Island
Cemmaes Hd
Pen-yr-Afr
Pwll Granant
Ceibwr Bay
Moylgrove
Monington
Glan-rhyd
Tre-dynst
Nevern
Tre-Wilym
Clgwyn
Whitechurch
Bryn-berian

Mount Ch.
Aber

Port Cardigan
Gwbert on the Sea
Penrhys

Verwick
Tremain
Nant Ark

CARDIGAN
St Dogmaels
Cilgerran
Llangoedmor
Castle Malgwyn

Neuadd

Bridell
Aber-Cych
Pantre
Newchapel
Eglwyswrw
Boncath
Bloenffos
Freni Fawr
Crymmych Arms
Afon Taf
Hermon
Pentre-galar
Derlwyn
Blaen

Llanfair Nant-gwyn Nevern

3

St David's Head
Whitesand Bay

St Davids
Solva
Trevine
Mathry
Jordanston
Castle Morris
Newbridge
Granston
Abercastle
Croes-goch
Llanrian
Triglemais
Trefio
Llanhowel
Llandeloy
Middle Mill
Rhodiad
Whitchurch
Cadfarchell
Llanreithan
St Lawrence
Welsh Hook
Wolf's Castle
Ambleston

Letterston
Scleddau
Tre-cwn
Punceston little Newcastle
Castleblythe
Tufton Inn
St Dogwells
Woodstock
New Moat
Henry's Moat
Llys-y-fran Res.
Maenclochog

Mynydd Kilkiffeth
Moryil Inn
Preselly Top or Foel Cwm Cerwyn

Mynydd Presel
Clyn Ford
Foel Drych
Rosebush
Mynachlog-ddu
Llangolman
Llanycefn

Glan-duad
Hebron
Llanglydwen
Llanboidy
Blaen-y-churig
Eglwys-fair-a-churig
Via Julia
Whitland

PEMBROKE

Hayscastle
Hayscastle Cross
Trelgarn
The Kell
Spittal
Trefgarn
Walton East
Llys-y-fran

Clarbeston
Clarbeston Road
Gelly
Pen-ffordd
Bletherston
Clynderwen
Llanfallteg
Rhyd-y-wroch
Cwm-felin-boeth

Login
Llanboidy

Llandissilio
Egremont
Llanfallteg
Castelldwyran

4

St Brides Bay

Garland Stone
Skomer
Mew Stone
Midland
Gateholm
The Stack
Skokholm
The Head
Broad Sound

Wooltack Pt
Marloes
St Brides
Talbenny
Rosepool
Walton West
Little Haven
Broad Haven
Haroldston West
Portfield Gate
Dreenhill
Broadway
Rosemarket
St Ishmael's
Herbrandston
Hubberston
Sandy Haven
Dale Pt
Dale
Thorn I.
Milford Haven

Rickets Head
Nolton Haven
Nolton
Keeston Br
Pelcomb Cross
Lambston
Portfield Gate
Merlin's Br
Steynton
Johnston
Freystrop Cross
Tiers Cross
Llangwm
Sardis
Hill Mountain
Houghton
Burton
Waterston
Neyland
Llanstadwell
Pembroke Ferry

Roch
Keeston
Simpson Cross
Tancredston
Crundale
Wiston
Clarbeston Road
Llawhaden
Canaston Br
Slebech
Picton Pk
The Rhos
Minwear
Martletwy
Yerbeston
Templeton
Begelly
Reynalton

Haverfordwest
Uzmaston
Woodbine
Lower Freystrop
Pope Hill
Freystrop
Landshipping
Landshipping
Martletwy
Cresswell
Lawrenny

Prendergast
Robeston Wathen
Canaston Br
Redstone Bank
Narberth
Cold Blow
Princes Gate
Ludchurch
Crunwear
Lampeter-Velfrey
Tavernspite
Red Roses
Pendin
Marros
Amroth
Lanteague
Eglwys-cymmin

Commercial
Crinow
Stepaside
Kilgetty
Saundersfoot
Saundersfoot Bay
Woodside
Monkstone Pt
New Hedges
Tenby Roads
Tenby
St Catherine's I.

5

Milford Haven
Dale Pt
Dale
Angle
Angle B.
Rhoscrowther
Pwllcrochan
Hundleton
Maiden Wells
Kingsfold
Newton
Castlemartin
Orielton
Cheriton
Freshwater West
Castlemartin
Blucks Pool
Warren
St Petrox
Merrion
Linney Hd

Milford Haven
Pembroke Dock
Pembroke
Lamphey
Hodgeston
Jameston
Manorbier
Old Castle Hd
St Margaret's I.

Waterloo
Milton
Carew
Carew Cheriton
St Florence
Gumfreston
Manorbier Sta
Lydstep
Penally
Giltar Pt
Caldy Sd
Caldy I.

CAR

Cosheston
Williamston
Redberth
Sageston

6

To Cork

F

The Wash
Bosherston
Buckspool
Saddle Hd
St Govan's Hd
Stackpole
Stackpole Hd
Broad Haven
Trewent Pt
Court

The Edinburgh Geographical Institute

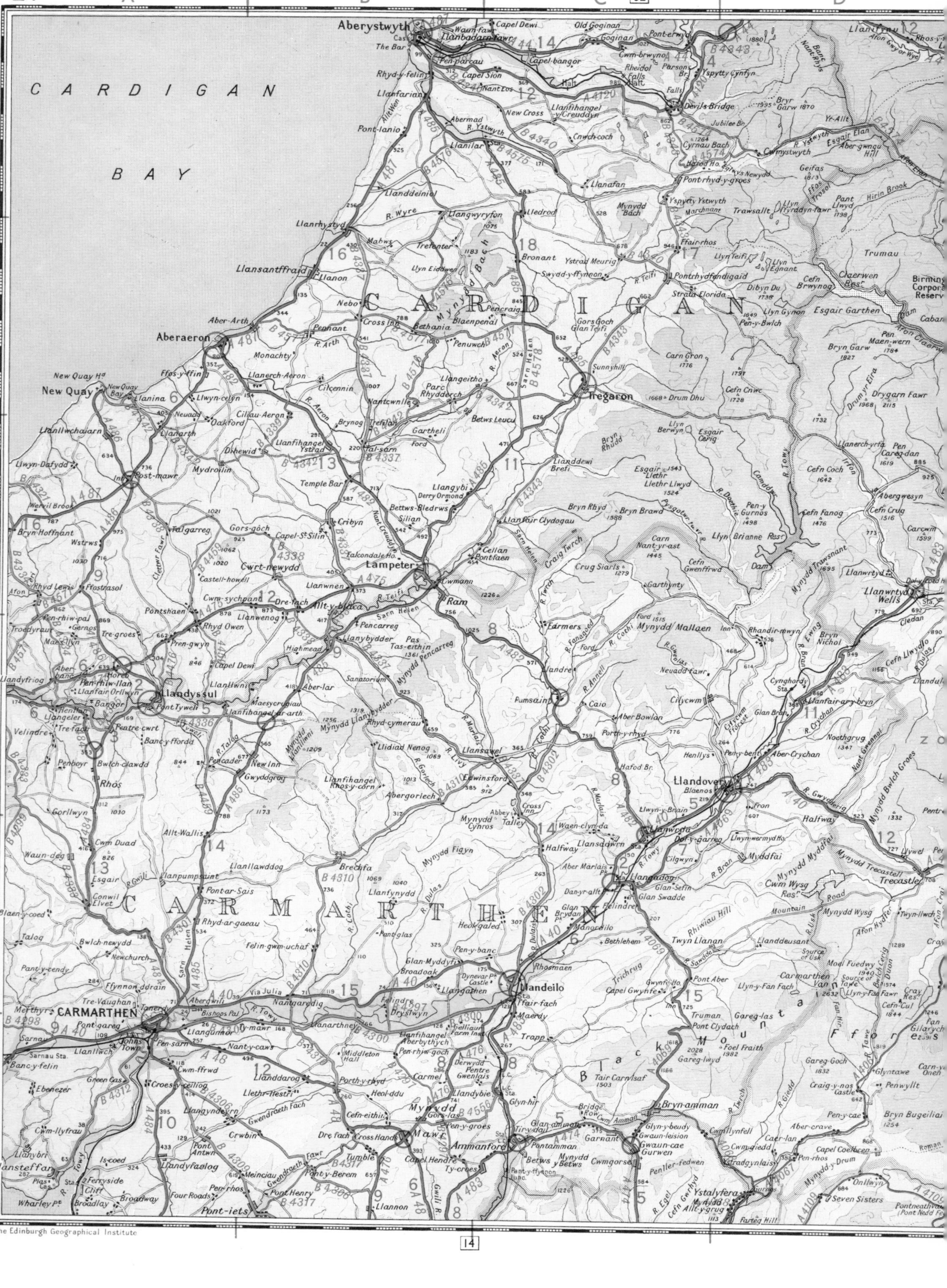

A   B   C   32   D

CARDIGAN

BAY

Aberystwyth

CARDIGAN

Aberaeron

New Quay

Tregaron

Lampeter

Llanwrtyd
Wells

Llandyssul

CARMARTHEN

Llandovery

Llandeilo

CARMARTHEN

Ammanford

23

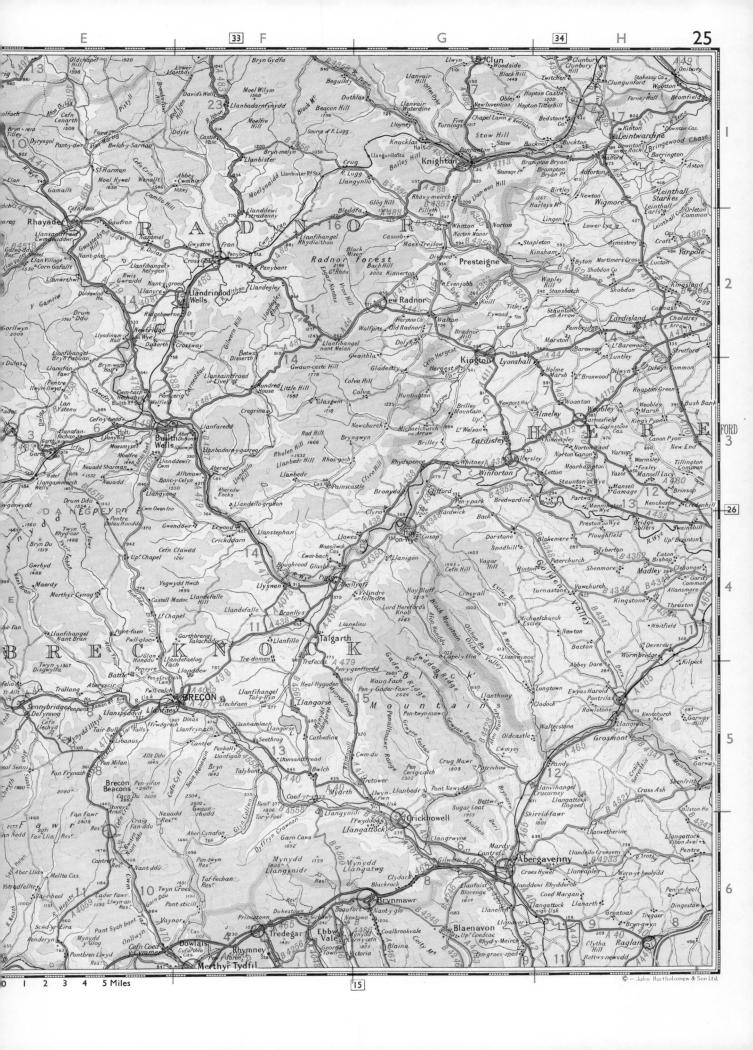

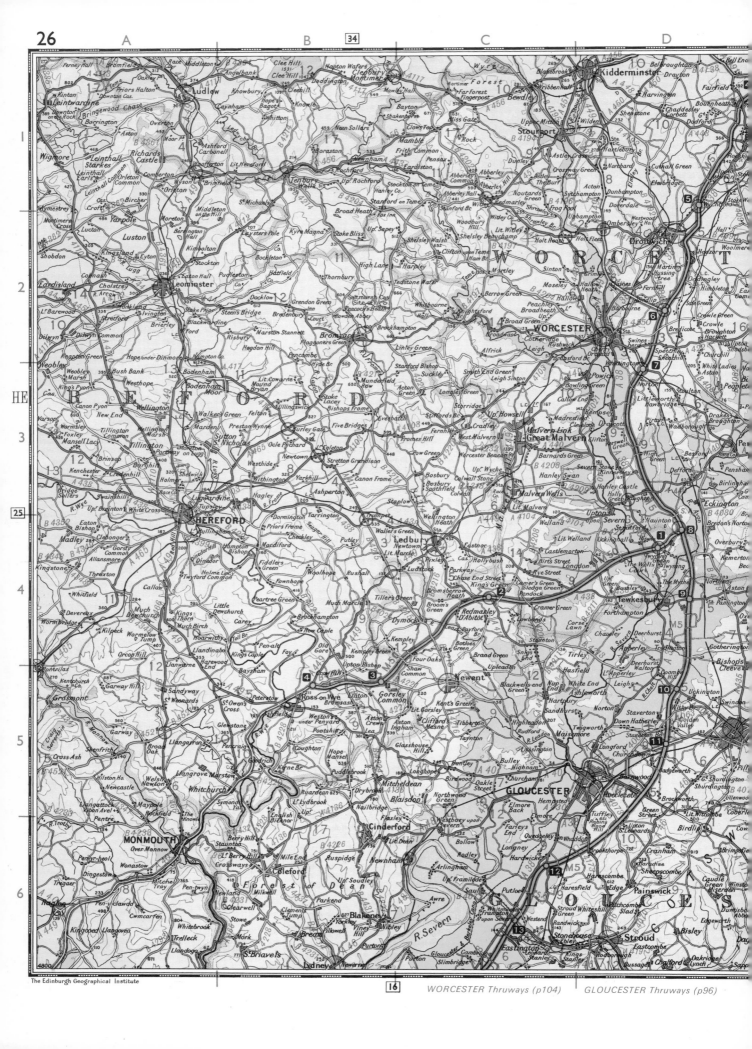

A   B   34   C   D

HE

25

16   *WORCESTER Thruways (p104)*   *GLOUCESTER Thruways (p96)*

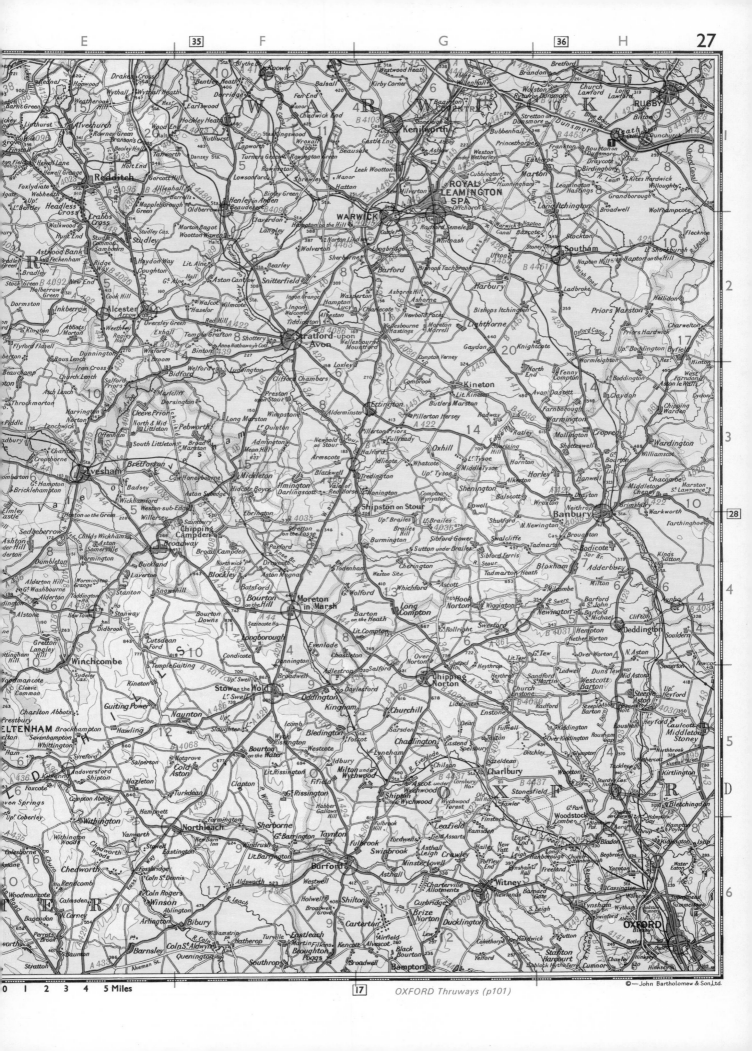

OXFORD Thruways (p101)

©—John Bartholomew & Son,Ltd.

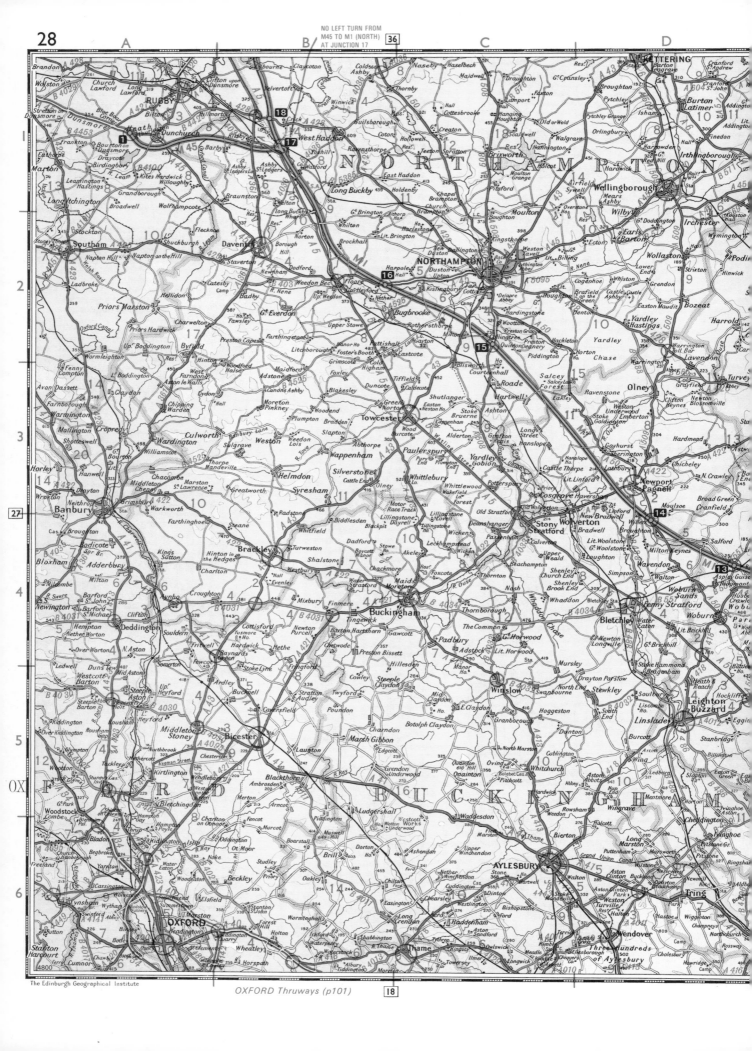

NO LEFT TURN FROM
M45 TO M1 (NORTH)
AT JUNCTION 17

OXFORD Thruways (p101)

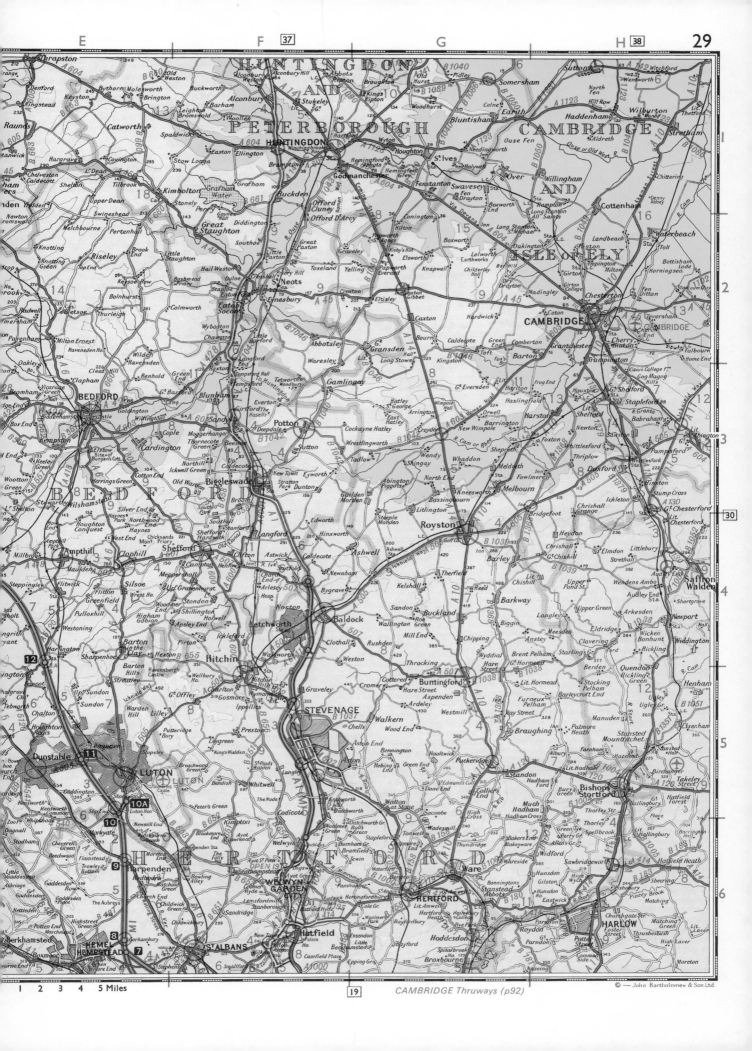

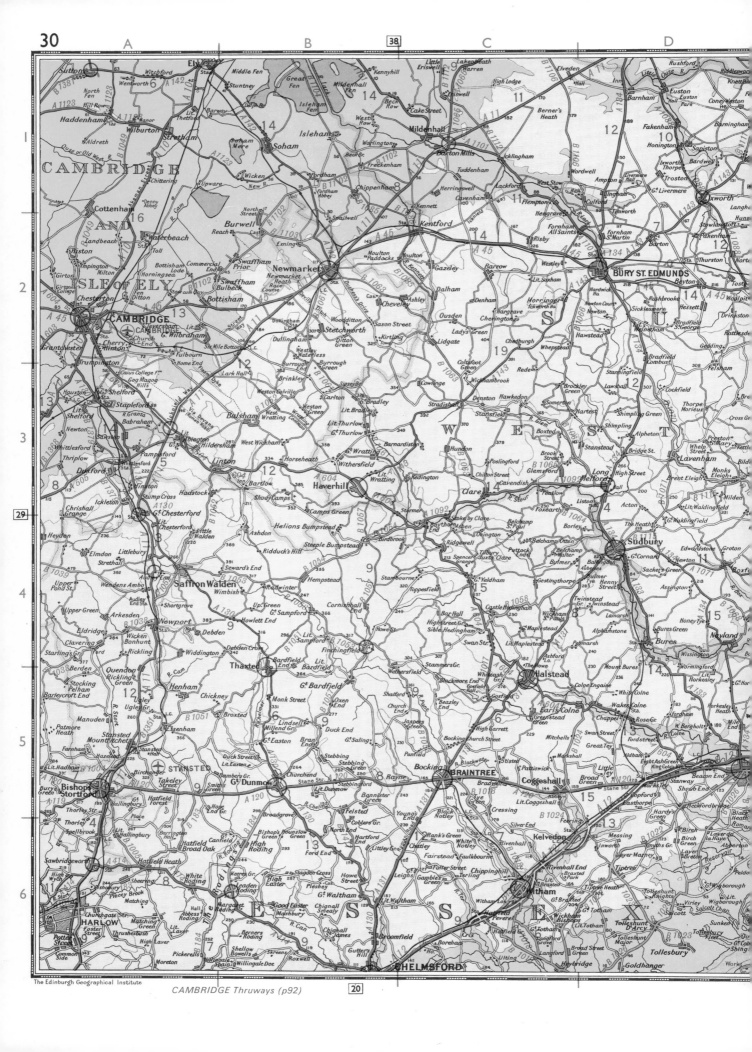

CAMBRIDGE Thruways (p92)

20

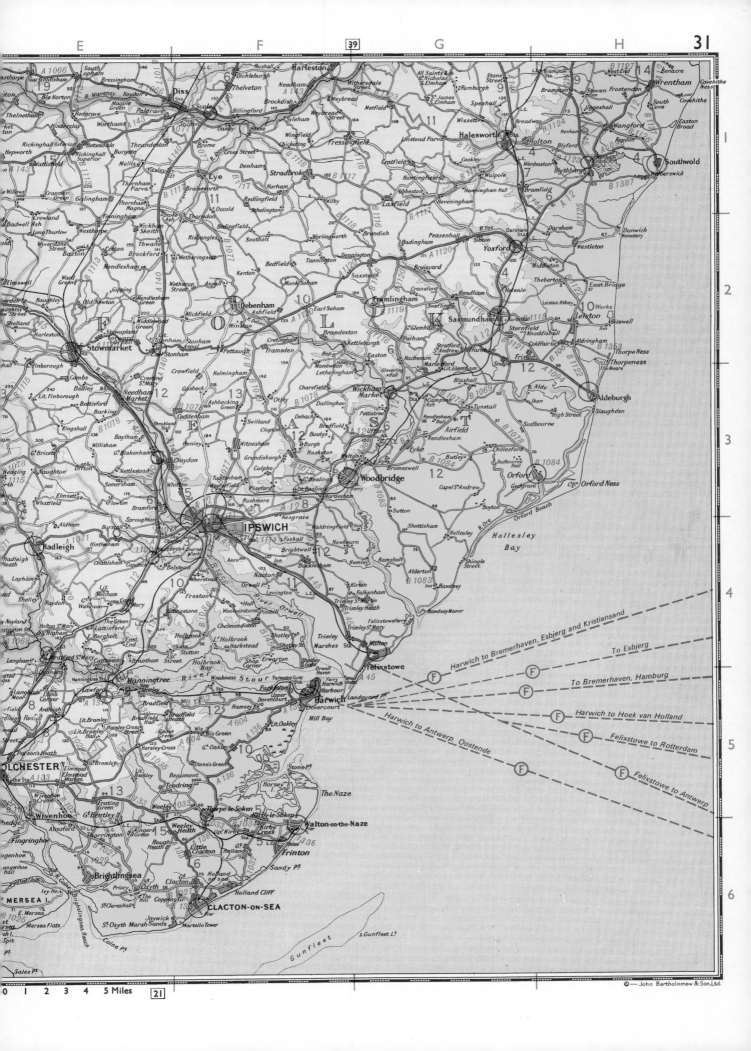

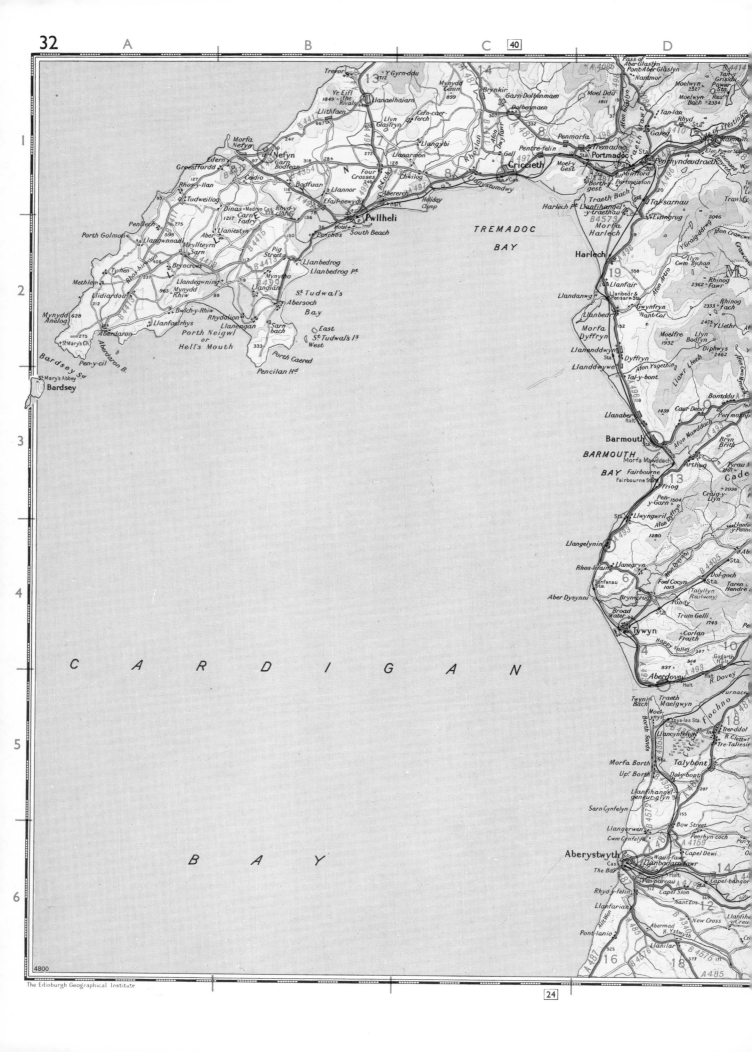

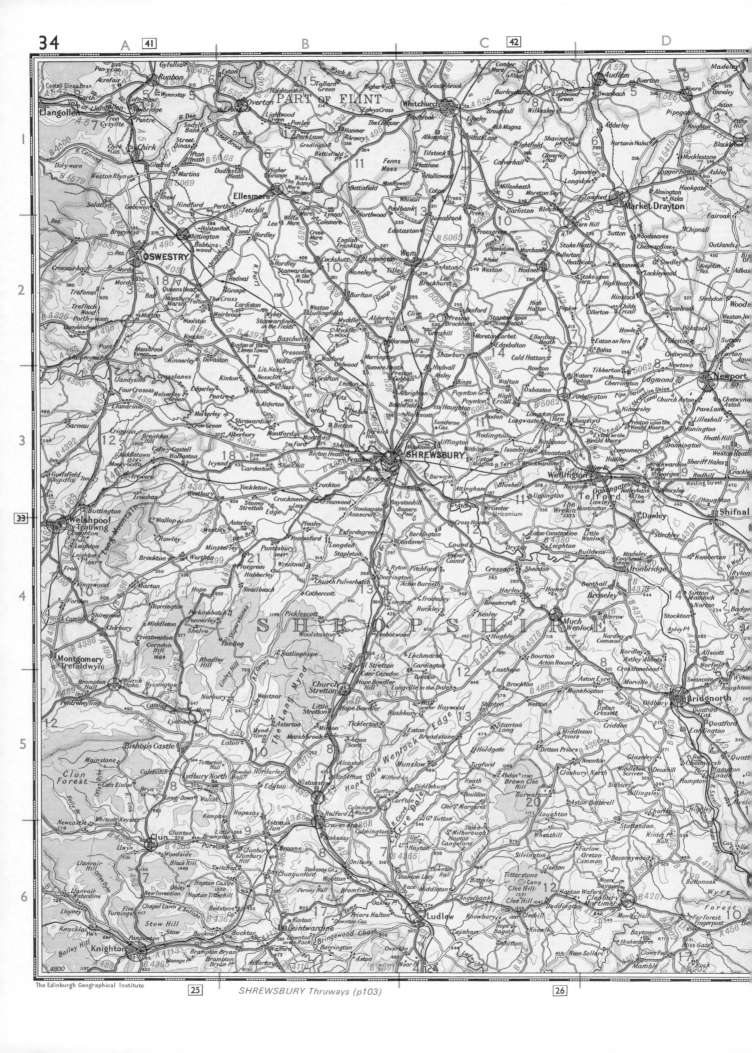

SHREWSBURY Thruways (p103)

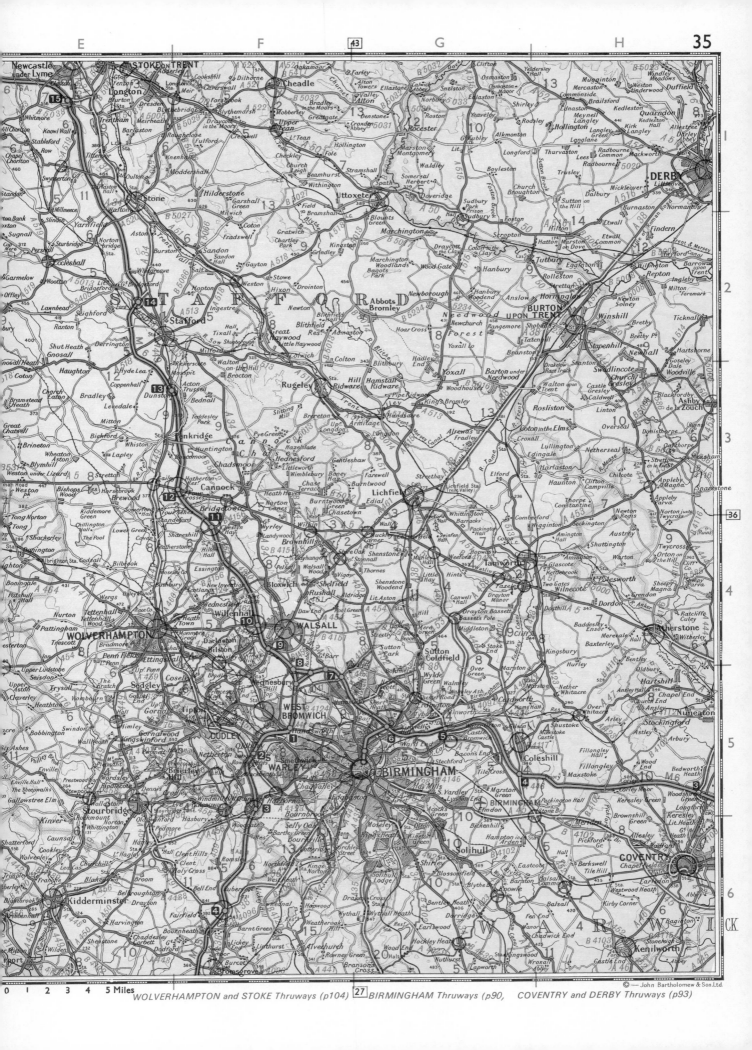

WOLVERHAMPTON and STOKE Thruways (p104)   BIRMINGHAM Thruways (p90,   COVENTRY and DERBY Thruways (p93)

© — John Bartholomew & Son.Ltd.

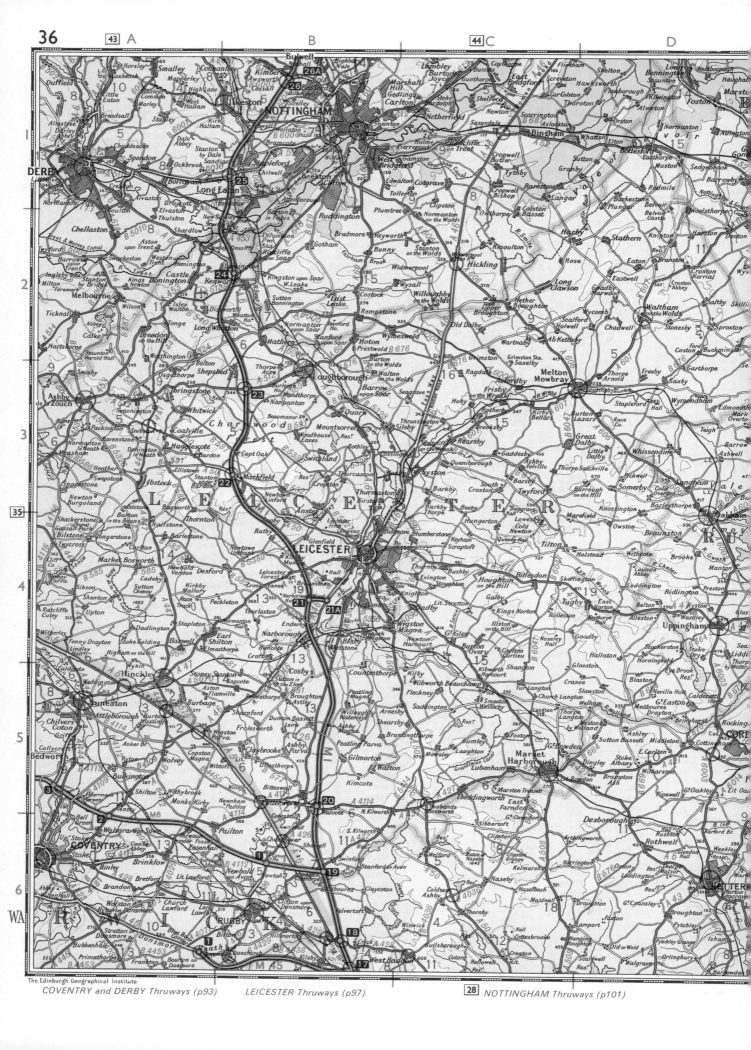

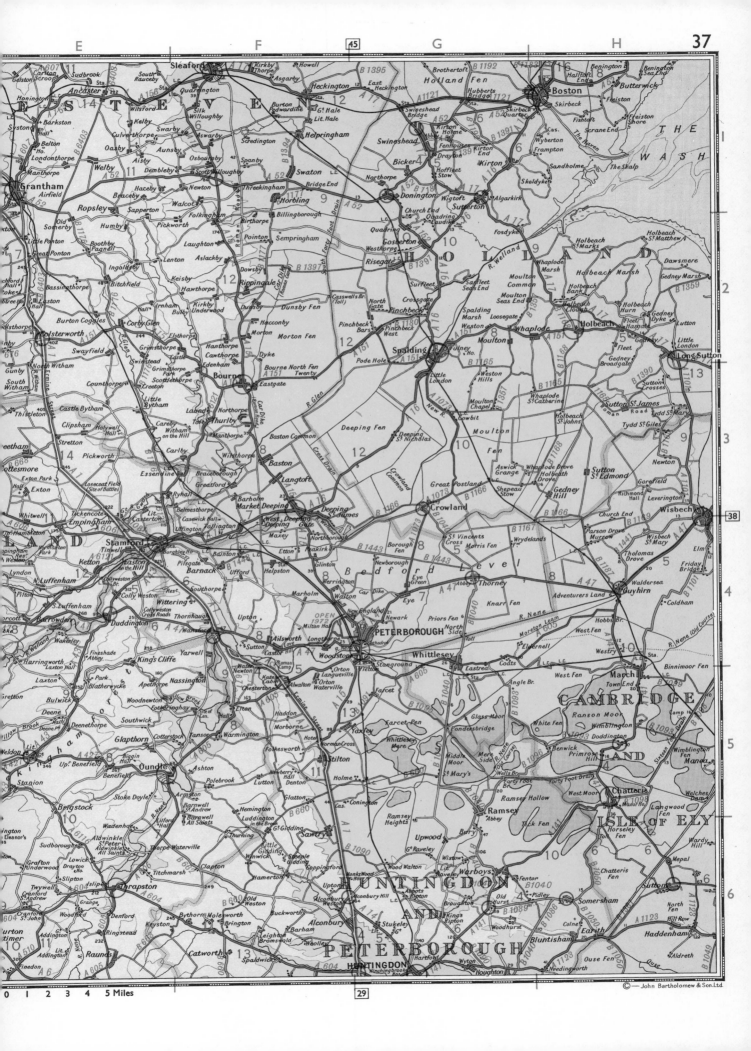

A B C D

THE WASH

1

2

3

37

4

5

6

Benington Sea End
Holbeach St Matthew
Dawsmere
Gedney Marsh
Gedney Drove End
Gedney Dyke
Lutton Marsh
Guy's Head
Lutton
Little London
Long Sutton
Sutton Bridge
Central Wingland
Crosskeys
Tydd St Mary
Tydd St Giles
Walpole St Andrews
Sutton Crosses
Newton
West Walton
Walpole St Peter
Leverington
Wisbech
Walsoken
Emneth
Elm
Friday Bridge
Coldham
Emneth Hungate
Needham Hall
Outwell
Laddus Fens
Upwell
North District
Three Holes
Nordelph
Christchurch
Euximoor Fen
Upwell Fen
South District
Binnimoor Fen
Lakes End
Upwell Fen
Welney
Nimblington Fen
Manea
CAMBRIDGE
Purls Bridge
Welches Dam
Langwood Fen
Wardy Hill
Coveney
Downham
Chettisham
AND Bedford Level
Wilburton
Witcham
Mepal
Sutton
Wentworth
Witchford
ISLE OF ELY
North Fen
Haddenham
Hill Row
Aldreth
Wilburton
Stretham
Soham Mere
Soham
Isleham

Terrington Marsh
Little London
Terrington St Clement
Clenchwarton Hall
Lovells Hall
Clenchwarton
Tilney All Saints
West Lynn
Tilney High End
Tilney cum Islington
Tilney St Lawrence
St John's Highway
Walpole Highway
Wiggenhall St Mary the Virgin
Wiggenhall St Peter
Marshland
West Walton Highway
St John's Fen End
Wiggenhall St Mary Magdalen
Marshland Drain
Marshland Fen
Stowbridge
Flood Relief Channel
Beaupre Hall
Stow Bardolph Fen
West Downham
Downham Market
Denver
Ryston Hall
Fordham
Hilgay
Ten Mile Bank
Wood Hall
Hilgay Fen
Southery
Lit. London
Southery Fens
Methwold Fens
Brandon Creek
Feltwell Fens
Queens Ground
Littleport Br.
Littleport
Burn
Padnal Fen
Hippea Bill Sta.
Shippea Hill
Ely
Middle Fen
Stuntney
Little Downham
Prickwillow
Great Fen
Kennyhill
Mildenhall Fen
Isleham Fen
Barway
Beck Row
West Row
Worlington
Barton Mills

New Hunstanton
Hunstanton
Hall
Heacham
Snettisham
Ingoldisthorpe
Sheringborne
Dersingham
Wolferton
Sandringham Ho.
N. Wootton
Castle Rising
Castle Rising Lo.
S. Wootton
King's Lynn
Gaywood
West Winch
North Runcton
Setchey
Saddle Bow
Wimbotsham
Bexwell
Crimplesham
Stradsett
West Dereham
Wereham
Stoke Ferry
Whittington
Northwold
Methwold
Feltwell
Hockwold cum Wilton
Hockwold Fens
Weeting
Brandon
Mile End
Lakenheath Sta.
Grime Fen
Wangford
Lakenheath
Little Eriswell
Lakenheath Warren
Eriswell
Cake Street
Mildenhall
Holme next the Sea
Thornham
Titchwell
Brancaster
Choseley
Kingstead
Summerfield
Docking
Fring
Sedgeford
Bircham Newton
G. Bircham
Bircham Tofts
Barwick
Anmer
Houghton
Harpley
West Rudham
East Rudham
Gayton
Gayton Thorpe
Grimston
Roydon
Hillington
East Winch
Middleton
Blackborough End
East Walton
West Bilney
Pentney
Narborough
West Acre
South Acre
Castle Acre
Newton
R. Nar
Wormegay
Marham
Shouldham
Shouldham Thorpe
Barton Bendish
Fincham
Swaffham
Beachamwell
Goderstone
Oxborough
Foulden
Didlington Hall
Cranwich
Mundford
Lynford Cottages
Stanford
West Tofts
Santon
Thetford Warren
Thetford
Thetford Sta.
Elveden
High Lodge
Berner's Heath
Honington

Brancaster Bay
Scolt Head
Norton Creek
Holkham Bay
Burnham Deepdale
Overy Staithe
Burnham Overy
Holkham
Wells next the Sea
Burnham Market
Burnham Thorpe
Holkham Park
Watham All Saints
Danish Camp
Wighton
N. Creake
Quarles
Crabbs Cas.
Binham
G. Walsingham
Little Walsingham
Egmere
Waterden
S. Creake
Barmer
Stanhoe
Barwick
Houghton St Giles
Thursford
Kettlestone
Croxton
Fakenham
Shereford
Hempton
Tattersett
Broomsthorpe
Tatterford
Toftrees
G. Ryburgh
Lit. Ryburgh
Colkirk
Dunton
Sculthorpe
N. Barsham
W. Barsham
Houghton
E. Barsham
Hindringham
Hindolveston
W. Raynham
E. Raynham
Oxwick
Whissonsett
Horningtoft
Wellingham
Weasenham All Saints
Weasenham St Peter
Lit. Massingham
G. Massingham
Airfield
S. Raynham
Gt. Dunham
Rougham
Lexham
West Lexham
Litcham
Mileham
Stanfield
North Elmham
Brisley
E. Bilney
Beetley
Gressenhall
East Dereham
Longham
Beeston
Scarning
Wendling
Little Dunham
Great Fransham
Little Fransham
Sporle
Necton
Ivy Todd
Holme Hale
North Pickenham
South Pickenham
Swaffham Heath
Ashill
Hilborough
Bodney
Great Cressingham
Little Cressingham
Saham Toney
Watton
Threxton
Merton
Thompson
Tottington
Stow Bedon
Breckles
Hockham
Shropham
Griston
Caston
Wayland
Ovington
Carbrooke
Watton Gr.
Cranworth
Shipdham
Bradenham
East Bradenham
Cockley Cley
Roman Remains

THE BATTLE AREA
BRECKLAND

Little Ouse R.
Brandon
Kilverstone
Brettenham
Shadwell
Rushford
Euston Park
Barnham
Coney Weston
Fakenham
Market Weston
Sapiston
Honington
Knettishall
Gasthorpe
West Harling Heath
Middle Harling
Bridgham
Roudham
Larling
Wretham
East Wretham
Snetterton
Illington
Eccles
Hargham

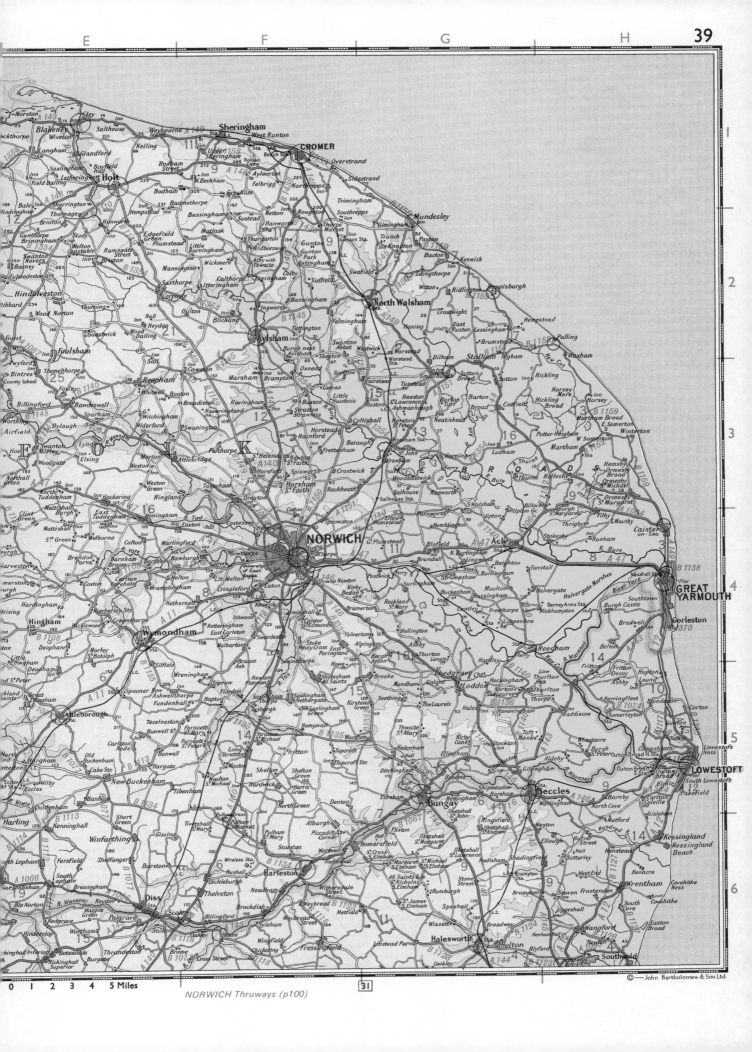

0 1 2 3 4 5 Miles

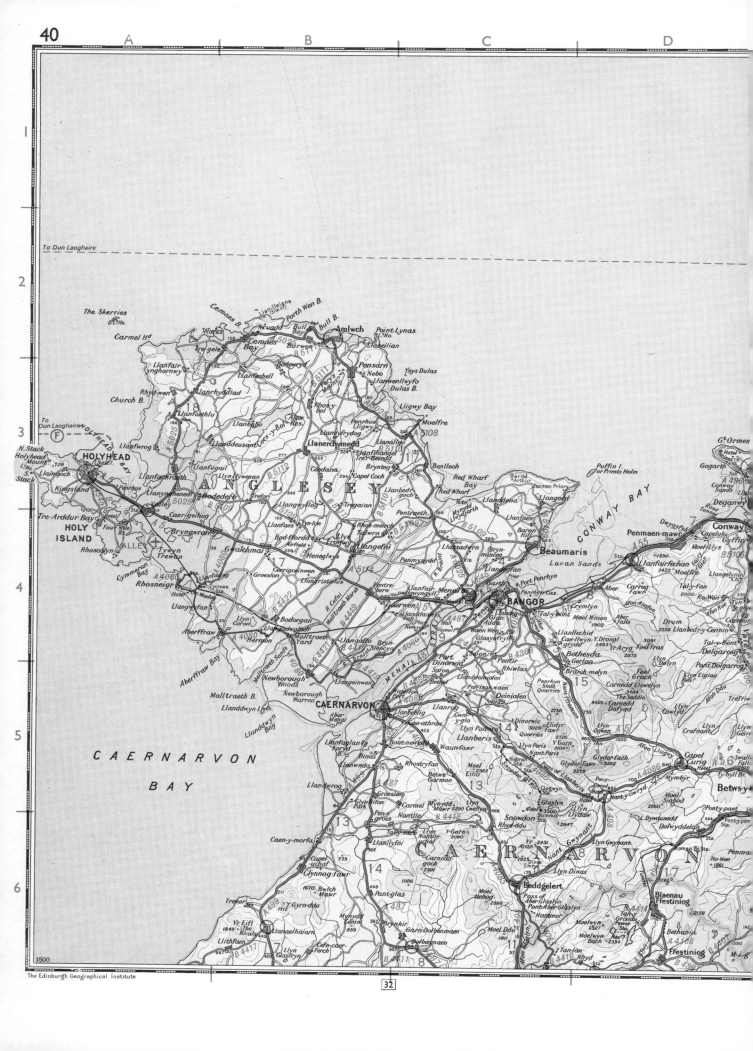

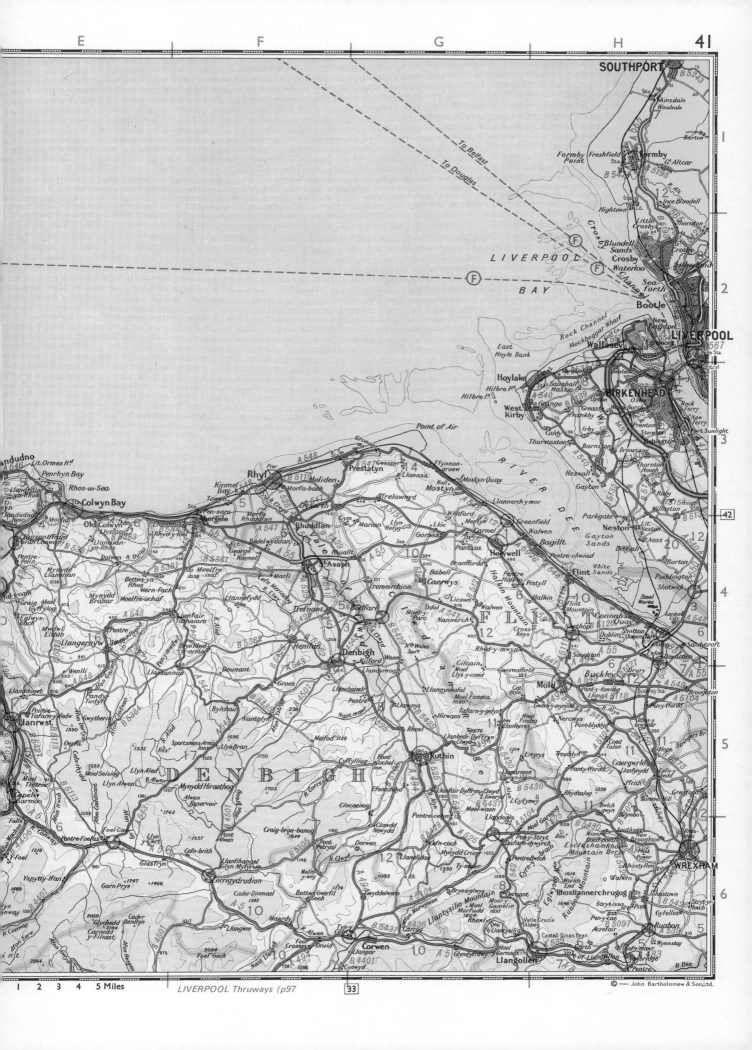

SOUTHPORT

LIVERPOOL BAY

Crosby Channel

LIVERPOOL

Bootle
New Brighton
Wallasey
BIRKENHEAD
Port Sunlight

Hoylake
West Kirby

RIVER DEE

Point of Air

Llandudno
Penrhyn Bay
Rhos-on-Sea
Colwyn Bay
Old Colwyn
Abergele

Rhyl
Meliden
Prestatyn
Llanasa
Mostyn

FLINT

Neston

Holywell
Bagillt
Flint
Connah's Quay
Shotton
Queensferry

St Asaph
Rhuddlan
Trefnant
Henllan

Denbigh

Ruthin

Mold
Buckley

DENBIGH

Corwen
Llangollen

Wrexham
Rhosllanerchrugog
Ruabon

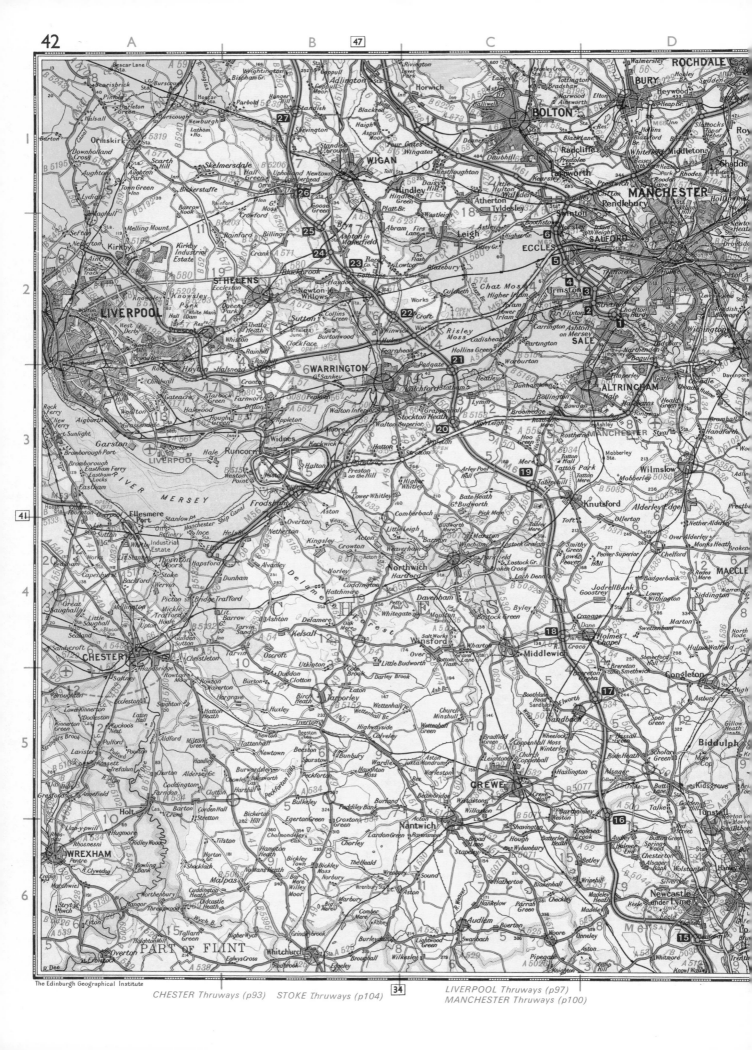

© —John Bartholomew & Son.Ltd.

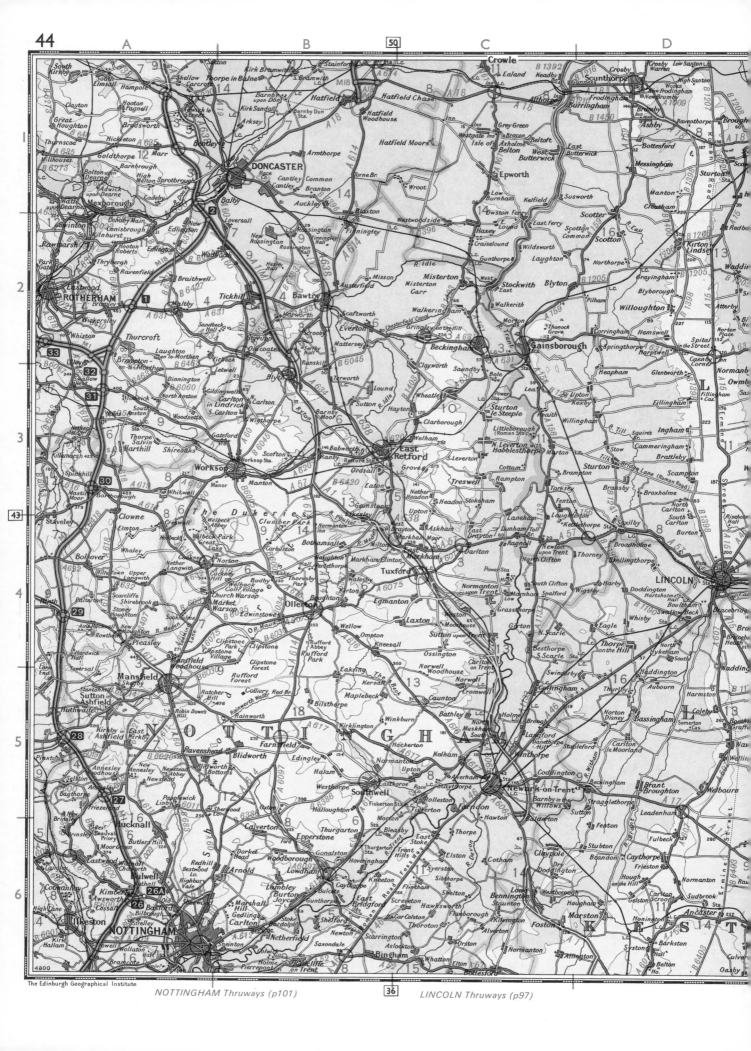

A   B   50   C   D

Crowle

Scunthorpe

DONCASTER

ROTHERHAM

Worksop

East Retford

Gainsborough

LINCOLN

Tuxford

Ollerton

Mansfield

Newark-on-Trent

Southwell

NOTTINGHAM

NOTTINGHAM Thruways (p101)

36

LINCOLN Thruways (p97)

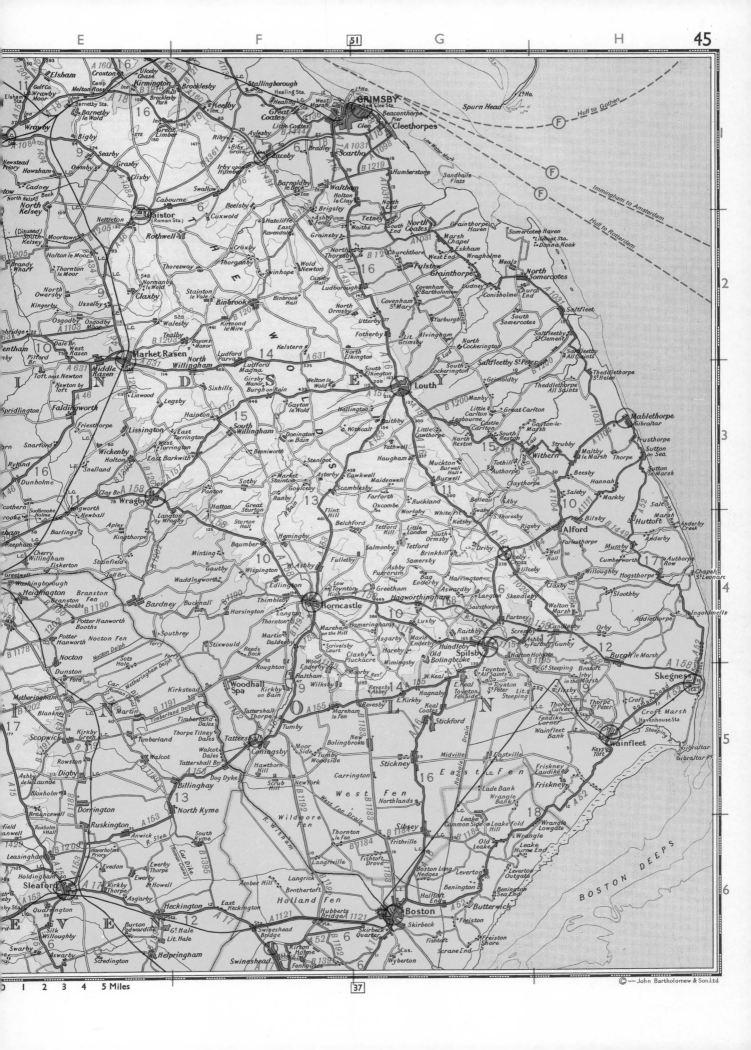

A   B   C   52   D

1

To Belfast

14

Whicham
Silecroft
Kirksanton
Haverigg
Haverigg Pt.
Hodbarrow
The Duddon Sands
Duddon Chan.
Scarth Chan.

Beck Side
The Side
Duddon Sands
Greenodd
Soutergate
Broughton
Beck
Arrad
Foot

Milton
Ireleth
Askam
Lindal
Marton
Newton
Dendron
Scales
Gleaston
Goldmire
Urswick
Birdsea
Dalcoats
Baycliff
Aldingham

DALTON
in Furness
Haycoat

ULVERSTON

Nth End
Nth Scale
New
Barrow
Abbey

BARROW

Leece
Roosecoate
Roosebeck
Ulverston Chan.
South Chan.

2

Vickerstown
Sth Vickerstown
WALNEY
ISLAND

Piel Pier
Sheep I.
Piel I.
Piel L. Cas.
Biggar
Roa I.
Rampside
Foulney I.

Mort
Bank

Hilpsford Pt.
Nth Scale Haws Pt.

3

Point of Ayre
Lighthouses

To Dun Laoghaire

F

Rue Point
The Ayres
Cranstal
Glentruan
Bride
Point Cranstal
(Shellag Point)

From Douglas to Ardrossan

Smeale
Ballathona
Johnodie

Sartfield
Jurby
Ascome
Sandygate
St Judes
Cronkglass
Regaby

FLEETWOO
Rossall Pt.

Andreas

Jurby Head
Crawyn
The Cronk
Sulby Glen Sta.
Wild Life Park
Sulby Br.
Sulby

Ramsey
Bay

Hydro
The Mooragh

RAMSEY

North
Wharf

Whiteside
Cleveleys

4

Orrisdale
Orrisdale Head
Bishops Court
Kirk Michael

Ballaugh
Mt Karrin
1084
Ravensdale
Slieau Curn
1153

Lezayre
Tableland Point
Port e Vullen
Maughold
N.Barrule
1860
Ballajora
Dreemskerry

Maughold Head

Slieau Monagh
1257

Slieau Dhoo
1139

Snaefell
2036
Hotel

Clagh
Ouyr
1806
Slieau
Lhean
Slieau
Ouyr
1483
Dhoon
Torraby

Lit. Bispham
Norbreck
A 584
Bispham

BLACKPOOL

Ballacarnane
Slieau
Freoaghane
1602
Sartfell
1490
Bungalow Hotel
Brainny
Phot.

Mullagh
Ouyr 1612

Abbeylands
Laxey
wheel
Minorca

North Shore

South Shore

F

Barregarrow
Ballabooye

Knocksharry

Peel
R?

Little
London

Hotel
Colden
1599

Injebreck
Res?

The
Garn
Cregny cowin

Laxey

Lonan Ch.
Laxey Head

Bulgham
Bay

To Larne and Belfast

ISLE OF MAN

St Patrick's Isle
Peel
PEEL
Contrary Head
Knockaloe
Patrick

Glen Helen
Slieau
Ruy
1570
St
Johns
Curraghglass

Slieau
Whaallian
Glenmaye

Baldwin
Greeba Cas.
Baldwin
Lands

Crosby
Marown Ch.
Union
Mills
Strang
Onchan

Abbey
Hillbery

Laxey Bay
Garwick Bay
Clay Head

Bank's Howe

5

Dalby
Dalby
Mt.
The Niarbyl

Foxdale
Barrule
739
S. Barrule
1585
Closeclark

Braaid
Kirk
Braddon

Cooil

Mount
Murray

Marine Dr.
DOUGLAS
Douglas Bay
Douglas Head

Niarbyl
Bay

Stuggadoo
St Marks
Ballavarre
Grenaby
Ballakilpheric
Ballabeg
Ballamodha
Ford

Port Soderick

Santon Head
Port Grenaugh

6

Fleshwick Bay
Bradda Mooar
Bradda Head
Port Erin
Four Roads
Cornvallie
Port
St Mary

Ballafesson
Colby
Croitecaley
Poolvash
B.
Cregneish

Malew
Ballabool
Ballasalla
ISLE OF MAN
(RONALDSWAY)
Derby Haven

Calf of
Man
Calf Sound
Perwick Bay
Spanish
Head
Castletown
Castletown
Bay
Langness
Point

ON THE SAME SCALE

SOUTHPORT

Caigher Point
Chicken R? L? Ho.

4800

The Edinburgh Geographical Institute

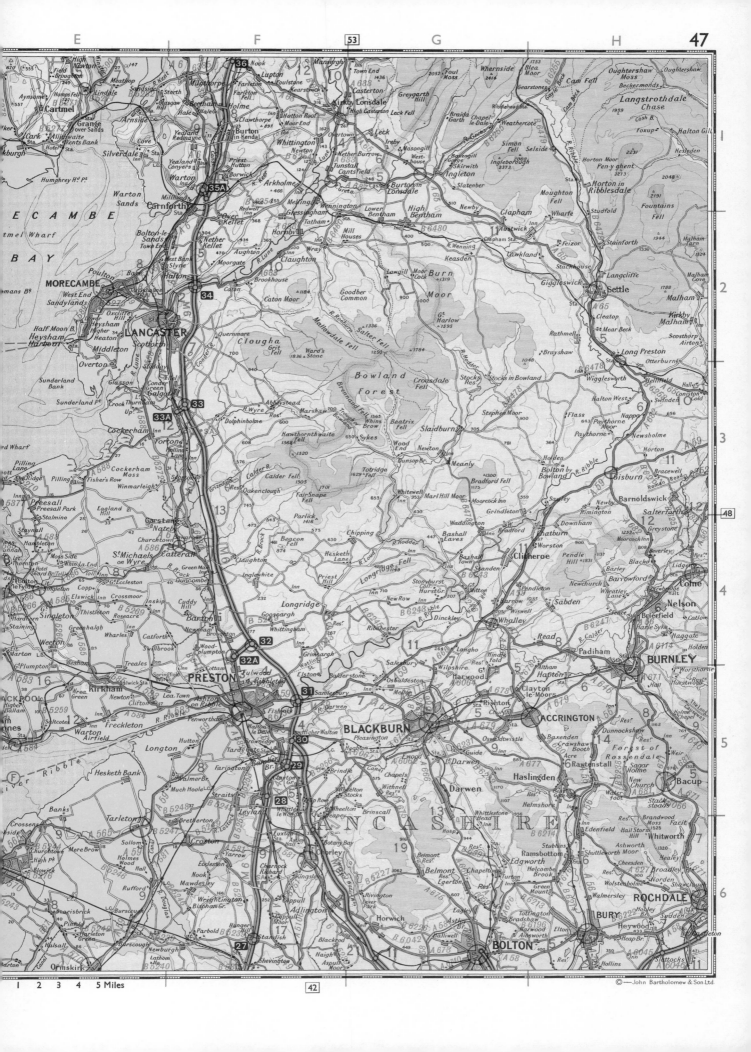

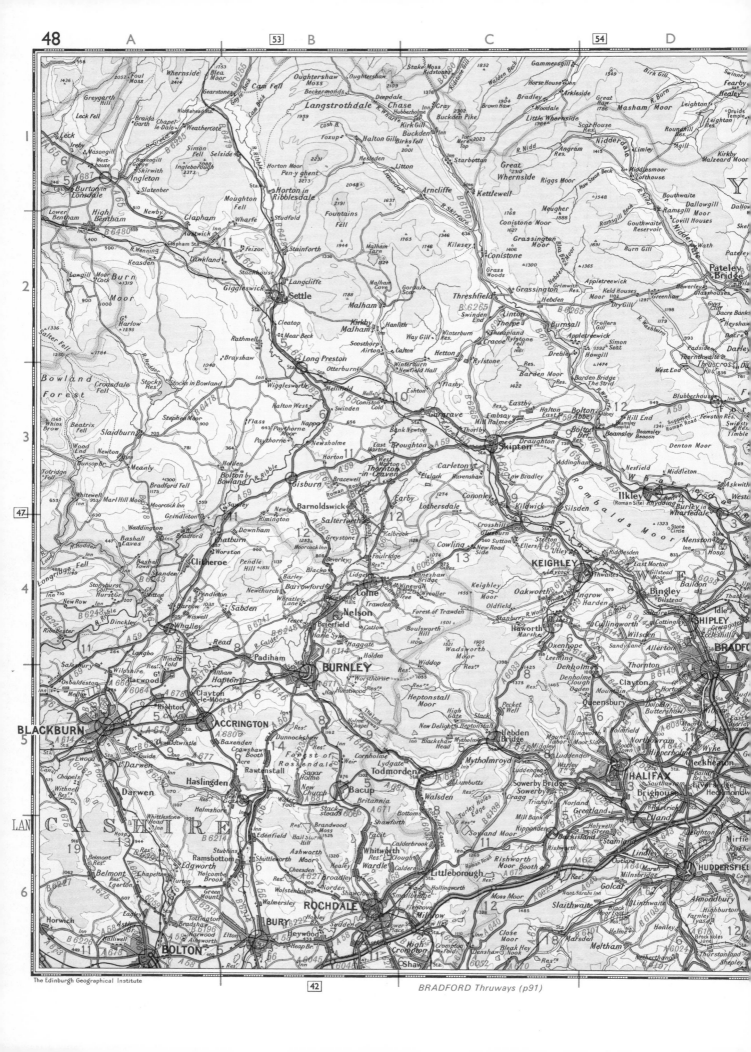

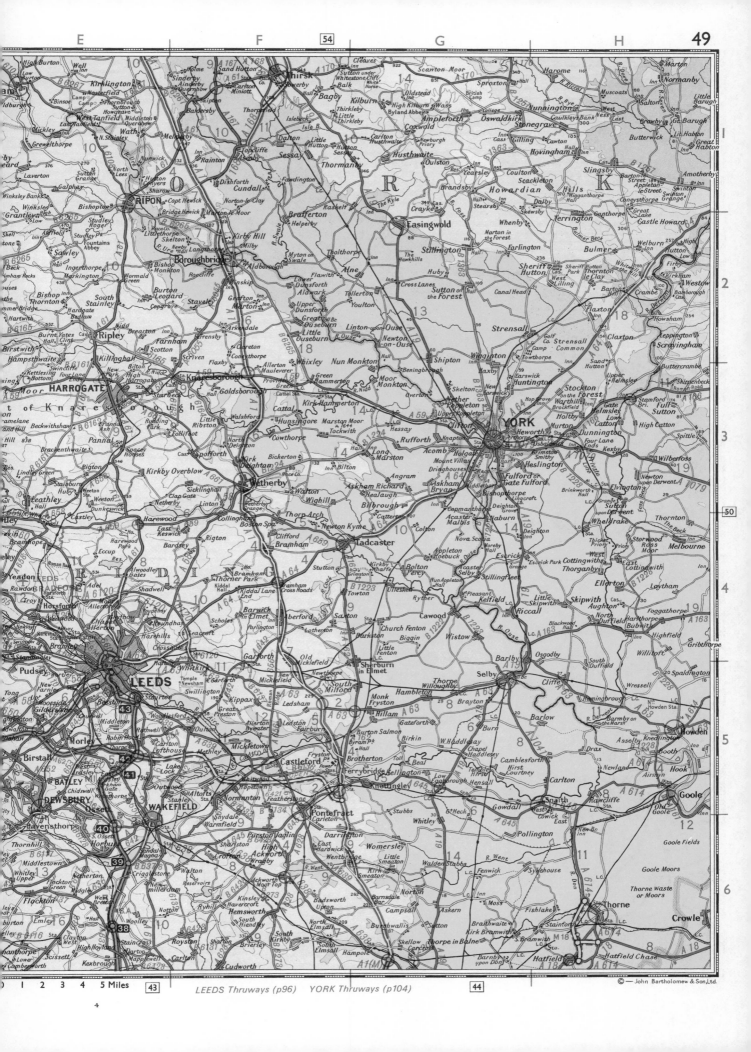

0 1 2 3 4 5 Miles

© — John Bartholomew & Son, Ltd.

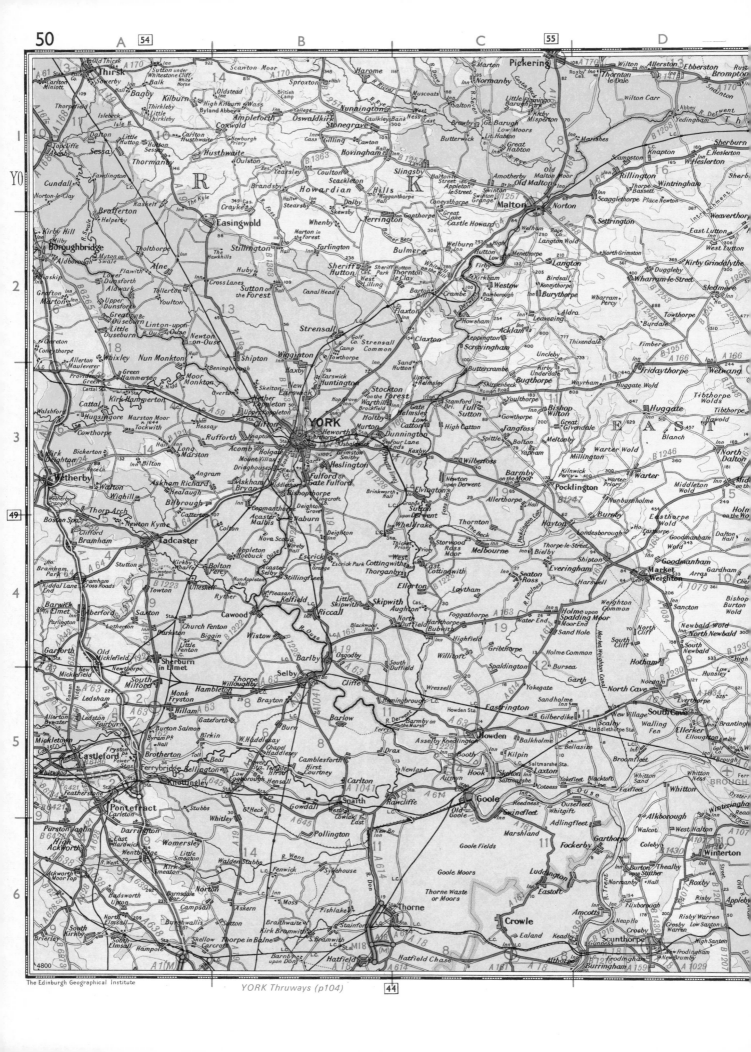

YORK Thruways (p104)

B R I D L I N G T O N

B A Y

RIVER

HUMBER

To Amsterdam

To Gothenburg

Spurn Head

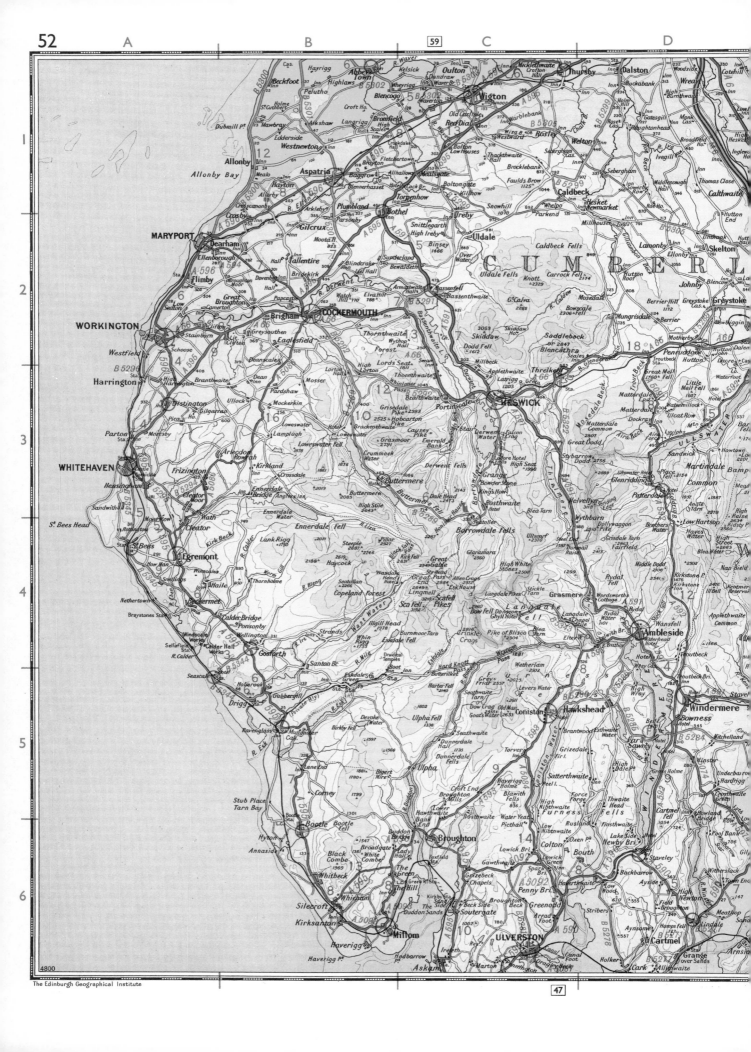

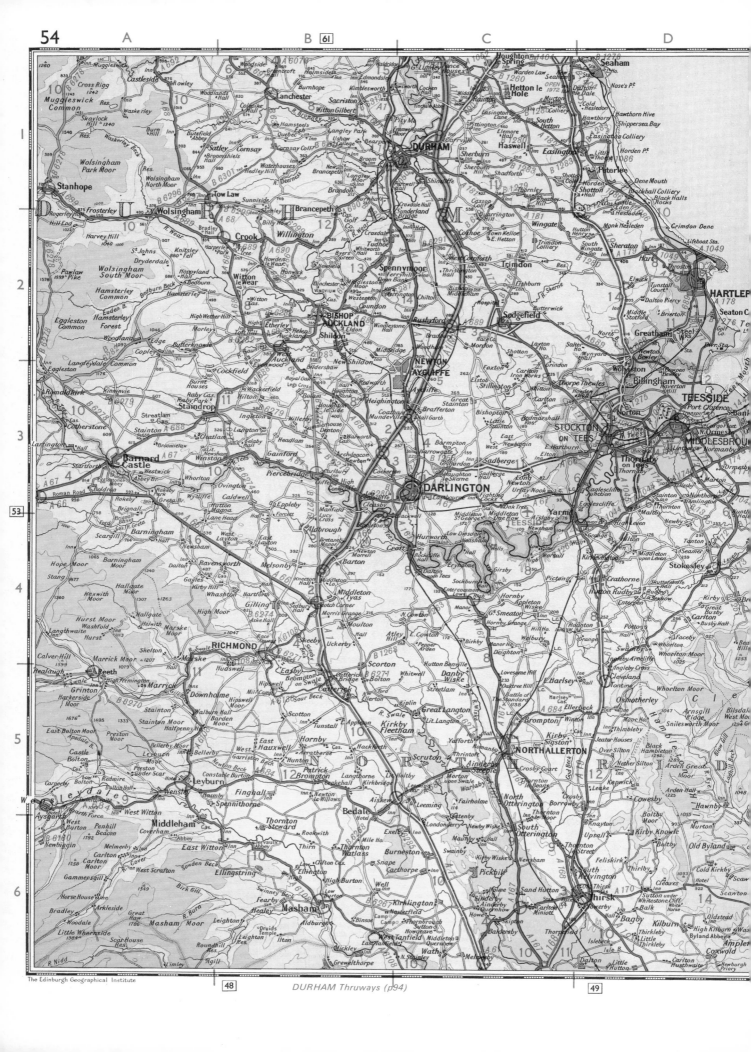

A   B   61   C   D

DURHAM

NORTH

DURHAM Thruways (p94)

The Edinburgh Geographical Institute

48   49

Stanhope
Wolsingham
Crook
Willington
Brancepeth
Lanchester
DURHAM
Sacriston
Witton Gilbert
Hetton le Hole
Seaham
Peterlee
Easington
Haswell
Trimdon
Sedgefield
Spennymoor
BISHOP AUCKLAND
Shildon
NEWTON AYCLIFFE
Wingate
HARTLEPOOL
Billingham
TEESSIDE
STOCKTON ON TEES
MIDDLESBROUGH
Norton
Thornaby on Tees
Yarm
DARLINGTON
Barnard Castle
Staindrop
Cockfield
Richmond
Catterick
NORTHALLERTON
Stokesley
Bedale
Leyburn
Middleham
Masham
Thirsk

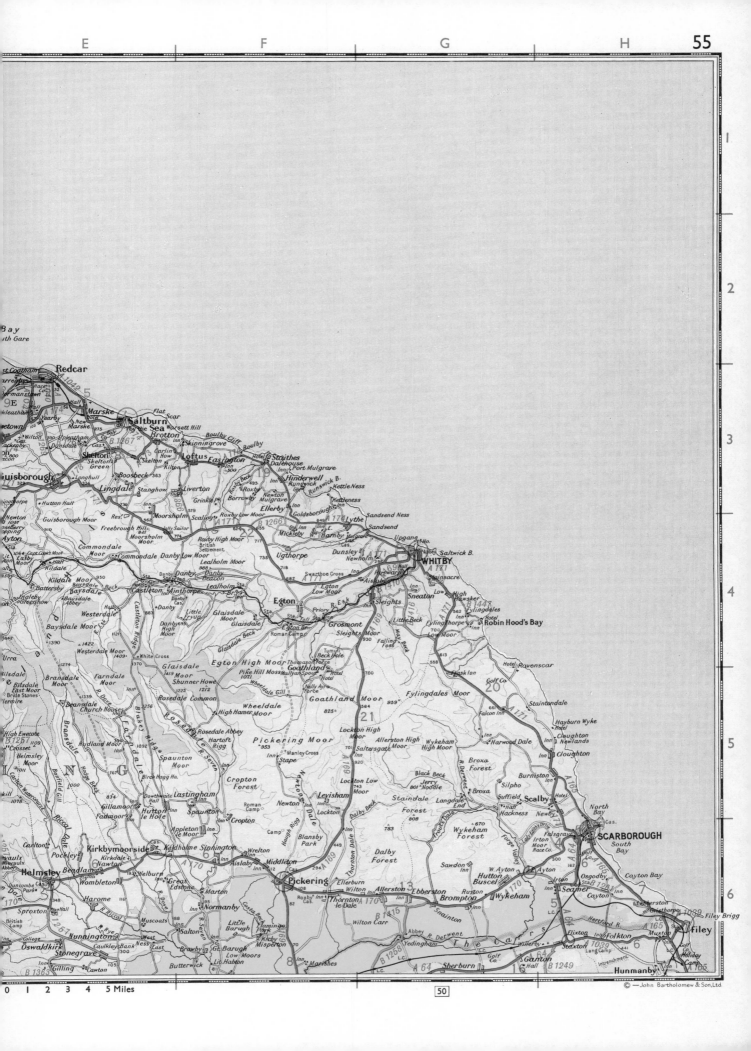

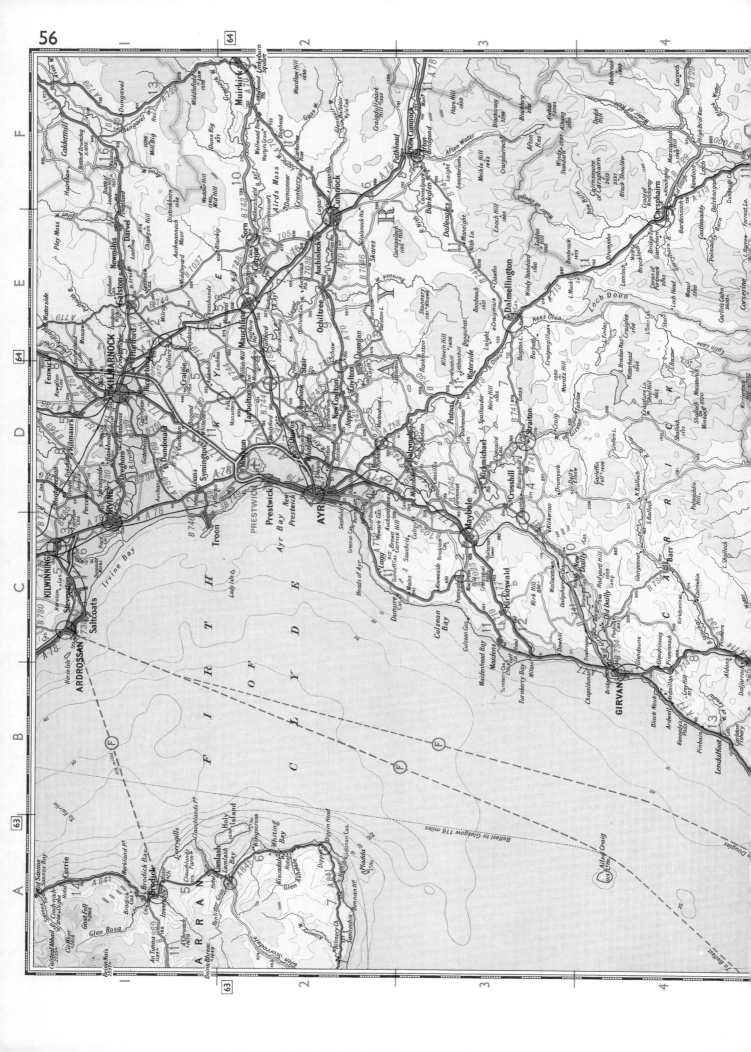

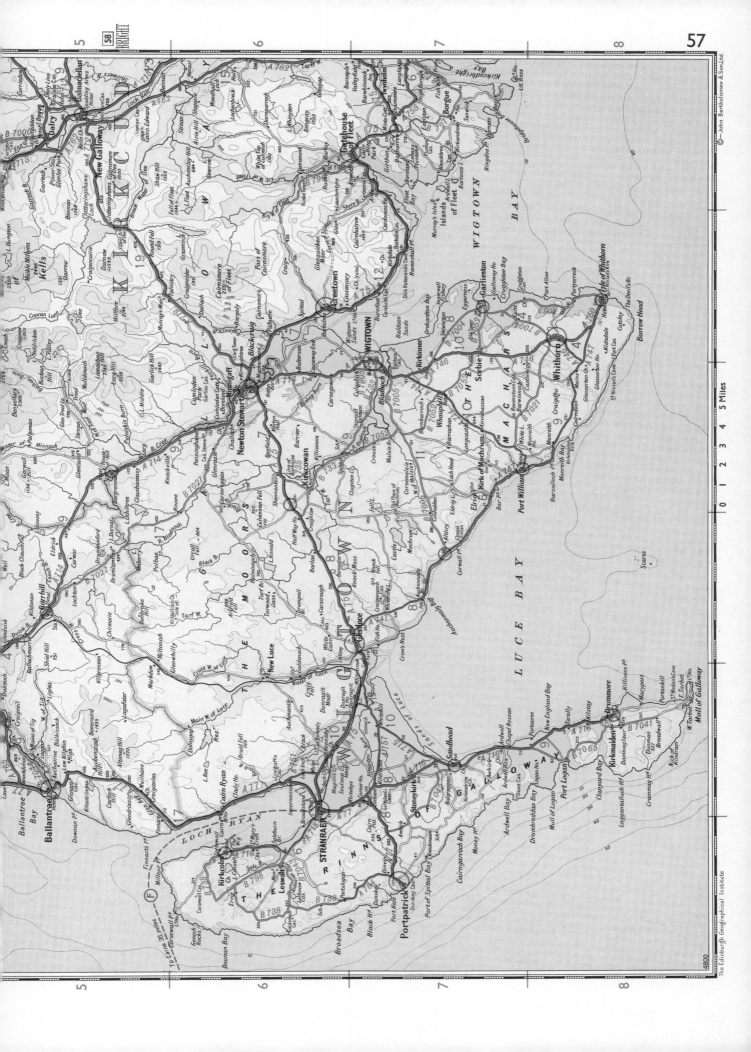

© John Bartholomew & Son,Ltd.

KIRKCUDBRIGHT

WIGTOWN BAY

LUCE BAY

MACHARS

THE MOORS

THE RINNS

OF GALLOWAY

Ballantrae Bay

LOCH RYAN

STRANRAER

Portpatrick

Newton Stewart

Kirkcowan

Glenluce

New Luce

New Galloway

Dalry

BalmaClellan

Gatehouse of Fleet

Creetown

WIGTOWN

Minnigaff

Kirkinner

Sorbie

Garlieston

Whithorn

Isle of Whithorn

Burrow Head

Port William

Sandhead

Port Logan

Kirkmaiden

Drummore

Mull of Galloway

Mull of Logan

Kirkcolm

Leswalt

Stoneykirk

Kells

Mull of Logan

0 1 2 3 4 5 Miles

to Larne 35 miles
Corsewall Pt.
Milleur Pt.
Finnart's Pt.

Cairn Ryan

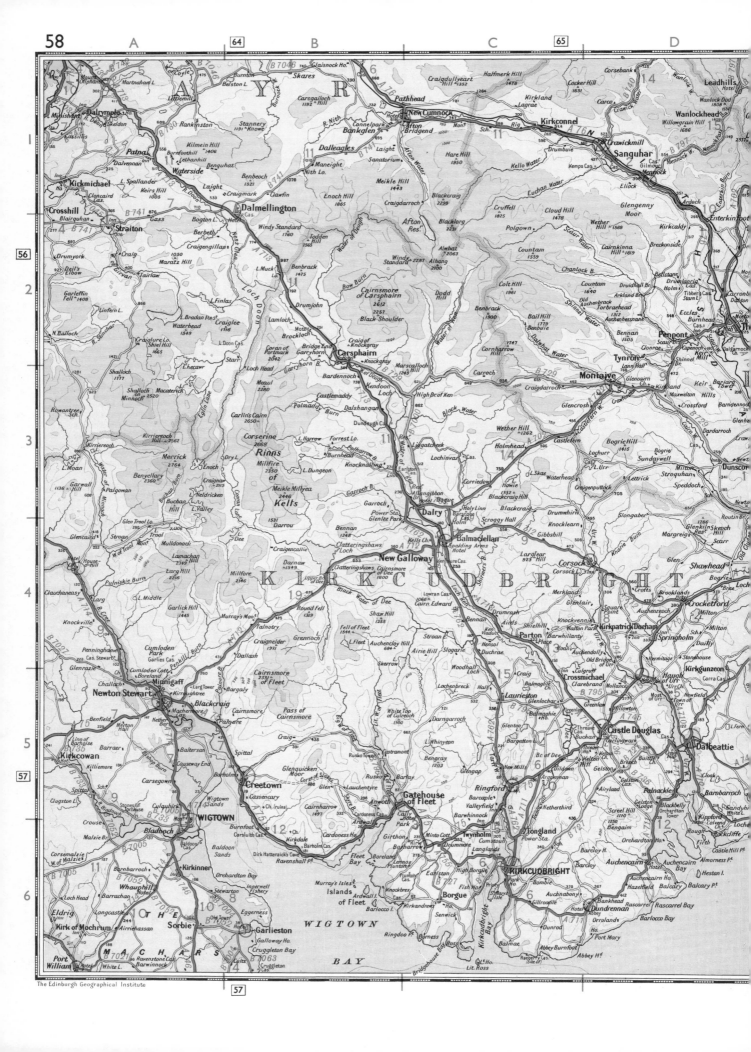

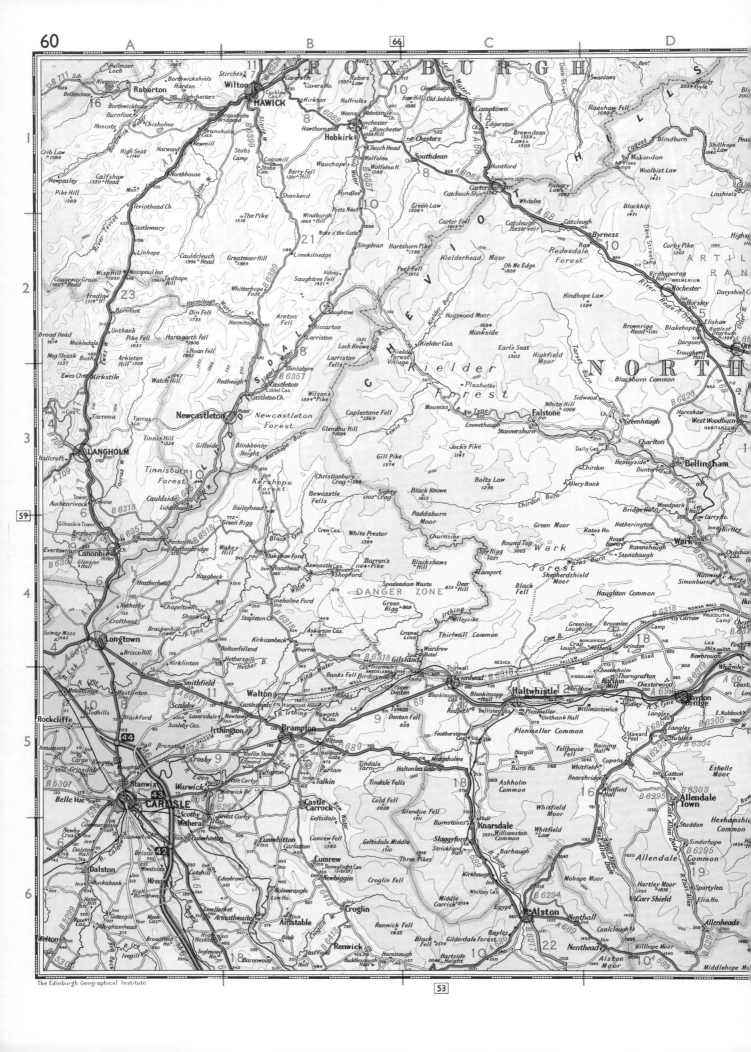

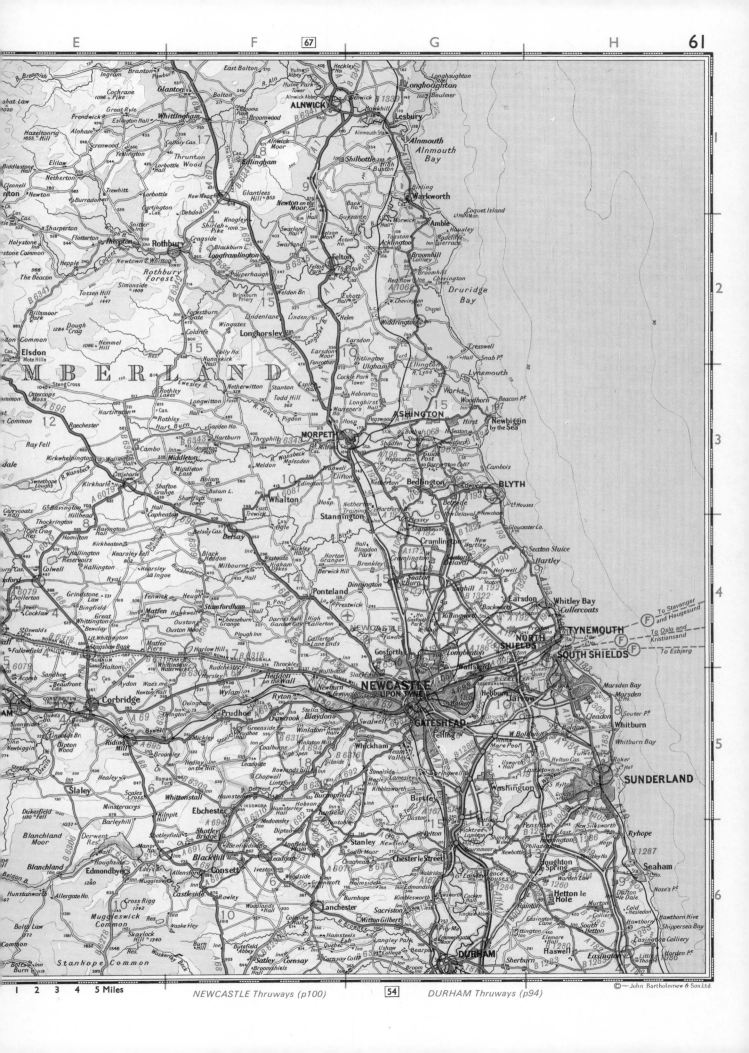

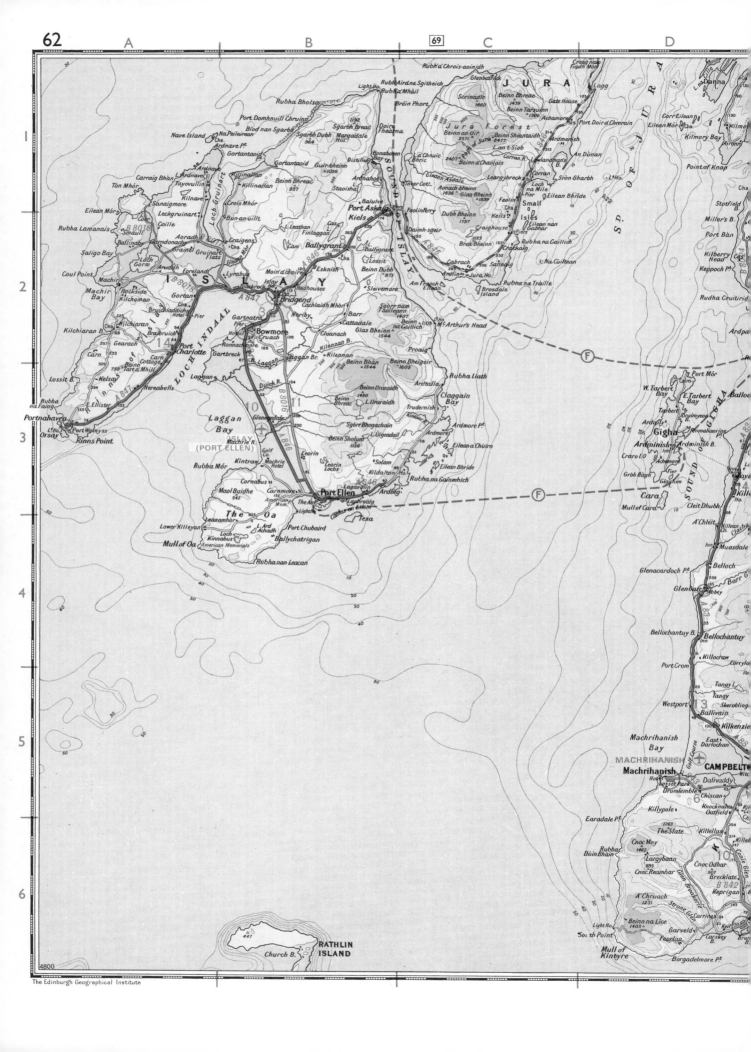

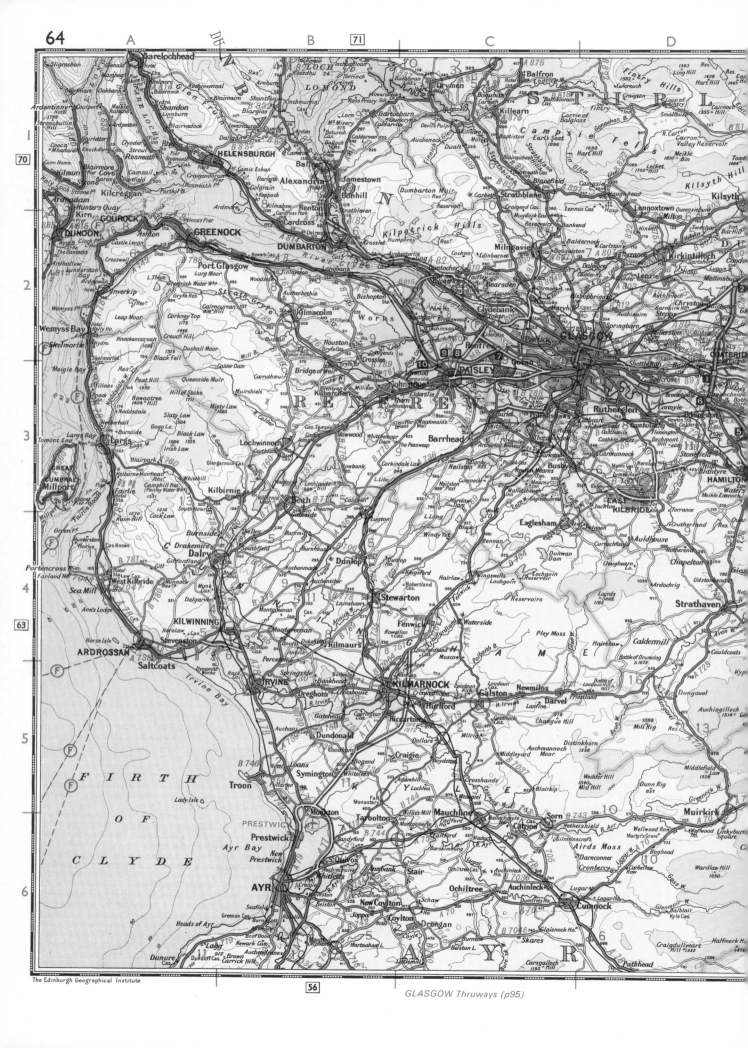

A   B   71   C   D

1

70

2

3

63

4

5

6

DUNBARTON

LOCH
LOMOND

STIRLING

Garelochhead
Hotel

Sligachan
Glenald
Manberg
Balernock
Oakbank
Blairmain
Blairglas
Shantron

Ardentinny
Hotel
Stronchullin
Hill
Coulport
Meikle
Rahane
Shandon
Linnburn
Hydro
Arkleston

HELENSBURGH
Cameron
Ho.
Balloch

Drymen
Boquhan
Endrick

Killearn

Campsie
Fells
Earl's Seat
1896

Fintry
Hills

Ling Hill
Hart Hill

STIRLING

Cairnoch
Hill

Balfron

Kilsyth

Lennoxtown
Milton

Kirkintilloch

Campsie
Hill

Kilsyth Hill

Alexandria

Jamestown
Bonhill
Renton
Cardross

Dumbarton Muir

Strathblane
Blanefield

Milngavie
Bearsden

GLASGOW

Clydebank

PAISLEY

Johnstone

RENFREW

Port Glasgow

GREENOCK

DUMBARTON

GOUROCK
DUNOON

Wemyss Bay

Skelmorlie

Largs

GREAT
CUMBRAE
Millport

West Kilbride

ARDROSSAN
Saltcoats

Kilwinning
Stevenston

IRVINE

Troon

PRESTWICK
Prestwick
New
Prestwick

AYR

Beith

Dalry

Kilbirnie

Lochwinnoch

Barrhead

Neilston

Stewarton

Fenwick

Kilmaurs

KILMARNOCK

Galston
Darvel

Newmilns

Muirkirk

Dundonald

Symington

Mauchline
Catrine
Sorn

Tarbolton

Ochiltree
Auchinleck

Cumnock

FIRTH

OF

CLYDE

AYR

RENFREW

HAMILTON

East
Kilbride

Rutherglen

COATBRIDGE

Eaglesham

Strathaven

Coylton

Strathblane

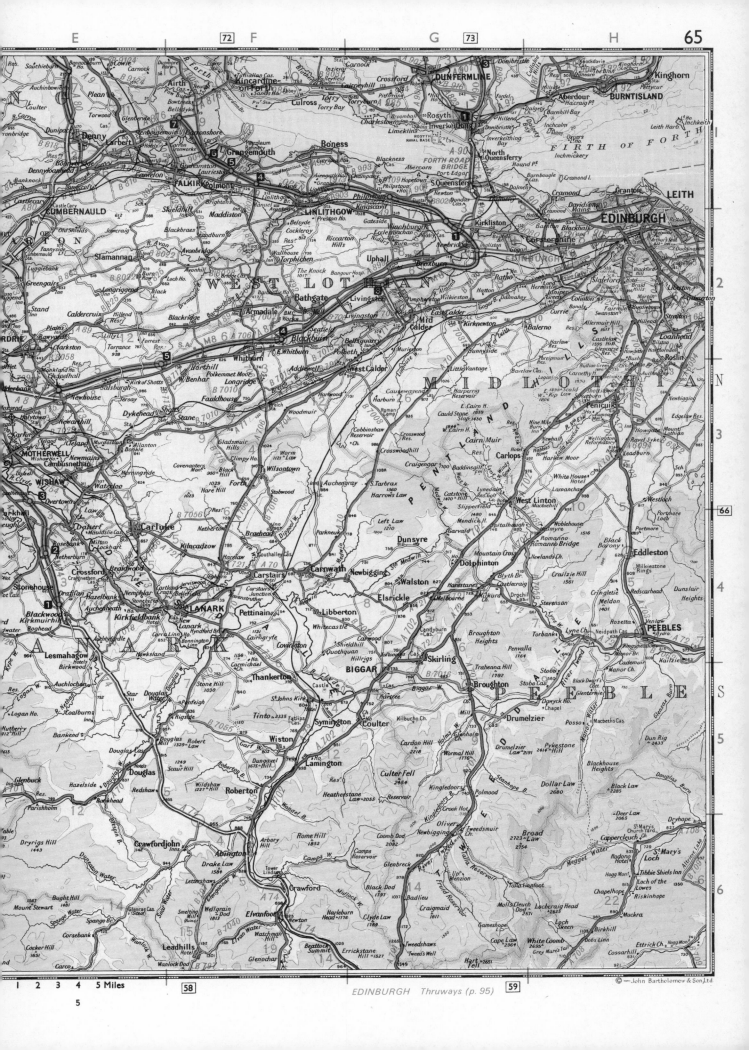

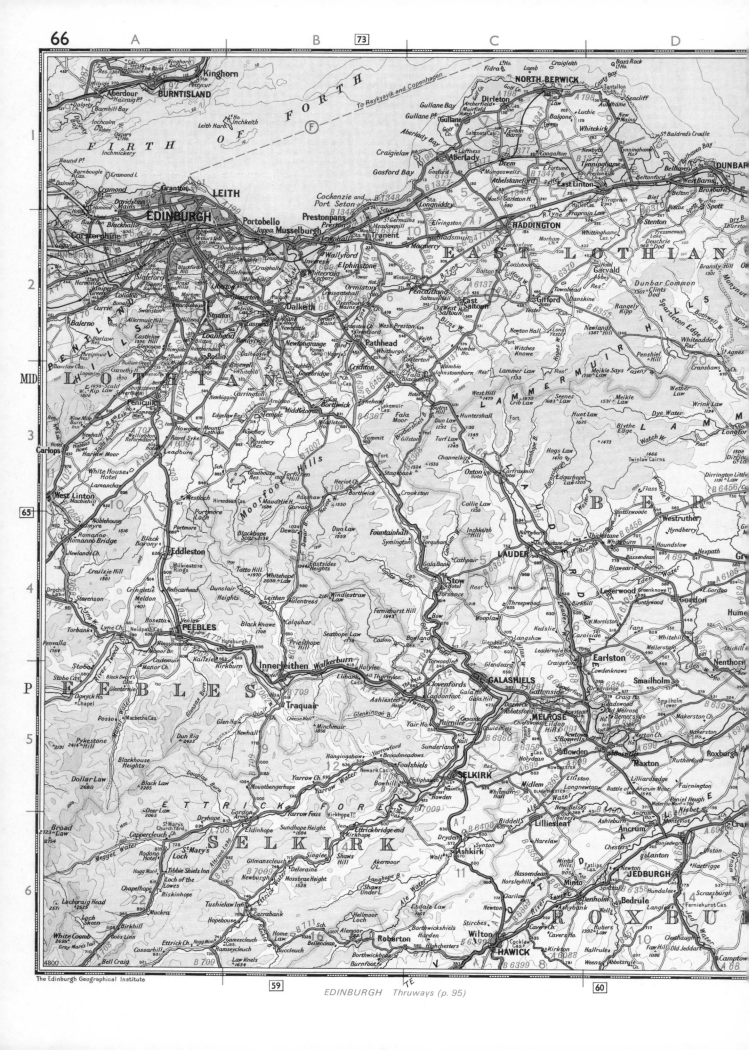

A   B   73   C   D

FIRTH OF FORTH

To Reykjavik and Copenhagen

NORTH BERWICK

DUNBAR

Kinghorn
Aberdour
BURNTISLAND

Inchkeith

Dirleton
Gullane Bay
Gullane Pt.
Gullane

Aberlady Bay
Gosford Bay
Craigielaw

Aberlady
Drem
Whitekirk
East Linton

GRANTON
LEITH
Portobello
Musselburgh
Prestonpans
Cockenzie and
Port Seton
Longniddry
Tranent
Elvingston

HADDINGTON

EAST LOTHIAN

EDINBURGH
Corstorphine
Slateford
Colinton
Currie
Balerno

Dalkeith
Elphinstone
Ormiston
Pencaitland
East Saltoun
West Saltoun
Gifford
Garvald
Dunbar Common

Penicuik
Loanhead
Roslin
Bonnyrigg
Gorebridge
Pathhead
Crichton
Fala
Humbie

LAMMERMUIR HILLS

MID LOTHIAN

West Linton
Carlops
Eddleston
Romanno Bridge

Temple
Middleton
Heriot
Fountainhall
Stow

Oxton
LAUDER

BERWICK

Westruther

PEEBLES

Innerleithen
Walkerburn
Traquair

Clovenfords
GALASHIELS
Earlston
Smailholm

PEEBLES

MELROSE
Abbotsford
St. Boswells
Bowden
Maxton
Roxburgh

SELKIRK

ETTRICK FOREST

Yarrow
Ashkirk
Lilliesleaf
Ancrum
JEDBURGH
Bedrule

ROXBURGH

HAWICK
Roberton
Wilton

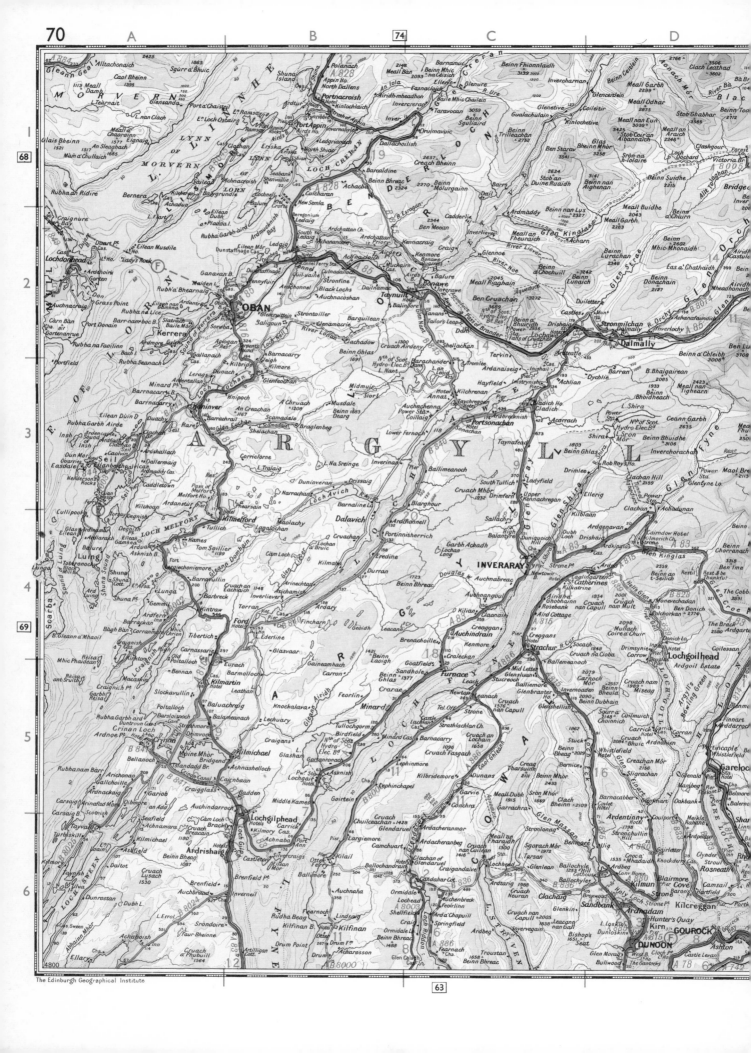

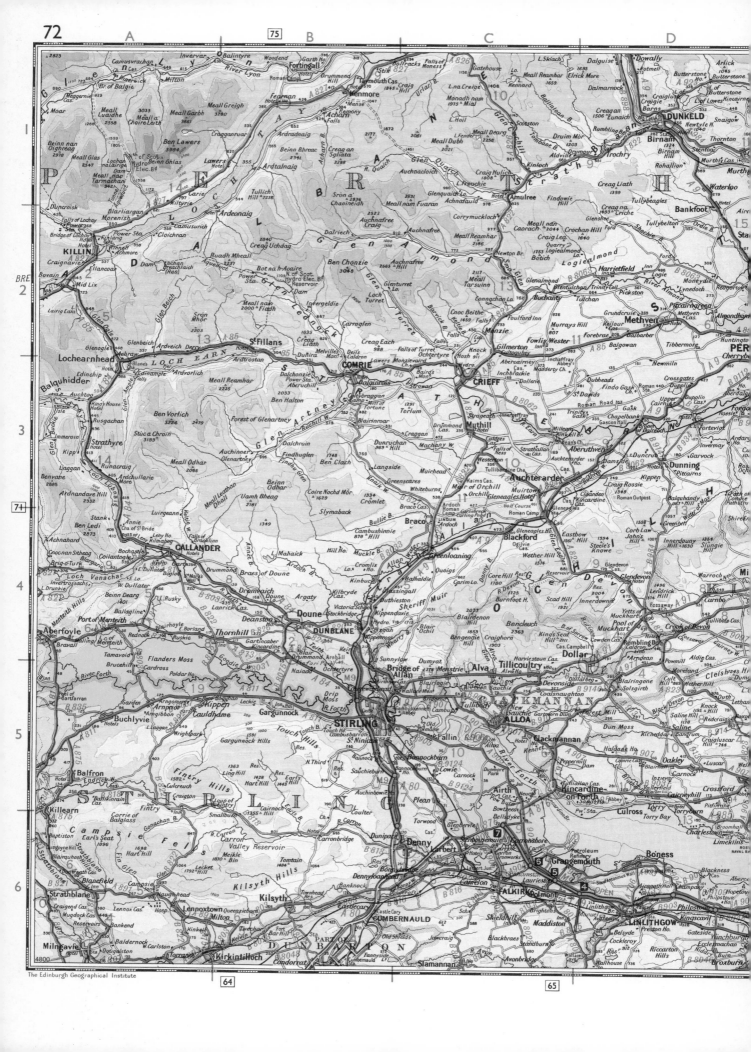

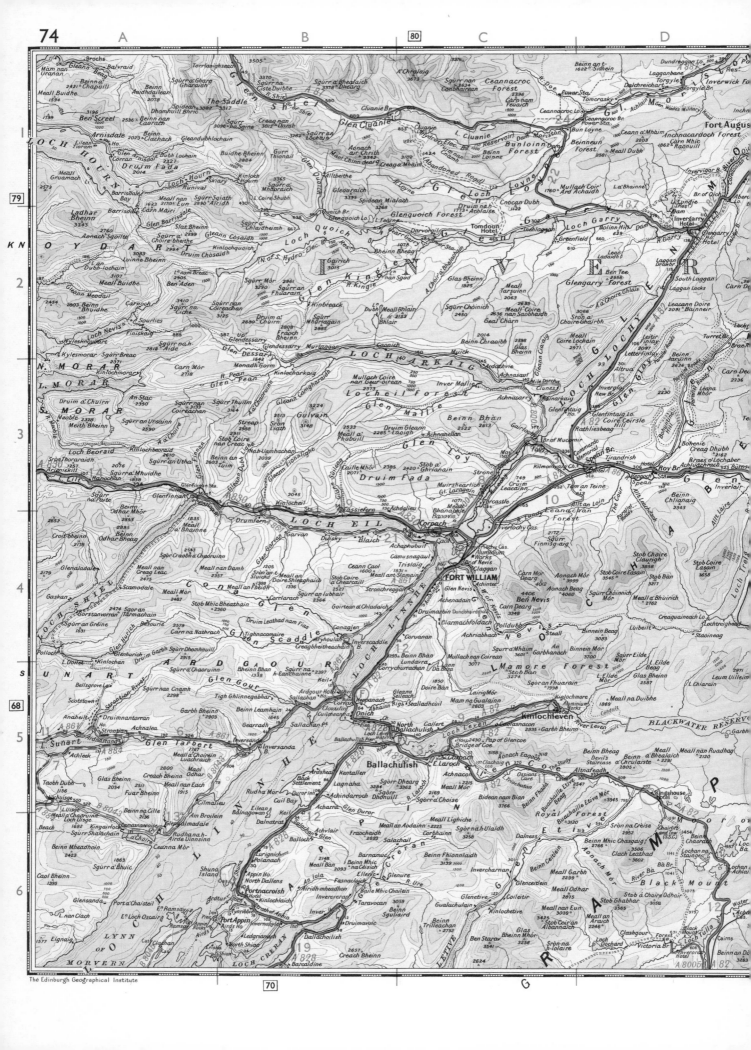

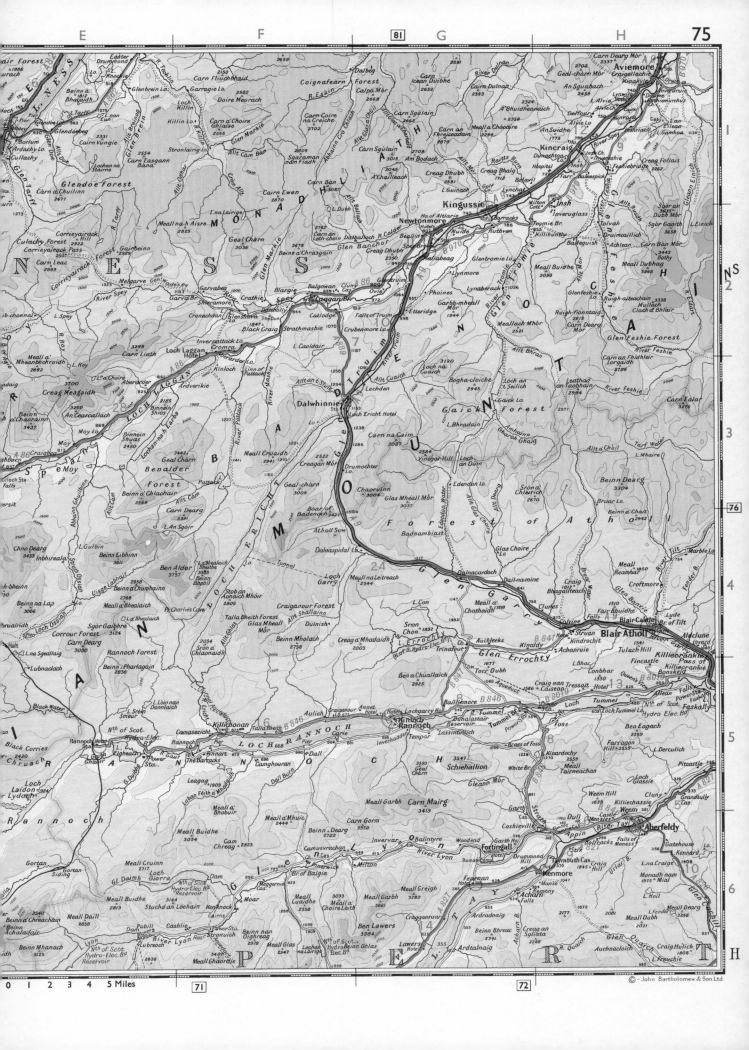

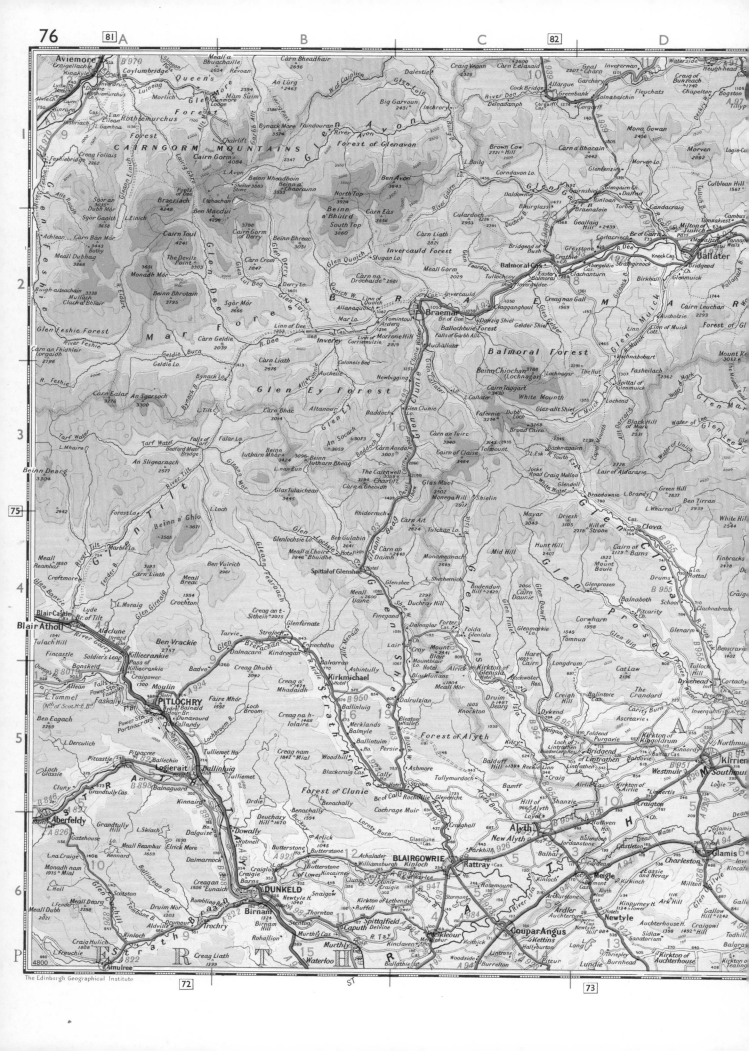

ABERDEEN

Girdle Ness
Nigg Bay

Cove Bay
Hare Ness
Earnsheugh Bay

Portlethen
Downies

Skateraw
Muchalls
Doonie Point
Cas. Rock of Muchalls

STONEHAVEN
Strathlethan Bay
Dunnottar Cas.
Thornyhive Bay
Trelung Ness

Crawton

Catterline
Todhead Pt

Kinneff

Inverbervie
Bervie Bay
Doolie Ness

FOREST OF BIRSE

KINCARDINE

MEARNS

HOWE OF THE MEARNS

Johnshaven
Milton Ness

St Cyrus
R. North Esk

Distillery

MONTROSE
R. South Esk
Scurdie Ness

Lunan Bay

Red Head

Whiting Ness
ARBROATH

Carlingheugh Bay
Auchmithie

ANGUS

FORFAR

BRECHIN

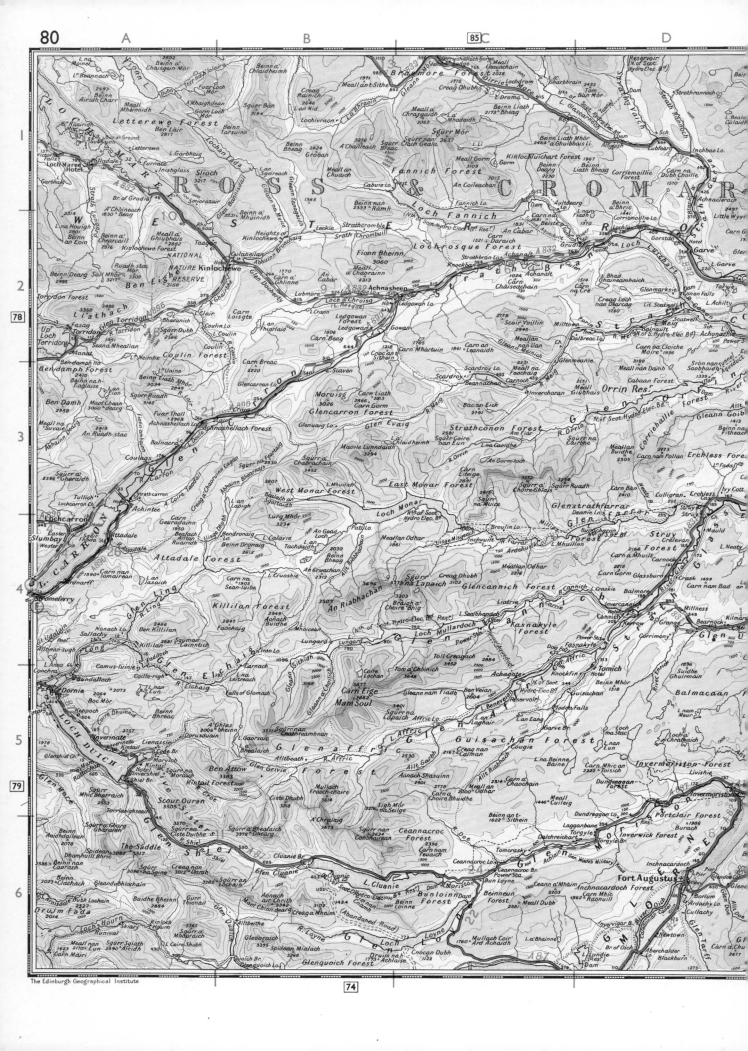

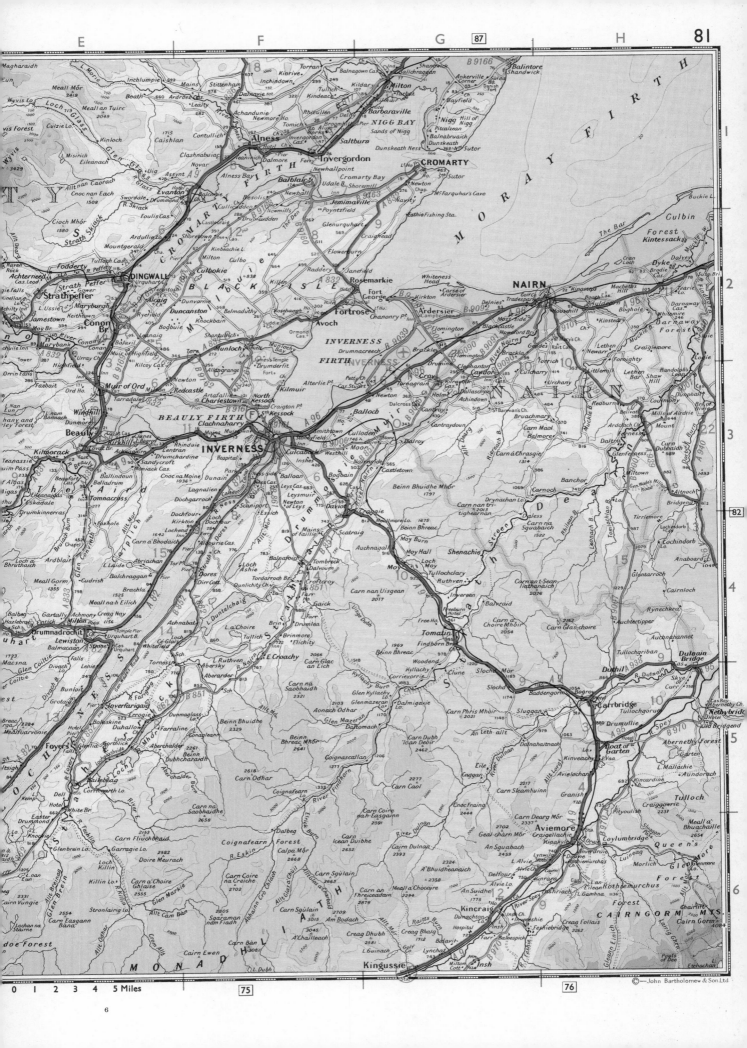

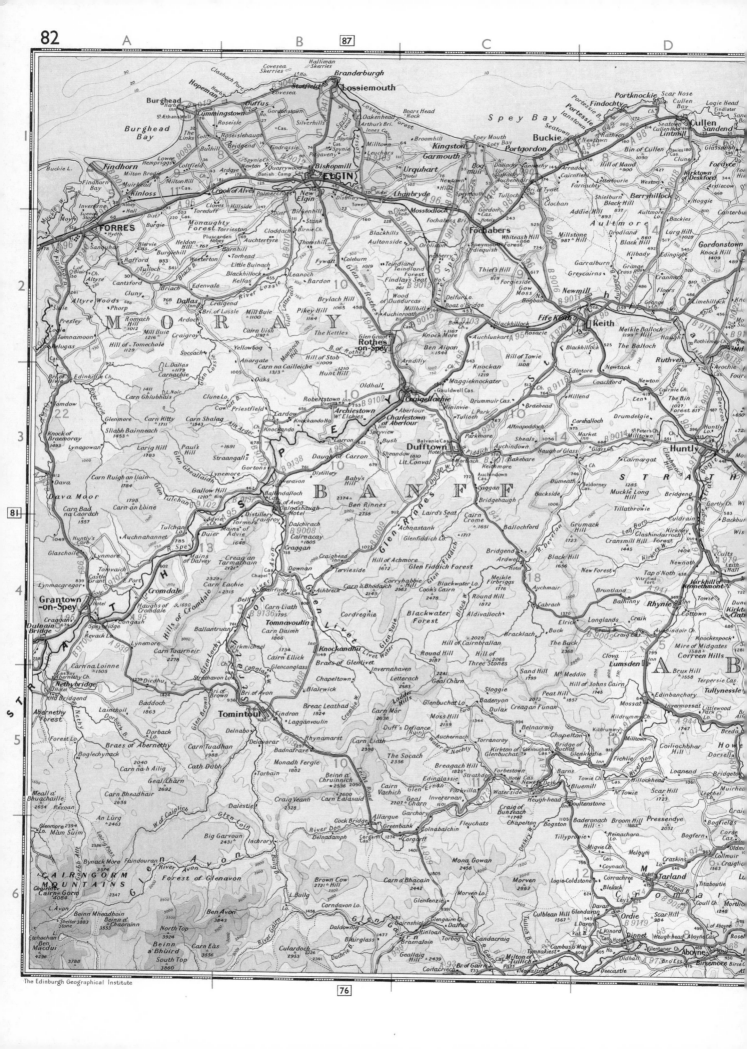

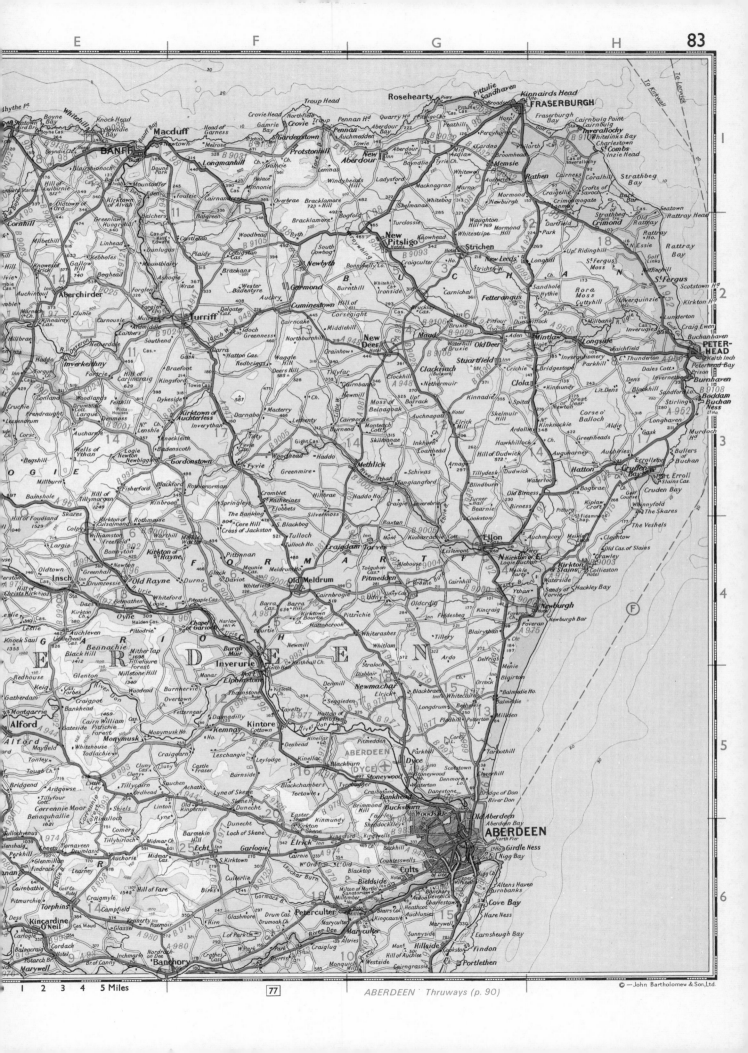

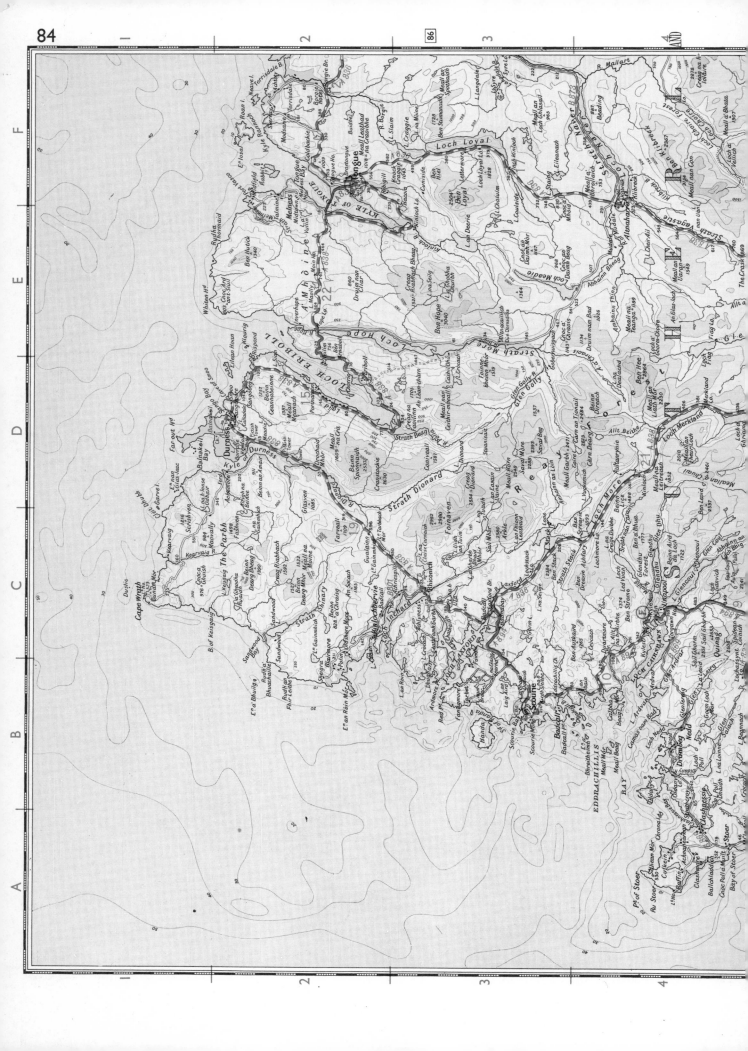

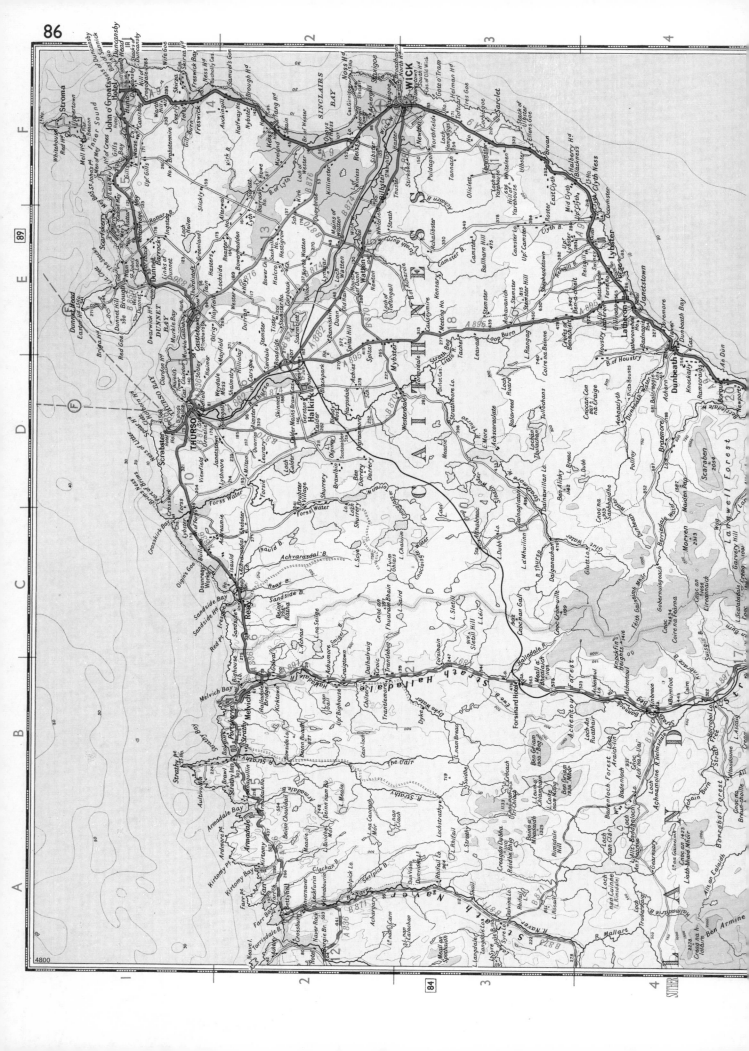

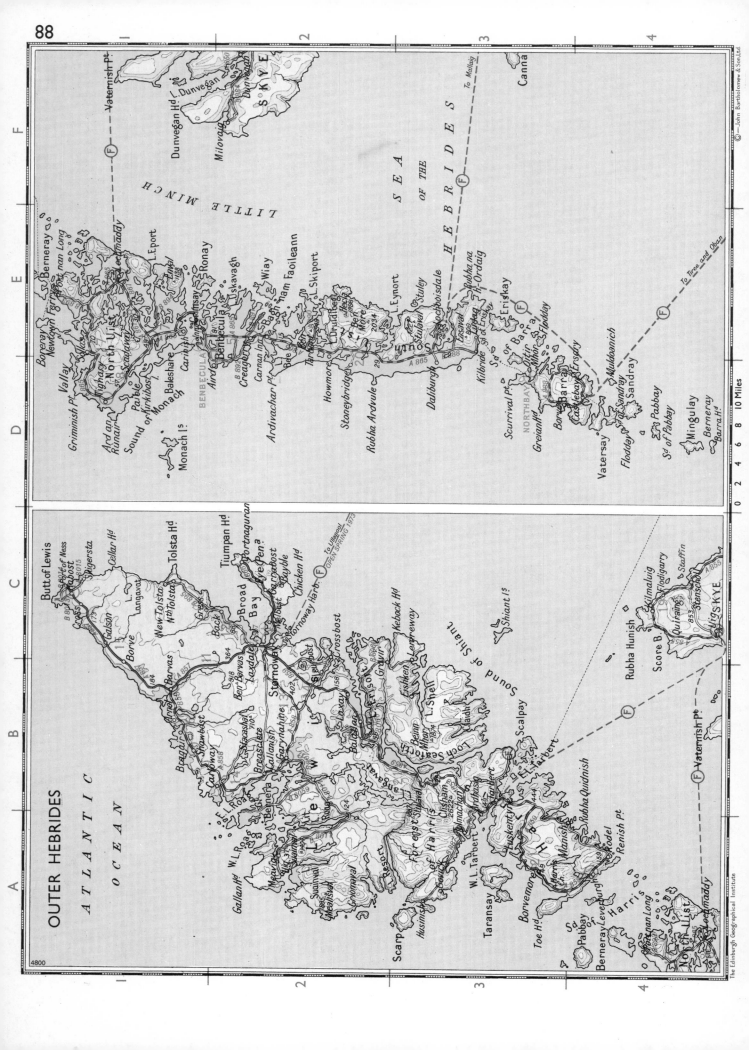

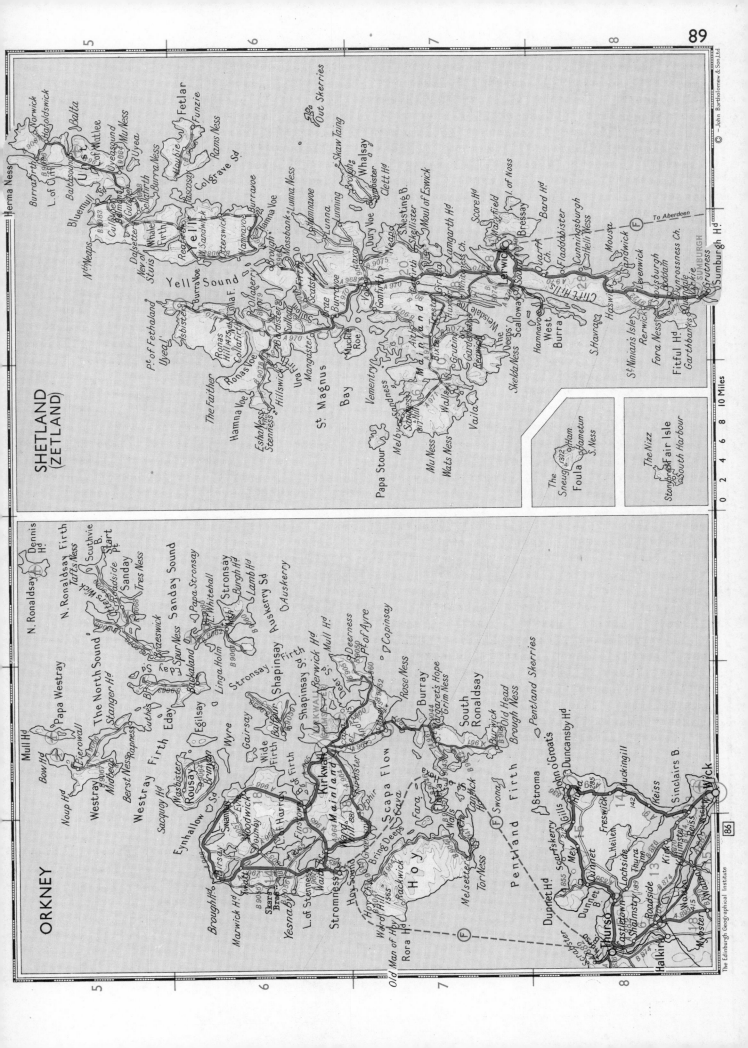

SHETLAND
(ZETLAND)

ORKNEY

Herma Ness

Norwick
Haroldswick
Balta
Burrafirth
L. of Cliff
Battlsound
Uyeasound
Mu Ness
U. of Matlee
Uyea
N. Neaps
Bluemull
Cullswick
Burra Ness
Haroldswick
Fetlar
Funzie
Rams Ness
Colgrave Sd.
Muckle
Haubie
Y e l l
Whale Firth
Mid Yell
Reafirth
Burravoe
Out Skerries
Dalsetter
Hev of Grind
Skaw Taing
Whalsay
W. Sandwick
Otterswick
Namavoe
Hamna Voe
Lunna Ness
Vidlin
Pt. of Fethaland
Ronas
Hill
Yell Sound
Colafirth
Yell
Brough
Boddam
Skellister
Nesting B.
Clett Hd.
Moul of Eswick
Scarf Hd.
I. of Noss
Bressay
Bard Hd.
To Aberdeen
Uyeal
Ura Firth
Hillswick
Ronas Voe
Sullom
Voe
Mangaster
Muckle
Roe
Voe
Gonfirth
Aith
Firth
Whiteness
Tingwall
Sound
Lerwick
Quarff
Fladdabister
Cunningsburgh
Helli Ness
Mousa
Sandwick
Lerwick
Dunrossness Ch.
SUMBURGH
Scatness
Grutness
Sumburgh Hd.
The Faither
Hamna Voe
Eshaness
Stenness
St. Magnus
Bay
Melby
Sandness
Vementry
Reawick
Tresta
Weisdale
Scalloway
Gardie
The
Deeps
Skelda Ness
Hamnavoe
West
Burra
S. Havra
St. Ninian's Isle
Fora Ness
Fitful Hd.
Garthbanks
Quendale
Ruvie
Papa Stour
Mu Ness
Wats Ness
Vaila
Walls
Sandness
Foula
The
Sneug
Ham
Hametun
S. Ness
The Nizz
Stonybrek
Fair Isle
South Harbour

0   2   4   6   8   10 Miles

N. Ronaldsay
Dennis Hd.
Tafts Ness
Start
Pt.
Sanday
Seal Skerry
N. Ronaldsay Firth
Scuthie B.
Broadside
Tres Ness
Mull Hd.
Bow Hd.
Papa Westray
Pierowall
Noup Hd.
The North Sound
Stanger Hd.
Midbea
Berst Ness
Sacquoy Hd.
Braeswick
Whitehall
Stronsay
Papa Stronsay
Lamb Hd.
Burgh Hd.
Sanday Sound
Spur Ness
Eday
Linga Holm
Auskerry
Westray Firth
Washister
Rousay
Wyre
Egilsay
Gairsay
Stronsay
Firth
Shapinsay Sd.
Shapinsay
Mull Hd.
Deerness
Auskerry
Pt. of Ayre
Rose Ness
Copinsay
Eynhallow
Brinyan
Wide
Firth
KIRKWALL
Deer
Ness
Berwick Hd.
Finstown
Orphir
Mainland
Birsay
Marwick Hd.
Dounby
Harray
Skara Brae
Yesnaby
L. of Stenness
Stromness
Hoy Sound
Graemsay
Scapa Flow
Walls
Cava
Flotta
Swona
Stroma
Burray
Margaret's Hope
Grim Ness
South Ronaldsay
Old Head
Brough Ness
Pentland Skerries
Brough Hd.
Ward Hill
Hoy
Melsetter
Tor Ness
Old Man of Hoy
Rora Hd.
Pentland Firth
Duncansby Hd.
John o'Groats
Gills
Scarfskerry
Mey
Dunnet Hd.
Dunnet
Castletown
Thurso
Halkirk
Freswick
Keiss
Sinclairs B.
Wick
Myster
Watten
Reiss

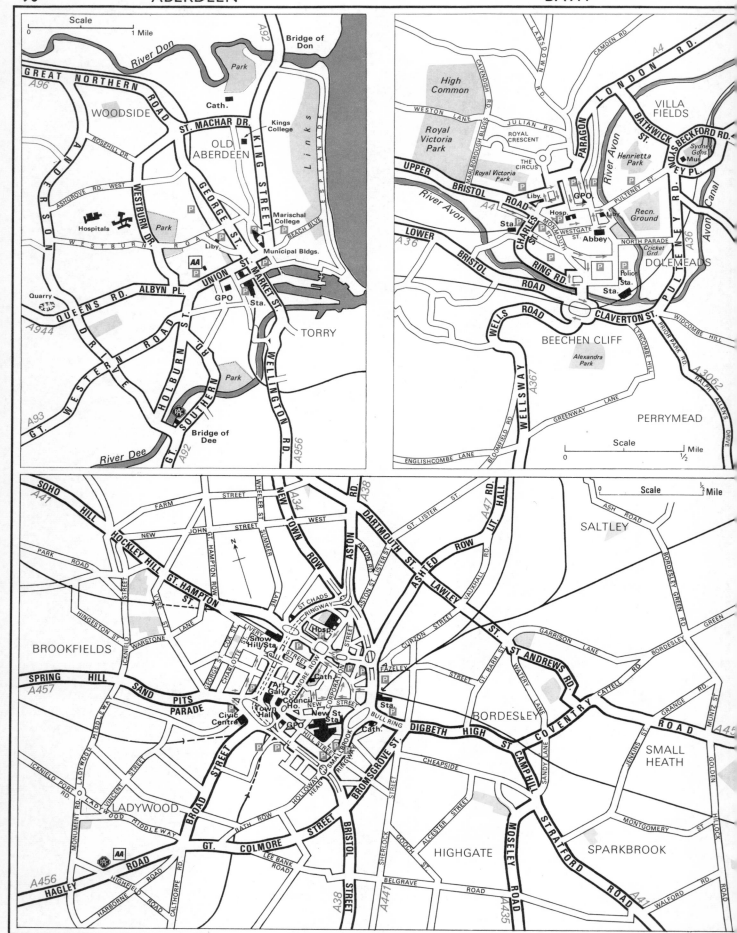

One-way Streets →   Car Parks   © John Bartholomew & Son Ltd

ABERDEEN

Scale 0 1 Mile

River Don
A92
Bridge of Don
Park
GREAT NORTHERN ROAD
A96
Cath.
WOODSIDE
ST. MACHAR DR.
Kings College
OLD ABERDEEN
Links
ROSEHILL DR.
ANDERSON
ASHGROVE RD. WEST
WESTBURN DR.
GEORGE ST.
KING STREET
ESPLANADE
Hospitals
Park
WESTBURN ROAD
P
Liby.
Marischal College
BEACH BLVD.
Municipal Bldgs.
AA P
UNION ST.
MARKET ST.
Quarry
QUEENS RD.
ALBYN PL.
GPO
Sta.
HOLBURN RD.
DRIVE
WESTERN ROAD
A944
A93
GT. SOUTHERN A92
TORRY
Park
WELLINGTON RD.
A456
Bridge of Dee
River Dee

BATH

A4
CAMDEN RD.
LANSDOWN RD.
LONDON RD.
VILLA FIELDS
High Common
WESTON LANE
CAVENDISH RD.
JULIAN RD.
PARAGON
BATHWICK ST.
BECKFORD RD.
Royal Victoria Park
MARLBOROUGH BLDGS.
ROYAL CRESCENT
THE CIRCUS
SYDNEY PL.
Sydney Gdns.
Mus.
UPPER BRISTOL ROAD
Royal Victoria Park
River Avon
Henrietta Park
River Avon
A41
Liby.
P
P
GPO
PULTENEY ST.
LOWER BRISTOL ROAD
A36
Hosp.
Sta.
CHARLES ST.
MONMOUTH
WESTGATE ST.
Liby.
Recn. Ground
PULTENEY RD.
BRISTOL
Abbey
NORTH PARADE
RING RD.
P
Cricket Grd.
DOLEMEADS
P
Police Sta.
A36
Sta.
Avon Canal
WELLS ROAD
CLAVERTON ST.
WIDCOMBE HILL
BEECHEN CLIFF
PRIOR PARK RD.
RALPH ALLEN'S DRIVE
WELLSWAY
A367
Alexandra Park
LYNCOMBE HILL
A3062
ENGLISHCOMBE LANE
BLOOMFIELD RD.
GREENWAY LANE
PERRYMEAD
Scale 0 ½ Mile

BIRMINGHAM

Scale 0 ½ Mile
SOHO HILL
A41
FARM STREET
WHEELER ST.
NEW TOWN ROW
A34
WEST
ASTON RD.
DARTMOUTH ST.
A38
GT. LISTER ST.
UT. HALL RD.
A47 RD.
ASH ROAD
SALTLEY
HOCKLEY HILL
NEW JOHN STREET WEST
GT. HAMPTON ROW
SUMMER LANE
ASTON ST.
ASHTED ROW
PARK ROAD
HINGESTON ST.
VYSE ST.
GT. HAMPTON ST.
ST. CHADS RINGWAY
LAWLEY ST.
BORDESLEY GREEN RD.
BROOKFIELDS
WARSTONE LANE
ICKNIELD ST.
LIVERY ST.
COX ST.
CHARLOTTE ST.
Hosp.
Snow Hill Sta.
CURZON STREET
VAUXHALL RD.
GARRISON LANE
ST. ANDREWS RD.
BORDESLEY
SPRING HILL
A457
SAND PITS PARADE
GEORGE ST.
COLMORE ROW
Art Galy.
Council Ho.
FAZELEY ST.
GT. BARR ST.
WATERY LANE
CATTELL RD.
COVENTRY ROAD
A45
Civic Centre
Town Hall
New St. Sta.
GPO
Cath.
BULL RING RINGWAY
Sta.
DIGBETH HIGH ST.
BORDESLEY
CAMPHILL
SMALL HEATH
ICKNIELD PORT RD.
LADYWOOD MIDDLEWAY
SMALLBROOK RINGWAY
BROMSGROVE ST.
CHEAPSIDE
SANDY LANE
JENKINS STREET
GRANGE RD.
MUNTZ ST.
GOLDEN
LADYWOOD
VINCENT STREET
BATH ROW
HOLLOWAY HEAD
BRISTOL STREET
SHERLOCK STREET
GOOCH STREET
ALCESTER STREET
MONTGOMERY ST.
STRATFORD ROAD
A41
SPARKBROOK
MONUMENT RD.
LADYWOOD MIDDLEWAY
BROAD STREET
GT. COLMORE STREET
LEE BANK ROAD
BELGRAVE ROAD
HIGHGATE
MOSELEY ROAD
A435
AA
HAGLEY ROAD
A456
HIGHFIELD ROAD
HARBORNE ROAD
CALTHORPE ROAD
A38
A441
WALFORD ROAD

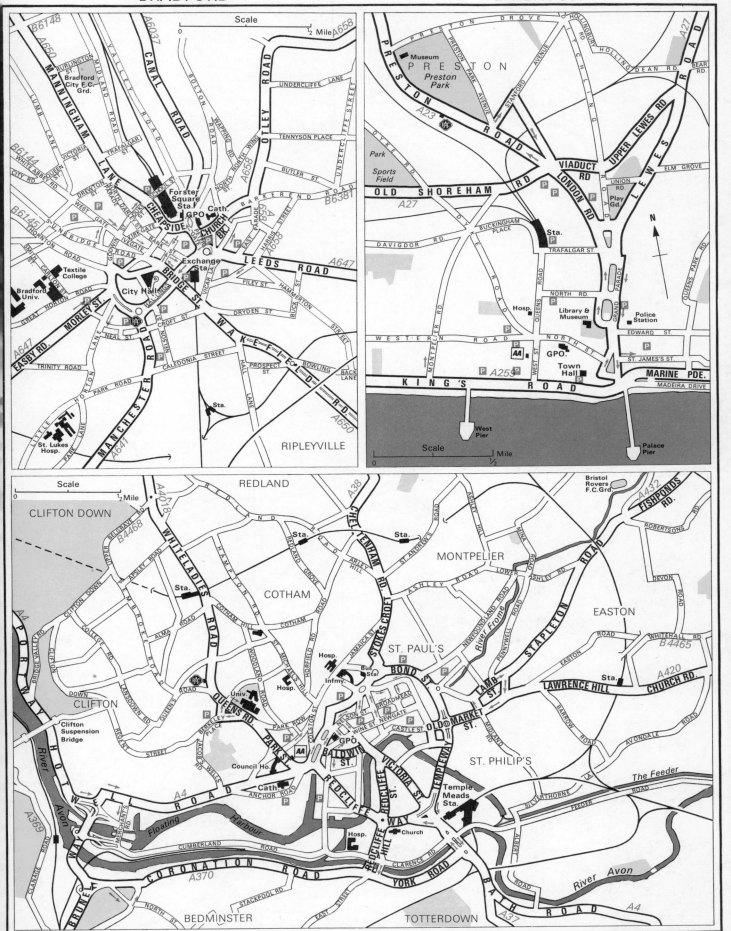

BRADFORD

Scale
0 ½ Mile

B6148 A6037 A658
B6150 MANNINGHAM LANE A650
BURLINGTON ST.
Bradford City F.C. Grd.
VALLEY ROAD
MIDLAND ROAD
CANAL ROAD
BOLTON ROAD
OTLEY ROAD
UNDERCLIFFE LANE
B6144
WHITE ABBEY ROAD
VICTORIA ST.
TRAFALGAR ST.
UNDERCLIFFE STREET
TENNYSON PLACE
B6145
CITY RD.
QUEEN ST.
THORNTON ROAD
SUNBRIDGE ROAD
GODWIN ST.
DREWTON ST.
NORTH PARADE
DARLEY ST.
SCHOOL ST.
Forster Square Sta.
CHEAPSIDE
GPO Cath.
CHURCH BK.
A658
WAPPING RD.
NORTH WING
BARKEREND ROAD
B6381
BUTLER ST.
WEST GATE
KIRK GATE
IVEGATE
BANK
EAST PARADE
HARRIS STREET
A658
Textile College
Exchange Sta.
BRIDGE ST.
VICAR LANE
LEEDS ROAD A647
FILEY ST.
HAMMERTON ST.
Bradford Univ.
GREAT HORTON RD.
CARLTON ST.
HALL INGS
City Hall
CROFT ST.
DRYDEN ST.
BUCK ST.
STREET
MORLEY ST.
NEAL ST.
CALEDONIA STREET
PROSPECT ST.
BOWLING BACK LANE
EASBY RD. A647
TRINITY ROAD
MANCHESTER ROAD
HORTON ROAD
PARK ROAD
HALL LANE
WAKEFIELD RD.
A650
LITTLE HORTON LANE
St. Lukes Hosp.
A641
Sta.
RIPLEYVILLE

BRIGHTON

PRESTON DROVE
HOLLINGBURY RD.
Museum
PRESTON
Preston Park
PRESTON PARK AVENUE
STANFORD AVENUE
PRESTON ROAD
DITCHLING
HOLLINGDEAN RD.
DEAN RD.
BEAR RD.
A27
A23
DYKE RD.
UPPER LEWES RD.
ELM GROVE
Park Sports Field
VIADUCT RD.
LONDON ROAD
LEWES ROAD
QUEENS PARK RD.
OLD SHOREHAM RD.
A27
UNION RD.
Play Gd.
DAVIGDOR RD.
BUCKINGHAM PLACE
Sta.
TRAFALGAR ST.
N
DYKE ROAD
Hosp.
QUEENS ROAD
NORTH RD.
GRAND PARADE
Police Station
EDWARD ST.
WESTERN ROAD
MONTPELIER ROAD
WEST ST.
NORTH ST.
Library & Museum
ST. JAMES'S ST.
AA
A259
GPO.
Town Hall
MARINE PDE.
KING'S ROAD
MADEIRA DRIVE
West Pier
Palace Pier
Scale
0 ½ Mile

BRISTOL

Scale
0 ½ Mile
REDLAND
A38
Bristol Rovers F.C. Grd.
A432
FISHPONDS RD.
CLIFTON DOWN
A4018
REDLAND ROAD
Sta.
CHELTENHAM RD.
Sta.
MONTPELIER
ROBERTSONS
B4468
WHITELADIES ROAD
ST. ANDREW'S
ASHLEY HILL
MINA ROAD
DEVON ROAD
UPPER BELGRAVE RD.
HAMPTON RD.
ARLEY HILL
COTHAM
REDLAND GROVE
ASHLEY ROAD
STAPLETON ROAD
EASTON
APSLEY ROAD
Sta.
COTHAM HILL
STOKES CROFT
LOWER ASHLEY RD.
River Frome
NEWFOUNDLAND ROAD
WHITEHALL RD.
B4465
EMBROKE
ALMA
COTHAM RD.
HORFIELD RD.
ST. MICHAEL'S
JAMAICA ST.
ST. PAUL'S
PENNYWELL ROAD
EASTON ROAD
A420
CLIFTON DOWN RD.
COLLEGE RD.
WOODLAND
Hosp.
BOND ST.
Sta.
LAWRENCE HILL
CHURCH RD.
A4
BRIDGE VALLEY RD.
LANSDOWN RD.
Univ.
Infmy.
Bus Sta.
LAMB ST.
BARROW ROAD
AVONDALE ROAD
CLIFTON
DOWN
QUEENS RD.
PARK ROW
NELSON ST.
BROADMEAD
NEWGATE
OLD MARKET ST.
ST. PHILIP'S
PORTWAY
RAC
Hosp.
PARK ST.
COLSTON ST.
WINE ST.
CASTLE ST.
MIDLAND ROAD
The Feeder
Clifton Suspension Bridge
BERKELEY PLACE
JACOB'S WELLS
REGENT STREET
AA
BALDWIN ST.
VICTORIA ST.
GPO
TEMPLE WAY
SILVERTHORNE
A369
River Avon
Council Ho.
ANCHOR ROAD
Cath.
REDCLIFFE WAY
Temple Meads Sta.
HOTWELL ROAD
MERCHANTS RD.
Floating Harbour
REDCLIFFE HILL
Church
BATH ROAD
FEEDER ROAD
CHANGE RD.
BRUNEL WAY
CUMBERLAND ROAD
Hosp.
CLARENCE RD.
River Avon
A370
CORONATION ROAD
YORK ROAD
ALBERT ROAD
NORTH ST.
STACKPOOL RD.
EAST ST.
BEDMINSTER
TOTTERDOWN
BATH ROAD
A37
A4

One-way Streets →   Car Parks P

© John Bartholomew & Son Ltd

CAMBRIDGE

CANTERBURY

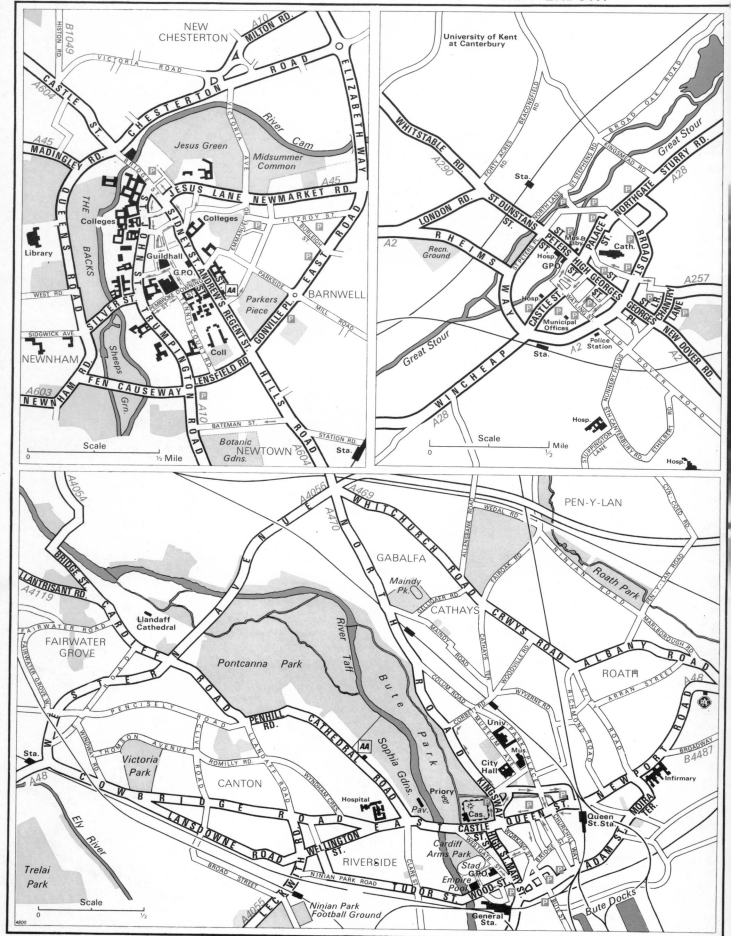

Car Parks P   One-way Streets →

© John Bartholomew & Son Ltd

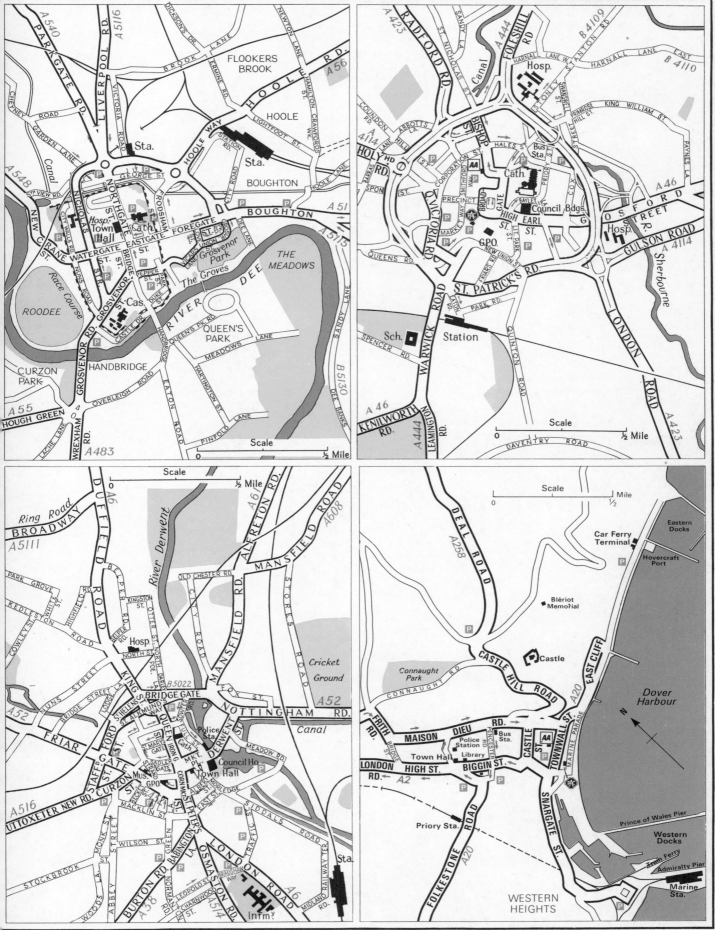

© John Bartholomew & Son Ltd

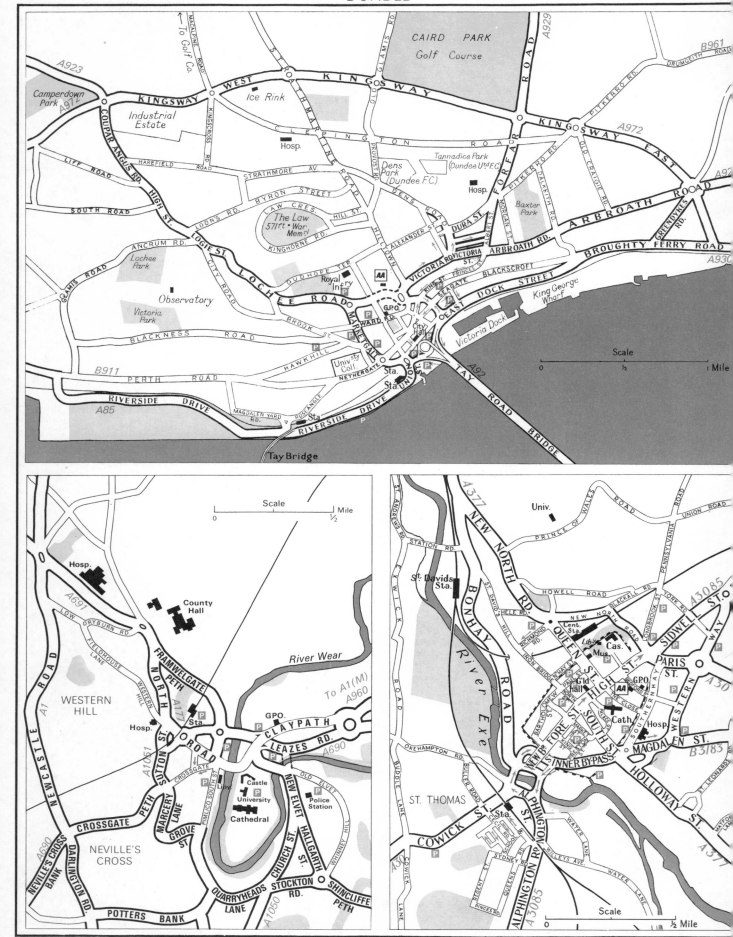

© John Bartholomew & Son Ltᵈ

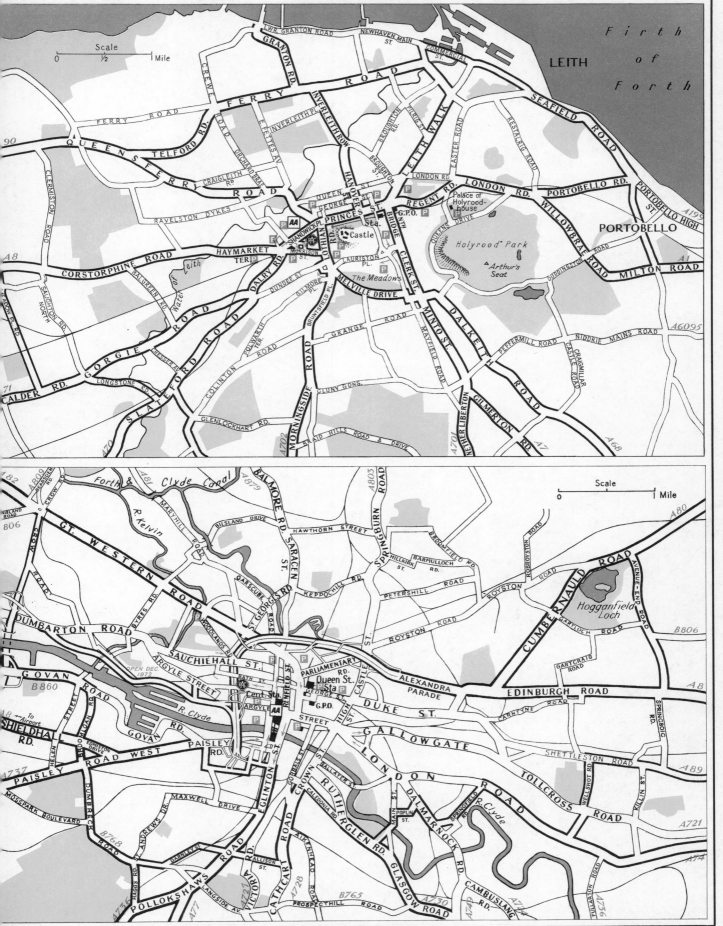

Scale
0 ½ 1 Mile

Firth of Forth

LEITH

PORTOBELLO

Palace of Holyroodhouse

Holyrood Park

Arthur's Seat

The Meadows

Castle

Scale
0 1 Mile

Forth & Clyde Canal

Hogganfield Loch

Queen St. Sta.

Cent. Sta.

R. Clyde

SHIELDHALL RD.

To Airport

One-way Streets →   Car Parks P

© John Bartholomew & Son Ltd

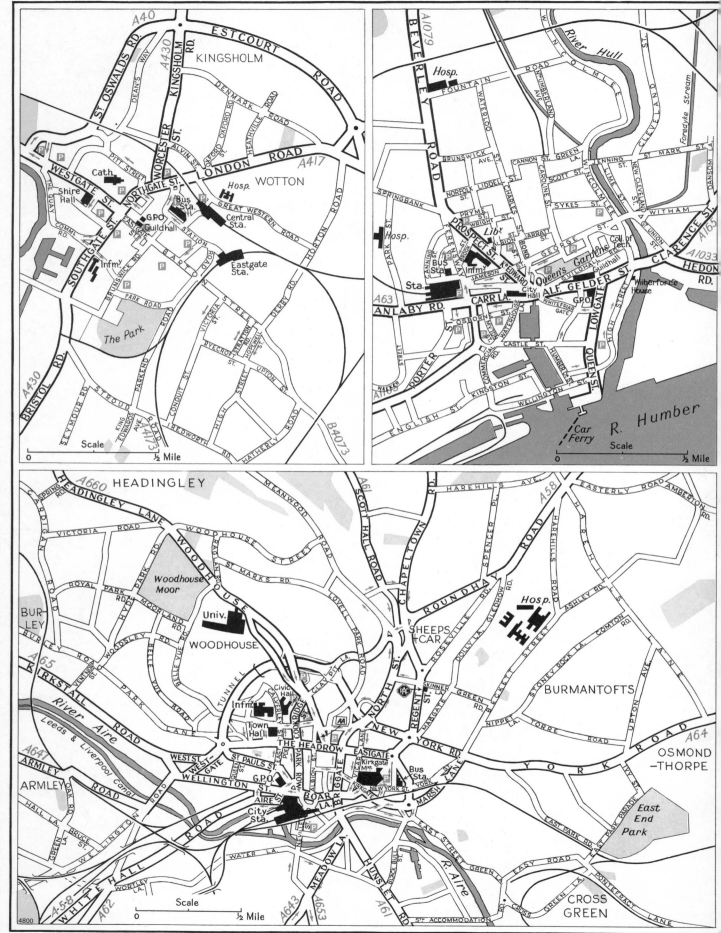

LEEDS

Car Parks **P**   One-way Streets →

© John Bartholomew & Son Ltd

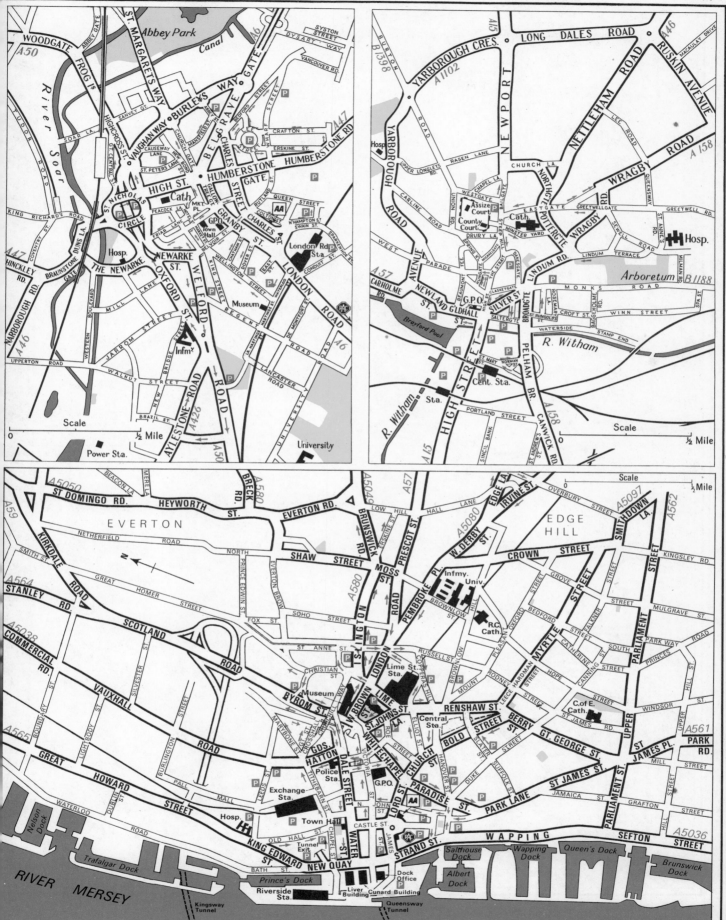

One-way Streets →   LIVERPOOL   Car Parks P

© John Bartholomew & Son Ltd

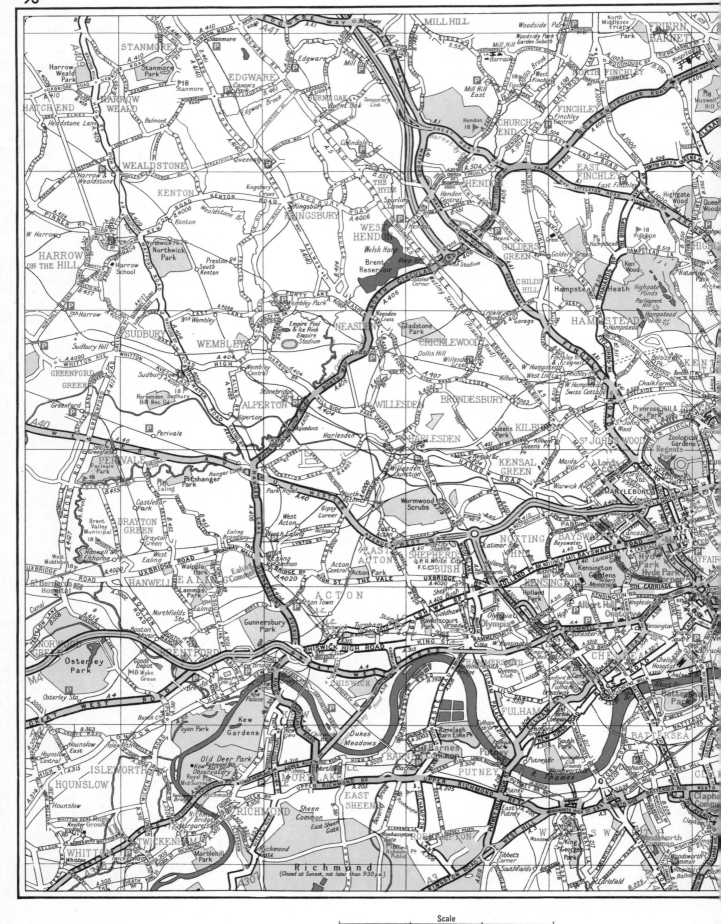

Scale

0   1   2   3 Miles

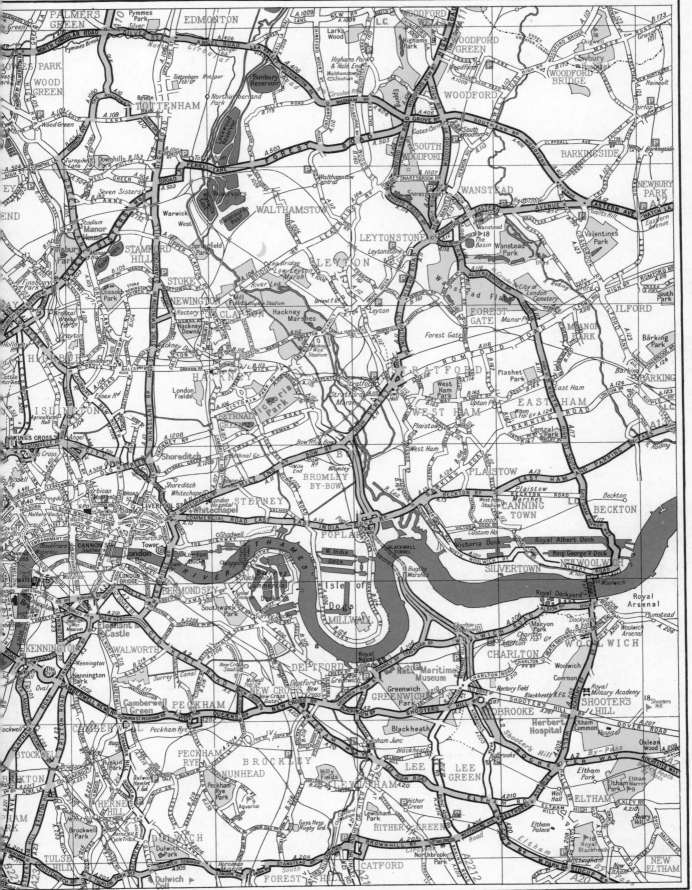

Recommended Through Routes ━━━━   One-way Streets →   Car Parks P

© John Bartholomew & Son Ltd

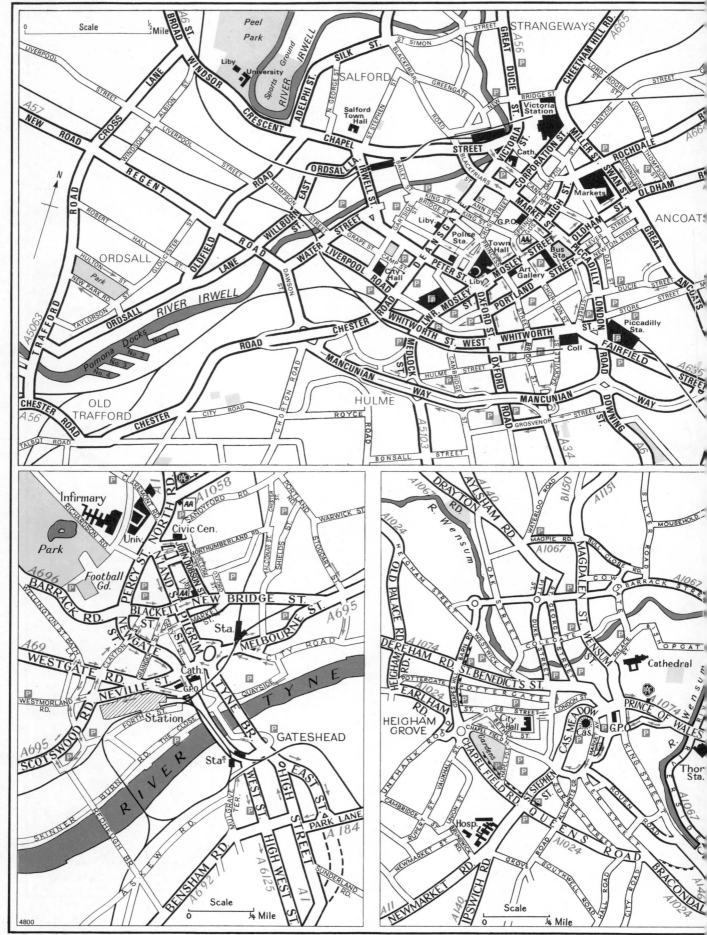

One-way Streets → Car Parks P

© John Bartholomew & S

MANCHESTER

Scale 0 ½ Mile

STRANGEWAYS

Peel Park

River Irwell

University
Liby
Sports Ground

SALFORD

Salford Town Hall

Victoria Station

Markets

NEW ROAD

CROSS LANE

WINDSOR

REGENT ROAD

CHAPEL STREET

ORDSALL LANE

ORDSALL

Hulton Park

TRAFFORD

RIVER IRWELL

Pomona Docks

OLD TRAFFORD

CHESTER ROAD

CHESTER ROAD

CITY ROAD

HULME

ROYCE ROAD

BONSALL STREET

DEANSGATE

PETER ST.

City Hall
Liby

Art Gallery

WHITWORTH ST. WEST

MEDLOCK ST.

OXFORD

CAMBRIDGE STREET

HULME

MANCUNIAN WAY

MANCUNIAN WAY

DOWNING ST.

Piccadilly Sta.

FAIRFIELD

Coll

PICCADILLY

ANCOATS

OLDHAM STREET

SWAN ST.

ROCHDALE RD.

CHEETHAM HILL RD.

Cath.

CORPORATION ST.

MARKET ST.

Town Hall
Police Sta.
G.P.O.

Bus Sta.

MOSLEY ST.

PORTLAND

LONDON RD.

GROSVENOR STREET

WHITWORTH STREET

NEWCASTLE UPON TYNE

Scale 0 ¼ Mile

Infirmary

Park

Football Gd.

BARRACK RD.

WESTGATE RD.

WESTMORLAND RD.

SCOTSWOOD RD.

A69

A695

A696

NORTH RD.

CLAREMONT RD.

RAC

AA

Civic Cen.

Univ.

NEW BRIDGE ST.

BLACKETT ST.

PILGRIM

NEWGATE

NEVILLE ST.

Cath.
G.P.O.

Station

THE CLOSE

TYNE BR.

Sta.

GATESHEAD

BENSHAM RD.

A692

HIGH WEST ST.

EAST ST.

HIGH STREET

PARK LANE

A184

SUNDERLAND RD.

RIVER TYNE

A1058

SANDYFORD RD.

PORTLAND RD.

CHESTER ST.

WARWICK ST.

NORTHUMBERLAND RD.

SHIELDS RD.

STODDART ST.

Sta.

MELBOURNE ST.

CITY ROAD

A695

Quayside

NORWICH

Scale 0 ¼ Mile

DRAYTON RD.

AYLSHAM RD.

R. Wensum

MAGPIE RD.

A1067

MAGDALEN ST.

MOUSEHOLD

BARRACK STREET

A1067

Cathedral

RAC

PRINCE OF WALES

R. Wensum

City Hall
Cas.
G.P.O.

OLD PALACE RD.

DEREHAM RD.

EARLHAM RD.

HEIGHAM GROVE

ST. BENEDICT'S ST.

POTTERGATE

ST. GILES STREET

CHAPEL FIELD RD.

Gardens

QUEENS ROAD

Hosp.

NEWMARKET RD.

IPSWICH RD.

A140

A11

SOUTHWELL ROAD

HALL ROAD

CITY ROAD

BRACONDALE

Thor Sta.

4800

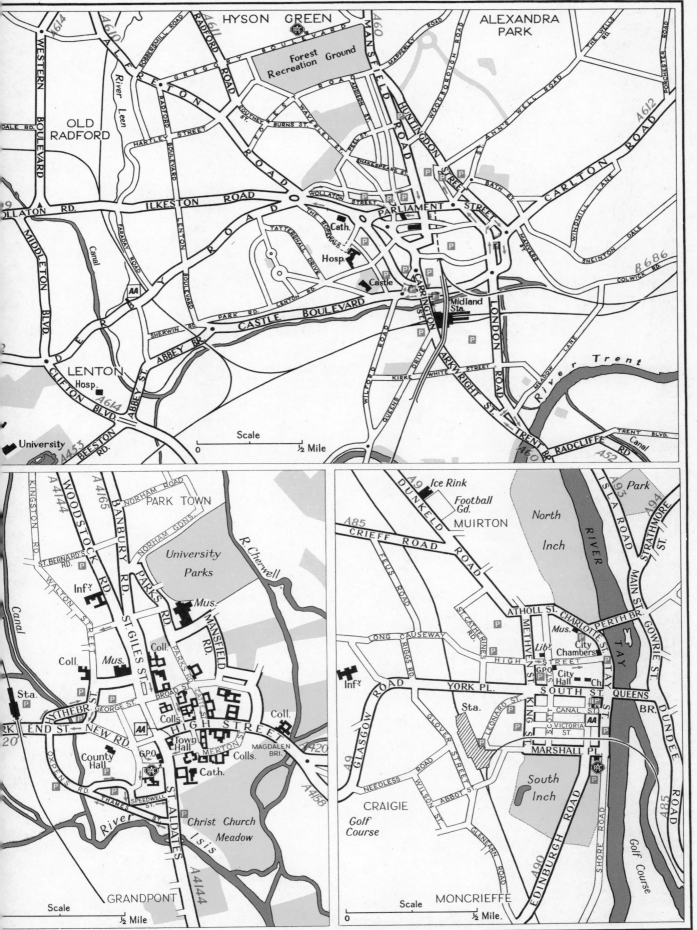

OXFORD   One-way Streets →   Car Parks P   PERTH

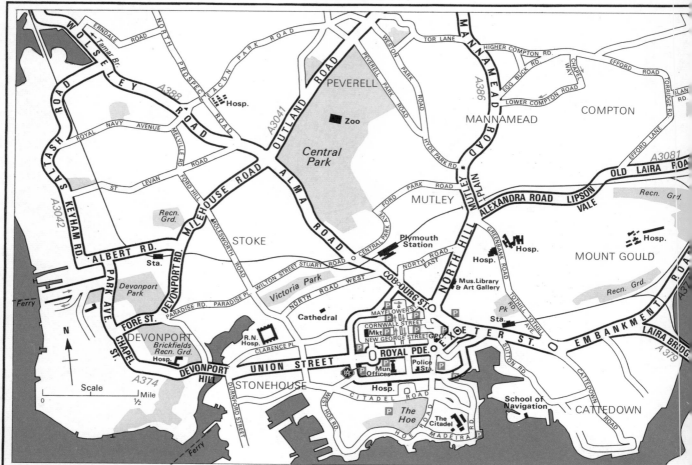

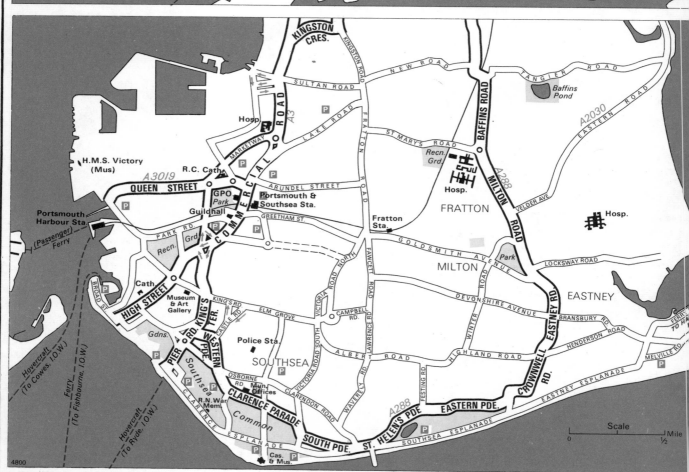

One-way Streets →

Car Parks P

© John Bartholomew & So

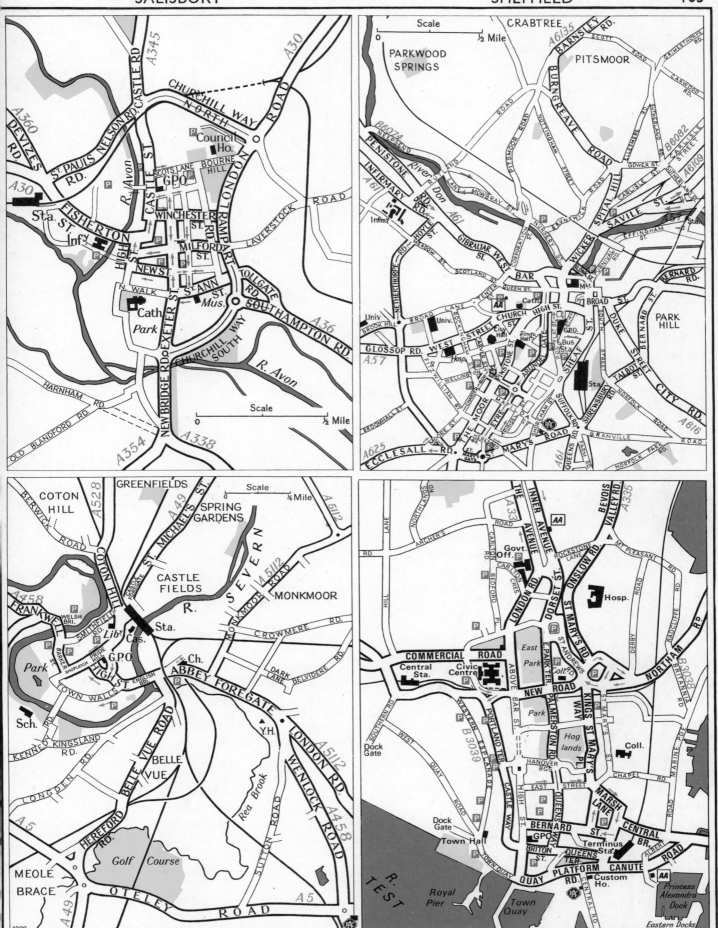

© John Bartholomew & Son Ltd

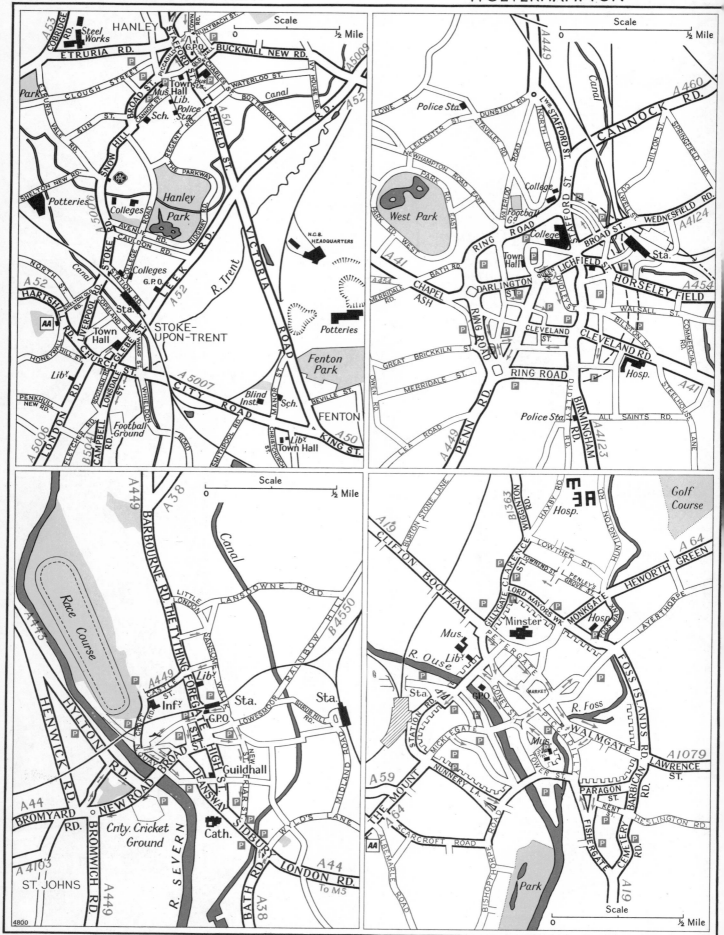

© John Bartholomew & Son Ltd

List of Counties and Abbreviations

A'deen	Aberdeen	—	Derby	—	Kinross	*Radn*	Radnor	B.	Bay
Angl	Anglesey	—	Devon	*Kirkcud*	Kirkcudbright	*Renf*	Renfrew	Br.	Bridge
—	Angus	—	Dorset	—	Lanark	*Ross*	Ross and Cromarty	C.	Cape
—	Argyll	*Dumf*	Dumfries	*Lancs*	Lancashire	*Rox*	Roxburgh	co.	County
—	Ayr	*Dunb*	Dunbarton	*Leics*	Leicester	*Rutl*	Rutland	div.	Division
—	Banff	—	Durham	*Lincs*	Lincoln	*Selk*	Selkirk	E.	East
Beds	Bedford	*E. Loth*	East Lothian	—	London	*Shet*	Shetland	Hd.	Head
Berks	Berkshire	—	Essex	*Mer*	Merioneth	*Shrops*	Shropshire (Salop)	I.	Island
—	Berwick	—	Fife	*M'loth*	Midlothian	*Som*	Somerset	L.	Lake, Loch, Lough
Brecon	Brecknock	—	Flint	*Mon*	Monmouth	*Staffs*	Stafford	mt.	Mountain
Bucks	Buckingham	*Glam*	Glamorgan	*Mont*	Montgomery	*Stirl*	Stirling	N.	North
—	Bute	*Glos*	Gloucester	—	Moray	*Suff*	Suffolk	Pen.	Peninsula
Caern	Caernarvon	*Hants*	Hampshire	—	Nairn	—	Surrey	Pt.	Point
Caith	Caithness	*Herefs*	Hereford	*Norf*	Norfolk	—	Sussex	R.	River
Cambs	Cambridge & I. of Ely	*Herts*	Hertford	*Northants*	Northampton	*Suth*	Sutherland	Res.	Reservoir
Card	Cardigan	*Hunts*	Huntingdon and	*N'land*	Northumberland	*Warks*	Warwick	S.	South
Carm	Carmarthen		Peterborough	*Notts*	Nottingham	*W. Loth*	West Lothian	St.	Saint
Ches	Cheshire	*I. of Man*	Isle of Man	—	Orkney	*W'land*	Westmorland	W.	West
Clack	Clackmannan	*I. of Wight*	Isle of Wight	*Oxon*	Oxford	*Wig*	Wigtown	=	Cross reference
Corn	Cornwall	*I'ness*	Inverness	*Peebl*	Peebles	*Wilts*	Wiltshire		
Cumb	Cumberland	—	Kent	*Pemb*	Pembroke	*Worcs*	Worcester		
Denb	Denbigh	*Kinc*	Kincardine	—	Perth	*Yorks*	Yorkshire		

Abbey St. Bathans *Berwick* **67 E3**
Abbey Town *Cumb* **59 F6**
Abbeystead *Lancs* **47 F3**
Abbots Bromley *Staffs* **35 G2**
Abbotsbury *Dorset* **8 D5**
Abbotsford *Selk* **66 C5**
Abbotsinch *Renf* **64 C2**
Aber Falls *Caern* **40 D4**
Aber Glaslyn, Pass of *Caern* **40 C6**
Aberaeron *Card* **24 A2**
Aberavon *Glam* **14 D3**
Aberbeeg *Mon* **15 G2**
Abercarn *Mon* **15 G2**
Aberchirder *Banff* **83 E2**
Aberdare *Glam* **15 E2**
Aberdaron *Caern* **32 A2**
Aberdeen *A'deen* **83 G6**
Aberdeenshire, co. **82 D4**
Aberdour *Fife* **73 E5**
Aberdovey *Mer* **32 D5**
Aberfeldy *Perth* **76 A6**
Aberffraw *Angl* **40 A4**
Aberford *Yorks* **49 F4**
Aberfoyle *Perth* **71 F4**
Abergavenny *Mon* **15 G1**
Abergele *Denb* **41 F4**
Abergwili *Carm* **24 A5**
Aberlady *E. Loth* **66 C1**
Aberllynfi *Brecon* **25 F4**
Aberlour *Banff* **82 B3**
Abernethy *Perth* **73 E3**
Aberporth *Card* **23 E1**
Abersoch *Caern* **32 B2**
Abersychan *Mon* **15 G1**
Aberthaw *Glam* **15 F4**
Abertillery *Mon* **15 G1**
Aberystwyth *Card* **32 D6**
Abingdon *Berks* **17 H2**
Abinger *Surrey* **11 G1**
Abington *Lanark* **65 F6**
Aboyne *A'deen* **77 E2**
Abram *Lancs* **42 B2**
Accrington *Lancs* **47 H5**
Acharacle *Argyll* **68 E2**
Achiltibuie *Ross* **85 A6**
Achnasheen *Ross* **80 C2**
Achray, Loch *Perth* **71 F4**
Achterneed *Ross* **81 E2**
Acle *Norf* **39 G4**
Acocks Green *Warks* **35 G5**
Acton *London* **19 F3**
Acton Turville *Glos* **16 C3**
Adderbury *Oxon* **27 H4**
Addlestone *Surrey* **19 E5**
Adlington *Lancs* **42 B1**
Adwick-le-Street *Yorks* **44 A1**
Ailort, Loch *I'ness* **68 E2**
Ailsa Craig, I. *Ayr* **56 A4**
Aintree *Lancs* **42 A2**
Aira Force, waterfall *Cumb* **52 D3**
Airedale *Yorks* **48 C4**
Aird of Sleat *Skye* **79 D7**
Airdrie *Lanark* **65 E2**
Aireborough *Yorks* **49 E4**
Airth *Stirl* **72 C5**
Alcester *Warks* **27 E2**
Alconbury *Hunts* **29 F1**
Aldbourne *Wilts* **17 G4**
Aldbrough *Yorks* **51 F4**
Aldeburgh *Suff* **31 H3**
Alderley Edge *Ches* **42 D3**
Aldermaston *Berks* **18 B5**
Alderney, I. *Channel Is.* **3 G4**
Aldershot *Hants* **18 C6**
Alderton *Suff* **31 G4**
Aldford *Ches* **42 A5**
Aldridge-Brownhills *Staffs* **35 F4**
Alexandra Park *London* **19 G3**
Alexandria *Dunb* **64 B1**
Alfold *Surrey* **11 F2**
Alford *A'deen* **83 E5**
Alford *Lincs* **45 H4**
Alfreton *Derby* **43 H5**
Alfriston *Sussex* **12 B6**
All Stretton *Shrops* **34 B4**
Allendale Town *N'land* **60 D5**
Allenheads *N'land* **53 G1**
Allerston *Yorks* **55 G6**
Allerton *Yorks* **48 D4**
Alloa *Clack* **72 C5**
Allonby *Cumb* **59 F6**
Alloway *Ayr* **56 D2**
Allt na Caillich, waterfall *Suth* **84 E3**
Alness *Ross* **81 F1**
Alnmouth *N'land* **61 G1**
Alnwick *N'land* **61 F1**
Alrewas *Staffs* **35 G3**
Alsager *Ches* **42 D5**
Alston *Cumb* **53 F1**
Altguish *Ross* **85 D8**
Altnacealgach *Suth* **85 C6**
Altnaharra *Suth* **84 F4**
Alton *Hants* **10 D1**
Altrincham *Ches* **42 D3**
Alva *Clack* **72 C5**
Alvechurch *Worcs* **27 E1**
Alwinton *N'land* **60 E1**
Alyth *Perth* **76 C6**
Amberley *Sussex* **11 F4**
Amble *N'land* **61 G2**
Ambleside *W'land* **52 D4**
Amersham *Bucks* **18 D2**
Amesbury *Wilts* **9 H1**
Amlwch *Angl* **40 B2**
Ammanford *Carm* **14 C1**
Ampleforth *Yorks* **50 B1**
Ampthill *Beds* **29 E4**
Amulree *Perth* **72 C1**
Ancaster *Lincs* **44 D6**
Ancrum *Rox* **66 D6**
Andover *Hants* **10 B1**
Angle *Pemb* **22 B5**
Anglesey, co. **40 A3**
Angmering-on-Sea *Sussex* **11 G5**
Angus, co. **76 D5**
Annan *Dumf* **59 G4**
Annfield Plain *Durham* **61 F6**
Anstruther *Fife* **73 H4**
Apperley *Glos* **26 D4**
Appersett *Yorks* **53 G5**
Appleby *W'land* **53 F3**
Applecross *Ross* **78 E4**
Appledore *Devon* **6 C2**
Appledore *Kent* **13 E4**
Arborfield Cross *Berks* **18 C4**
Arbroath *Angus* **73 H1**
Archiestown *Moray* **82 B3**
Ardeonaig *Perth* **72 B2**
Ardersier *I'ness* **81 G2**
Ardessie, waterfall *Ross* **85 A7**
Ardgay *Ross* **85 F7**
Ardgour *Argyll* **74 B5**
Ardleigh *Essex* **31 E5**
Ardlui *Dunb* **71 E3**
Ardnamurchan *Argyll* **68 C3**
Ardrishaig *Argyll* **70 A6**
Ardrossan *Ayr* **64 A4**
Ardsley *Yorks* **43 H1**
Ardvasar *Skye* **79 E7**
Argyll, co. **70 A3**
Arisaig *I'ness* **68 E1**
Arkaig, Loch *I'ness* **74 B2**
Arksey *Yorks* **44 B1**
Arlingham *Glos* **16 C1**
Armadale *Suth* **86 A2**
Armadale *W. Loth* **65 F2**
Arnisdale *I'ness* **79 F7**
Arnold *Notts* **44 B6**
Arnside *W'land* **47 E1**
Arran, I. *Bute* **63 F4**
Arrochar *Dunb* **71 E4**
Arthur's Seat, hill *M'loth* **65 H2**
Arundel *Sussex* **11 F4**
Ascog *Bute* **63 G2**
Ascot *Berks* **18 D4**
Ashbourne *Derby* **43 F6**
Ashburton *Devon* **4 D4**
Ashbury *Berks* **17 G3**
Ashby-de-la-Zouch *Leics* **35 H3**
Ashby Woulds *Leics* **35 H3**
Ashdale Falls *Bute* **63 G5**
Ashdown Forest *Sussex* **12 B4**
Ashford *Kent* **13 F3**
Ashford *Surrey* **19 E4**
Ashington *N'land* **61 G3**
Ashkirk *Selk* **66 C6**
Ashley *Staffs* **34 D1**
Ashover *Derby* **43 H4**
Ashtead *Surrey* **19 F5**
Ashton-in-Makerfield *Lancs* **42 B2**
Ashton-under-Lyne *Lancs* **43 E2**
Askam *Lancs* **46 D1**
Askrigg *Yorks* **53 H5**
Aspatria *Cumb* **52 B1**
Aspull *Lancs* **42 B1**
Assynt, Loch *Suth* **85 C5**
Aston Cross *Glos* **26 D4**
Atherstone *Warks* **35 H4**
Atherton *Lancs* **42 C1**
Attleborough *Norf* **39 E5**
Attlebridge *Norf* **39 F3**
Auchenblae *Kinc* **77 G3**
Auchinleck *Ayr* **64 C6**
Auchmithie *Angus* **77 F6**
Auchterarder *Perth* **72 C3**
Auchterderran *Fife* **73 E5**
Auchtermuchty *Fife* **73 E3**
Audenshaw *Lancs* **42 D2**
Audlem *Ches* **34 D1**
Audley End *Essex* **30 A4**
Auldearn *Nairn* **81 H2**
Aultbea *Ross* **78 F1**
Aultguish, waterfall *I'ness* **80 D6**
Aust *Glos* **16 B3**
Avebury *Wilts* **17 E4**
Avening *Glos* **16 D2**
Aveton Gifford *Devon* **4 D5**
Aviemore *I'ness* **81 H6**
Avoch *Ross* **81 F2**
Avonmouth *Glos* **16 A4**
Awbridge *Hants* **10 A2**
Awe, Loch *Argyll* **70 B4**
Axbridge *Som* **15 H5**
Axe Edge *Derby-Staffs* **43 E4**
Axminster *Devon* **5 H1**
Aycliffe *Durham* **54 C3**
Aylesbury *Bucks* **18 C1**
Aylesford *Kent* **12 D1**
Aylsham *Norf* **39 F2**
Aymestrey *Herefs* **25 H1**
Ayr *Ayr* **56 D2**
Ayrshire, co. **56 D2**
Aysgarth *Yorks* **53 H5**
Aysgarth Force, waterfall *Yorks* **54 A5**
Ayton *Berwick* **67 F3**
Babbacombe *Devon* **5 E4**
Bacup *Lancs* **47 H5**
Badachro *Ross* **78 E2**
Badcall *Suth* **84 B3**
Bagillt *Flint* **41 H4**
Baginton *Warks* **35 H6**
Bagshot *Surrey* **18 D5**
Baildon *Yorks* **48 D4**
Baillieston *Lanark* **64 D3**
Bainbridge *Yorks* **53 H5**
Bakewell *Derby* **43 G4**
Bala *Mer* **33 F1**
Balallan *Lewis* **88 B2**
Balby *Yorks* **44 B1**
Baldock *Herts* **29 F4**
Baldwin *Isle of Man* **46 B5**
Balerno *M'loth* **65 H2**
Balfron *Stirl* **64 C1**
Balintore *Ross* **81 G1**
Ballachulish *Argyll* **74 C5**
Ballagan, Spout of, waterfall *Stirl* **64 C1**
Ballantrae *Ayr* **57 B5**
Ballasalla *Isle of Man* **46 B6**
Ballater *A'deen* **76 D2**
Ballaugh *Isle of Man* **46 B4**
Ballindalloch Castle *Banff* **82 B3**
Ballinluig *Perth* **76 A5**
Balloch *Dunb* **64 B1**
Balmacara *Ross* **79 F5**
Balmaclellan *Kirkcud* **58 F3**
Balmoral Castle *A'deen* **76 C2**
Balquhidder *Perth* **71 F3**
Balsham *Cambs* **30 B3**
Bamber Bridge *Lancs* **47 F5**
Bamburgh *N'land* **67 H5**
Bampton *Devon* **7 G3**
Bampton *Oxon* **17 G2**
Banavie *I'ness* **74 C4**
Banbury *Oxon* **27 H3**
Banchory *Kinc* **77 F2**
Banff *Banff* **83 E1**
Banffshire, co. **82 B3**
Bangor *Caern* **40 C4**
Bankend *Dumf* **59 E4**
Bankfoot *Perth* **72 D2**
Bannockburn *Stirl* **72 C5**
Banstead *Surrey* **19 F5**
Bardney *Lincs* **45 E4**
Bardon Mill *N'land* **60 D5**
Bardsea *Lancs* **46 D1**
Bardsey, I. *Caern* **32 A3**
Barford *Warks* **27 G2**
Barking *London* **19 H3**
Barlborough *Derby* **44 A3**
Barmouth *Mer* **32 D3**
Barnard Castle *Durham* **54 A3**
Barnby Moor *Notts* **44 B3**
Barnet *London* **19 F2**
Barnoldswick *Yorks* **47 H3**
Barnsley *Yorks* **43 G1**
Barnstaple *Devon* **6 D2**
Barr *Ayr* **56 C4**
Barra, I. *I'ness* **88 D3**
Barrhead *Renf* **64 C3**
Barrhill *Ayr* **57 C5**
Barrow-in-Furness *Lancs* **46 D2**
Barrowford *Lancs* **48 B4**
Barry *Angus* **73 G1**
Barry *Glam* **15 F4**
Barton in the Clay *Beds* **29 E4**
Barton-upon-Humber *Lincs* **51 E5**
Barton-under-Needwood *Staffs* **35 G3**
Baschurch *Shrops* **34 B2**
Basildon *Essex* **20 D3**
Basingstoke *Hants* **18 B6**
Baslow *Derby* **43 G4**
Bass Rock *E. Loth* **73 H5**
Bassenthwaite *Cumb* **52 C2**
Bassingbourn *Cambs* **29 G3**
Bath *Som* **16 C5**
Bathgate *W. Loth* **65 F2**
Batley *Yorks* **49 E5**
Battle *Sussex* **12 D5**
Battlesbridge *Essex* **20 D2**
Bawdeswell *Norf* **39 E3**
Bawdsey *Suff* **31 G4**
Bawtry *Yorks* **44 B2**
Baycliff *Lancs* **46 D1**
Baythorn End *Essex* **30 C4**
Beachley *Glos* **16 B3**
Beachy Head *Sussex* **12 C6**
Beaconsfield *Bucks* **18 D3**
Beaminster *Dorset* **8 C4**
Bearsden *Dunb* **64 C2**
Beattock *Dumf* **59 F2**
Beaulieu *Hants* **10 B4**
Beauly *I'ness* **81 E3**
Beaumaris *Angl* **40 C4**
Bebington *Ches* **41 H3**
Beccles *Suff* **39 H5**
Beckenham *London* **19 G4**
Beckingham *Notts* **44 C2**
Beckington *Som* **16 C6**
Bedale *Yorks* **54 B5**
Beddgelert *Caern* **40 C6**
Bedford *Beds* **29 E3**
Bedfordshire, co. **29 E3**
Bedgebury *Kent* **12 D3**
Bedlington *N'land* **61 G3**
Bedwas *Mon* **15 G3**
Bedwellty *Mon* **15 G2**
Bedworth *Warks* **36 A5**
Beeley *Derby* **43 G4**
Beer *Devon* **5 G2**
Beeston *Notts* **36 B1**
Beeston *Yorks* **49 E5**
Begelly *Pemb* **22 D5**
Beinn Dearg, mt. *Perth* **75 H3**
Beith *Ayr* **64 B3**
Belford *N'land* **67 G5**
Bellingham *N'land* **60 D3**
Belper *Derby* **43 H6**
Belsay *N'land* **61 F4**
Belvoir *Leics* **36 D1**
Bembridge *I. of Wight* **10 D5**
Ben Alder, mt. *I'ness* **75 F4**
Ben Cruachan, mt. *Argyll* **70 C2**
Ben Hope, mt. *Suth* **84 E3**
Ben Lawers, mt. *Perth* **71 G1**
Ben Lomond, mt. *Stirl* **71 E4**
Ben Macdui, mt. *A'deen* **76 A2**
Ben More, mt. *Mull* **69 D5**
Ben More, mt. *Perth* **71 F3**
Ben More Assynt, mt. *Suth* **85 D5**
Ben Nevis, mt. *I'ness* **74 C4**
Ben Vorlich, mt. *Dunb* **71 E4**
Ben Vorlich, mt. *Perth* **72 A3**
Ben Wyvis, mt. *Ross* **85 E8**
Benbecula, I. *I'ness* **88 E2**
Benfleet *Essex* **20 D3**
Benington *Lincs* **37 H1**
Benson *Oxon* **18 B2**
Bentley *Yorks* **44 B1**
Bentworth *Hants* **10 D1**
Berkeley *Glos* **16 B2**
Berkhamsted *Herts* **18 E1**
Berkshire, co. **18 A4**
Berneray, I. *I'ness* **88 A4**
Bernisdale *Skye* **78 B4**
Berriedale *Caith* **87 D5**
Berwick-upon-Tweed *N'land* **67 G3**
Berwickshire, co. **66 D3**

Clydach Glam 14 C2
Clyde, R. Dunb-Renf 64 B2
Clyde, Falls of Lanark 65 F4
Clydebank Dunb 64 C2
Coalville Leics 36 A3
Coatbridge Lanark 64 D2
Cock Bridge A'deen 82 B6
Cockburnspath Berwick 67 E2
Cockenzie E. Loth 66 B1
Cockerham Lancs 47 E3
Cockermouth Cumb 52 B2
Coggeshall Essex 30 C5
Colchester Essex 31 E5
Cold Ashton Glos 16 C4
Cold Norton Essex 21 E2
Coldingham Berwick 67 F2
Coldstream Berwick 67 E4
Coleford Glos 16 B1
Coleshill Warks 35 G5
Colinsburgh Fife 73 G4
Colintraive Argyll 63 G1
Coll, I. Argyll 68 A3
Collingham Notts 44 C5
Colmonell Ayr 57 B5
Colne Lancs 47 H4
Colne Valley Yorks 60 D7
Colonsay, I. Argyll 69 C7
Coltishall Norf 39 G3
Colwinston Glam 15 E4
Colwyn Bay Denb 41 E3
Colyton Devon 5 G2
Combe Martin Devon 6 D1
Comrie Perth 72 B3
Congleton Ches 42 D5
Congresbury Som 16 A5
Coningsby Lincs 45 F5
Conisbrough Yorks 44 A2
Coniston Lancs 52 C5
Connah's Quay Flint 41 H4
Connel Argyll 70 B2
Conon Bridge Ross 81 E2
Consett Durham 61 F6
Constantine Corn 2 C5
Contin Ross 81 E2
Conway Caern 40 D4
Conwil Elvet Carm 23 E3
Cookham Berks 18 D3
Coombe Bissett Wilts 9 H2
Corbridge N'land 61 E5
Corby Northants 36 D5
Corby Glen Lincs 37 E2
Corfe Castle Dorset 9 G6
Cornhill-on-Tweed N'land 67 F4
Cornwall, co. 3 E2
Cornwood Devon 4 C4
Corpach I'ness 74 C4
Corran Argyll 74 B5
Corrie Arran 63 G3
Corsham Wilts 16 D4
Corstopitum N'land 61 E5
Corwen Mer 33 G1
Coryton Essex 20 D3
Coseley Staffs 35 F5
Cosham Hants 10 D4
Cotswold Hills Glos 16 D1
Cottenham Cambs 29 H1
Cottesmore Rutl 37 E3
Cottingham Yorks 51 E5
Coulter Lanark 65 G5
Coupar-Angus Perth 73 E1
Cove Dunb 70 D6
Coventry Warks 35 H6
Coverack Corn 2 D6
Cowbridge Glam 15 E4
Cowdenbeath Fife 73 E5
Cowes I. of Wight 10 B5
Cowfold Sussex 11 H3
Cowley Oxon 18 A1
Cradley Worcs 35 F5
Craggie I'ness 81 G3
Craigellachie Moray 82 C3
Craighouse Jura 62 C2
Craignure Mull 68 E4
Crail Fife 73 H4
Cramlington N'land 61 G4
Cranborne Dorset 9 G3
Cranbrook Kent 12 D3
Cranfield Beds 28 D3
Cranleigh Surrey 11 F1
Cranwell Lincs 45 E6
Crarae Argyll 70 C5
Crathie Church A'deen 76 C2
Craven Arms Shrops 34 B6
Crawford Lanark 65 F6
Crawley Sussex 11 H2
Credenhill Herefs 26 A3
Crediton Devon 4 D1
Creetown Kirkcud 57 E6
Cressage Shrops 34 C4
Crewe Ches 42 C5
Crewkerne Som 8 C3
Crianlarich Perth 71 E3
Criccieth Caern 32 C1
Crickhowell Brecon 25 G6
Cricklade Wilts 17 E2
Crieff Perth 72 C3
Crimond A'deen 83 H2
Croft Yorks 54 C4
Cromarty Ross 81 G1
Cromdale Moray 82 A4
Cromer Norf 39 F1
Cromford Derby 43 G5
Crompton Lancs 43 E1
Crook Durham 54 B2
Crook of Alves Moray 82 A1
Crook of Devon Kinross 72 D4
Crooklands W'land 53 E6
Crosby I. of Man 46 B5
Crosby Lancs 41 H2
Cross Gates Radn 25 F2
Cross Hands Carm 24 B6
Crossford Lanark 65 E4
Crossgates Fife 73 E5
Crosshill Ayr 56 D3
Crosshills Yorks 48 C4
Cross-in-Hand Sussex 12 B4
Crossway Green Worcs 26 D1
Croston Lancs 47 F6
Crowborough Sussex 12 B4
Crowland Lincs 37 G3
Crowle Lincs 44 C1
Crown Hill Devon 4 B5
Crowthorne Berks 18 C5
Croxley Green Herts 19 E2
Croyde Devon 6 C2
Croydon London 19 G5
Cruachan, Falls of Argyll 70 B4
Cruden Bay A'deen 83 H3
Crudgington Shrops 34 C4
Crummock Water Cumb 52 B3
Cuckfield Sussex 11 H3
Cuckney Notts 44 A4
Cudworth Yorks 43 H1
Cuillin Hills Skye 79 C6
Culbin Sandhills Moray 81 H1
Cullen Banff 82 D1
Cullingworth Yorks 48 D4
Culloden Moor I'ness 81 G3
Cullompton Devon 7 G4
Culmstock Devon 7 H4
Culross Fife 72 D5
Cults A'deen 77 H1
Culworth Northants 28 B3
Culzean Castle Ayr 63 H6
Cumberland, co. 52 C2
Cumbernauld Dunb 65 E2
Cumnock Ayr 56 F2
Cupar Fife 73 F3
Curragh, The I. of Man 46 B4
Cwmamman Carm 15 E2
Cwmbran Mon 15 G2
Dagenham London 19 H3
Dalbeattie Kirkcud 58 D5
Dalcross I'ness 81 G3
Dalegarth Force = Stanley Force
Dalkeith M'loth 66 B2
Dallas Moray 82 A2
Dalmally Argyll 70 D2
Dalmellington Ayr 56 E3
Dalmeny W. Loth 65 G1
Dalnaspidal Perth 75 G4
Dalry Ayr 64 A4
Dalry Kirkcud 58 C3
Dalrymple Ayr 56 D3
Dalston Cumb 59 H6
Dalton Dumf 59 F4
Dalton in Furness Lancs 46 D1
Dalwhinnie I'ness 75 F3
Darfield Yorks 43 H1
Darlaston Staffs 35 F4
Darlington Durham 54 C3
Dartford Kent 19 H4
Dartmoor Devon 4 C3
Dartmouth Devon 5 E5
Darton Yorks 43 G1
Darvel Ayr 64 C5
Darwen Lancs 47 G5
Datchet Bucks 19 E4
Daventry Northants 28 B2
Dawley Shrops 34 D4
Dawlish Devon 5 F3
Deal Kent 13 H2
Dean, Forest of Glos 16 B1
Dearham Cumb 52 B2
Dearne Yorks 43 H1
Debden Essex 30 A4
Debenham Suff 31 F2
Deddington Oxon 27 H4
Dee, R. A'deen 77 G2
Dee, Linn of, waterfall A'deen 76 B2
Deepcar Yorks 43 G2
Deeping St. James Lincs 37 F3
Delamere Forest Ches 42 B4
Denbigh Denb 41 F4
Denbighshire, co. 41 F5
Denby Dale Yorks 43 G1
Denham Bucks 19 E3
Denholme Yorks 48 D4
Dennington Suff 31 G2
Denny Stirl 65 E1
Denton Lancs 43 E2
Deptford Wilts 9 G1
Derby Derby 36 A1
Derbyshire, co. 43 G4
Dervaig Mull 68 C4
Derwen Denb 41 G6
Desborough Northants 36 D5
Devauden Mon 16 A2
Devil's Beef Tub Dumf 59 F1
Devil's Bridge Card 33 E6
Devil's Dyke Sussex 11 H4
Devil's Elbow Derby 43 E2
Devil's Elbow Perth 76 C3
Devizes Wilts 17 E5
Devon, co. 4 C1
Devon, Falls of Perth 72 D4
Devonport Devon 3 H3
Dewsbury Yorks 49 E5
Didcot Berks 18 A3
Didmarton Glos 16 C3
Digby Lincs 45 E5
Dinas Mawddwy Mer 33 F3
Dingwall Ross 81 E2
Dirleton E. Loth 66 C1
Dishforth Yorks 49 F1
Diss Norf 31 F1
Dittisham Devon 5 E5
Ditton Priors Shrops 34 C5
Doddington Cambs 37 H5
Doddington N'land 67 G5
Dodworth Yorks 43 G1
Dolgarrog Caern 41 E4
Dolgarrog Cascade Caern 40 D4
Dolgellau Mer 33 E3
Dollar Clack 72 D4
Dolphinton Lanark 65 G4
Dolwyddelan Caern 40 D6
Doncaster Yorks 44 B1
Donington Lincs 37 G1
Dorchester Dorset 8 D5
Dores I'ness 81 F4
Dorking Surrey 19 F6
Dornie Ross 80 A5
Dornoch Suth 87 B7
Dorset, co. 8 D4
Douglas I. of Man 46 B5
Douglas Lanark 65 E5
Doune Perth 72 B4
Dounreay Caith 86 C2
Dove Dale Derby-Staffs 43 F5
Dover Kent 13 H3
Dovercourt Essex 31 F5
Dowally Perth 76 B6
Dowlais Glam 15 F1
Downham Market Norf 38 B4
Downton Hants 10 A5
Downton Wilts 9 H2
Downton Devon 4 B2
Dreghorn Ayr 64 B5
Drigg Cumb 52 B5
Droitwich Worcs 26 D2
Dronfield Derby 43 H3
Droylsden Lancs 42 D2
Drumbeg Suth 84 B4
Drumelzier Peebl 65 G5
Drumlithie Kinc 77 G3
Drummore Wig 57 B8
Drumnadrochit I'ness 81 E4
Drumochter, Pass of I'ness 75 G3
Dryburgh Abbey Berwick 66 D5
Drymen Stirl 64 C1
Drynoch Skye 79 C5
Ducklington Oxon 17 G1
Duddington Northants 37 E4
Dudley Worcs 35 F5
Duffield Derby 36 A1
Dufftown Banff 82 C3
Duich, Loch Ross 80 A5
Dukeries, The Notts 44 A3
Dukestown Mon 15 F1
Dukinfield Ches 43 E2
Dulnain Bridge Moray 81 H4
Dumbarton Dunb 64 B2
Dumfries Dumf 59 E4
Dumfriesshire, co. 58 D3
Dunbar E. Loth 66 D1
Dunbartonshire, co. 65 D2
Dunbeath Caith 86 E4
Dunblane Perth 72 B4
Duncansby Caith 86 F1
Dunchurch Warks 27 H1
Dundee Angus 73 F2
Dundonald Ayr 64 B5
Dundonnell Ross 85 B7
Dundrennan Kirkcud 58 D6
Dunfermline Fife 73 E5
Dungeness Kent 13 F5
Dunipace Stirl 65 E1
Dunkeld Perth 72 D1
Dunlop Ayr 64 B4
Dunnet Caith 86 E1
Dunning Perth 72 D3
Dunnottar Castle Kinc 77 H3
Dunoon Argyll 63 H1
Duns Berwick 67 E3
Dunscore Dumf 58 D3
Dunsfold Surrey 11 F2
Dunsop Bridge Yorks 47 G3
Dunstable Beds 29 E5
Dunstaffnage Castle Argyll 70 B2
Dunster Som 7 G1
Dunsyre Lanark 65 G4
Duntulm Skye 78 C2
Dunvegan Skye 78 A4
Durham Durham 54 C1
Durham, co. 54 A1
Durness Suth 84 D2
Durnford Wilts 9 H1
Dursley Glos 16 C2
Durston Som 8 B2
Duthil I'ness 81 H5
Duxford Cambs 29 H3
Dyce A'deen 83 G5
Dyffryn Mer 32 D2
Dymchurch Kent 13 F4
Dymock Herefs 26 C4
Dysart Fife 73 F5
Eaglesfield Dumf 59 G4
Eaglesham Renf 64 C4
Ealing London 19 F3
Earby Yorks 48 B3
Eardisley Herefs 25 G3
Earith Hunts 29 G1
Earl Shilton Leics 36 A4
Earls Colne Essex 30 C5
Earlsferry Fife 73 G4
Earlston Berwick 66 D4
Earn, Loch Perth 72 A3
Earsdon N'land 61 G4
Eas-Coul-Aulin, waterfall Suth 84 C4
Easebourne Sussex 11 E3
Easington Durham 54 C1
Easingwold Yorks 49 G2
East Cowes I. of Wight 10 C5
East Dereham Norf 38 D3
East Grinstead Sussex 12 A3
East Ham London 20 B3
East Harling Norf 39 E6
East Kilbride Lanark 64 D3
East Linton E. Loth 66 D1
East Lothian, co. 66 C2
East Markham Notts 44 C4
East Retford Notts 44 B3
East Riding, div. Yorks 50 D3
East Wemyss Fife 73 F5
Eastbourne Sussex 12 C6
Eastington Glos 16 C1
Eastleigh Hants 10 B3
Eastry Kent 13 H2
Eastwood Notts 44 A6
Eaton Norf 39 F4
Eaton Socon Hunts 29 F2
Ebbw Vale Mon 15 F1
Ebchester Durham 61 F5
Ecclefechan Dumf 59 G4
Eccles Berwick 67 E4
Eccles Lancs 42 C2
Ecclesfield Yorks 43 H2
Eccleshall Staffs 35 E2
Echt A'deen 77 G1
Eckford Rox 66 D5
Eckington Derby 43 H3
Eddleston Peebl 66 A4
Edenbridge Kent 12 B2
Edgbaston Warks 35 F5
Edgware London 19 F2
Edinburgh M'loth 65 H2
Edlingham N'land 61 F1
Edmondbyers Durham 61 E6
Edmonton London 19 G2
Edzell Angus 77 F4
Egham Surrey 19 E4
Eglingham N'land 67 G6
Egmanton Notts 44 C4
Egremont Cumb 52 A4
Egton Yorks 55 F4
Eil, Loch I'ness 74 B4
Eilean, Loch an I'ness 81 H6
Elderslie Renf 64 C3
Elgin Moray 82 B1
Elgol Skye 79 D7
Elie Fife 73 G4
Elland Yorks 48 D6
Ellesmere Shrops 34 B1
Ellesmere Port Ches 42 A4
Ellington N'land 61 G3
Ellon A'deen 83 G4
Ellsley Berks 17 H3
Elmdon Warks 35 G5
Elphin Suth 85 C6
Elrick A'deen 83 F6
Elsdon N'land 61 E2
Elstree Herts 19 F2
Eltham London 19 H4
Elvington Yorks 50 C3
Ely Cambs 38 A6
Embleton N'land 67 H6
Empingham Rutl 37 E4
Emsworth Hants 10 D4
Enard B. Ross 85 A5
Enfield London 20 A2
Ennerdale Water Cumb 52 B3
Epping Essex 19 H2
Epping Forest 20 B2
Epsom Surrey 19 F5
Epworth Lincs 44 C1
Erdington Warks 35 G5
Eriboll, Loch Suth 84 D2
Ericht, Loch I'ness 75 F4
Eriskay, I. I'ness 88 E3
Erith London 19 H4
Ermine Street Lincs 44 D3
Errol Perth 73 F2
Erskine Renf 64 C2
Esher Surrey 19 F5
Eskdale Cumb 52 C4
Essex, co. 20 C1
Eston Yorks 54 D3
Etive, Loch Argyll 70 C2
Eton Bucks 18 D4
Ettington Warks 27 G3
Ettrick Church Selk 66 A6
Euston Suff 38 D6
Evanton Ross 81 F1
Evesham Worcs 27 E3
Evesham, Vale of Worcs 27 E3
Ewe, Loch Ross 78 F1
Ewell Surrey 19 F5
Exeter Devon 5 E2
Exmoor Som-Devon 7 E1
Exmouth Devon 5 F3
Eyam Derby 43 G3
Eye Suff 31 F1
Eye, pen. Ross 88 C2
Eyemouth Berwick 67 F2
Eynort, Loch S. Uist 88 E3
Eynsford Kent 20 B5
Failsworth Lancs 42 D1
Fair Oak Hants 10 C3
Fairford Glos 17 F2
Fairlie Ayr 63 H2
Fairwood Common Glam 14 B3
Fakenham Norf 38 D2
Falkirk Stirl 72 C6
Falkland Fife 73 F4
Falmouth Corn 2 D5
Falstone N'land 60 C3
Fannich, Loch Ross 80 C2
Fareham Hants 10 C4
Faringdon Berks 17 G2
Farnborough Hants 18 D6
Farne Is. N'land 67 H4
Farnham Surrey 18 C6
Farningham Kent 20 C5
Farnsfield Notts 44 B5
Farnworth Lancs 42 C1
Farrington Gurney Som 16 B5
Farsley Yorks 49 E4
Faversham Kent 13 F1
Fearn Ross 87 B8
Featherstone Yorks 49 F5
Felixstowe Suff 31 G4
Felling Durham 61 G5
Feltham London 19 E4
Felton N'land 61 F2
Feltwell Norf 38 B5
Fender, Falls of Perth 75 H4
Fenny Stratford Bucks 28 D4
Fenwick Ayr 64 C4
Fern Down Dorset 9 G4
Fernhurst Sussex 11 E2
Ferrybridge Yorks 50 A5
Ferryden Angus 77 G5
Ferryfield Kent 13 F5
Fettercairn Kinc 77 F4
Ffestiniog Mer 33 E1
Fforestfach Glam 14 C2
Fife, co. 73 F4
Filey Yorks 51 F1
Filton Glos 16 B3
Finchingfield Essex 30 B4
Finchley London 19 F3
Findhorn Moray 82 A1
Findochty Banff 82 D1
Findon Kinc 77 H2
Findon Sussex 11 G4
Finella Fall Kinc 77 G4
Fingal's Cave Argyll 69 B5
Finningham Suff 31 E2
Finningley Notts 44 B2
Fintry, Loup of, waterfall Stirl 64 D1
Fishbourne Sussex 11 E4
Fishguard Pemb 22 B2
Fittleworth Sussex 11 F3
Flamborough Hd. Yorks 51 G2
Fleet Hants 18 C6
Fleetwood Lancs 46 D3
Fletching Sussex 12 B4
Flimby Cumb 52 A2
Flint Flint 41 H4
Flintshire, co. 41 G4
Flockton Yorks 49 E6
Flodden Field N'land 67 F5
Flookburgh Lancs 47 E1
Fobbing Essex 20 D3
Fochabers Moray 82 C2
Folkestone Kent 13 G3
Folkingham Lincs 37 F2
Fontwell Sussex 11 F4
Fordingbridge Hants 9 H3
Fordwich Kent 13 G2
Forfar Angus 77 E5
Formby Lancs 41 H1
Forres Moray 82 A2
Fort Augustus I'ness 74 D1
Fort George I'ness 81 G2
Fort William I'ness 74 C4
Forth Br. 65 G1
Forth, R. 72 C5
Fortingall Perth 75 G6
Fortrose Ross 81 F2
Fortuneswell Dorset 9 E6
Foss Way Notts 36 C3
Foulness I. Essex 21 F3
Fountains Abbey Yorks 49 E2
Four Crosses Caern 32 B1
Fowey Corn 3 F3
Foyers I'ness 81 E5
Framlingham Suff 31 G2
Frampton Cotterell Glos 16 B3
Frant Sussex 12 C3
Fraserburgh A'deen 83 H1
Freckleton Lancs 47 E5
Freshwater I. of Wight 10 B5

Fressingfield Suff 31 F1
Freswick Caith 86 F1
Frimley Surrey 18 D5
Frinton Essex 31 F6
Friockheim Angus 77 F5
Fritham Hants 10 A3
Frizington Cumb 52 A3
Frodsham Ches 42 B3
Frome Som 16 C6
Fulford Yorks 50 B3
Fulwood Lancs 47 F5
Fyne, Loch Argyll 70 B5
Fyvie A'deen 83 F3
Gailey Staffs 35 E3
Gainsborough Lincs 44 C2
Gairloch Ross 78 F2
Galashiels Selk 66 C5
Galgate Lancs 47 F3
Galloway Kirkcud/Wig 57 C6
Galston Ayr 64 C5
Gamlingay Cambs 29 F3
Gamston Notts 44 B3
Garboldisham Norf 39 E6
Garelochhead Dunb 70 D5
Garforth Yorks 49 F4
Gargunnock Stirl 72 B5
Garlieston Wig 57 E7
Garmouth Moray 82 C1
Garry, Loch I'ness 74 D2
Garstang Lancs 47 F4
Garston Lancs 42 A3
Garth Brecon 25 E3
Garthmyl Mont 33 H4
Garton-on-the-Wolds Yorks 51 E2
Garvald E. Loth 66 D2
Garve Ross 80 D2
Garw Glam 14 D4
Garynahine Lewis 88 B2
Gateacre Lancs 42 A3
Gatehouse-of-Fleet Kirkcud 58 C5
Gateshead Durham 61 G5
Gatley Ches 42 D3
Gelligaer Glam 15 F2
Gerrards Cross Bucks 18 D3
Gifford E. Loth 66 C2
Gilfach Glam 15 F2
Gillingham Dorset 9 E2
Gillingham Kent 20 D4
Gilsland Cumb/N'land 60 C4
Girvan Ayr 56 B4
Gisburn Yorks 47 H3
Glamis Angus 73 F1
Glamorganshire, co. 14 D2
Glas Maol, mt. Angus 76 C3
Glascarnoch Res. Ross 80 C1
Glasgow Lanark 64 C2
Glass Houghton Yorks 49 F5
Glastonbury Som 8 C1
Glen Affric I'ness 80 C5
Glen Almond Perth 72 B2
Glen Coe Argyll 74 C5
Glen Garry Perth 74 C2
Glen Lyon Perth 71 G1
Glen Moriston I'ness 80 C6
Glen Shee Perth 76 B4
Glen Shiel Ross 80 A6
Glen Trool Kirkcud 57 D5
Glenboig Lanark 64 D2
Glenbuck Ayr 65 E5
Glendevon Perth 72 D4
Gleneagles Perth 72 C3
Glenelg I'ness 79 F6
Glenfarg Perth 73 E3
Glenfinnan I'ness 74 A3
Glengarry I'ness 74 D2
Glenisla Angus 76 C5
Glenluce Wig 57 C7
Glenridding W'land 52 D3
Glenrothes Fife 73 F4
Glomach, Falls of Ross 80 B5
Glossop Derby 43 E2
Gloucester Glos 26 C5
Gloucestershire, co. 26 C6
Glyn Neath Glam 14 D1
Glyncorrwg Glam 14 D2
Glyndebourne Sussex 12 B5
Goat Fell, mt. Arran 63 F3
Goathland Yorks 55 F4
Godalming Surrey 18 D6
Godmanchester Hunts 29 F1
Godshill I. of Wight 10 C6
Golborne Lancs 42 B2
Golcar Yorks 48 D6
Golden Valley Herefs 25 H4
Golspie Suth 87 B6
Gomersal Yorks 49 E5
Goodwick Pemb 22 B2
Goodwood Sussex 11 E4
Goole Yorks 49 H5
Gordonstown A'deen 82 F3
Gordonstown Banff 82 D2
Gorebridge M'loth 66 B3
Goring Oxon 18 B3
Goring Sussex 11 G5
Gorleston Norf 39 H4
Gorseinon Glam 14 B2
Gosforth Cumb 52 B4
Gosforth N'land 61 G4
Gosport Hants 10 C4
Gourock Renf 63 H1
Govan Lanark 64 C2
Gower Pen. Glam 14 E3
Gowerton Glam 14 B2
Gramisdale I'ness 88 E2
Grampound Corn 3 E3
Grange Lancs 47 E1
Grangemill Derby 43 G5
Grangemouth Stirl 64 F1
Grantchester Cambs 29 H2
Grantham Lincs 37 E1
Granton M'loth 65 H1
Grantown-on-Spey Moray 82 A4
Grantshouse Berwick 67 E2
Grasmere W'land 52 D4
Gravesend Kent 20 C4
Grays Thurrock Essex 20 C4
Grayshott Hants 11 F2
Great Ayton Yorks 55 E4
Great Casterton Rutl 37 E3
Great Chesterford Essex 30 A3
Great Cumbrae, I. Bute 63 H2
Great Driffield Yorks 51 E3
Great Dunmow Essex 30 B5
Great Gidding Hunts 37 F6
Great Grimsby = Grimsby, Great
Great Harwood Lancs 47 G5
Great Limber Lincs 45 E1
Great Malvern Worcs 26 C3
Great Missenden Bucks 18 D2
Great Orme's Head Caern 40 D3
Great Orton Cumb 59 H5
Great Salkeld Cumb 53 E2
Great Shefford Berks 17 G4
Great Shelford Cambs 30 A3
Great Staughton Hunts 29 F2
Great Torrington Devon 6 D3
Great Wakering Essex 21 E3
Great Waltham Essex 20 D1
Great Witchingham Norf 39 E3
Great Witley Worcs 26 C1
Great Yarmouth Norf 39 H4
Greatham Durham 54 D2
Greatham Hants 11 E2
Greenfield Flint 41 G4
Greenhead N'land 60 C5
Greenhithe Kent 20 C4
Greenlaw Berwick 66 D4
Greenock Renf 63 H1
Greenwich London 19 G4
Gretna Dumf 59 G4
Gretna Green Dumf 59 G4
Grey Mare's Tail, waterfall Dumf 59 F1
Grey Mare's Tail, waterfall Kirkcud 57 E6
Greystoke Cumb 52 D2
Griffithstown Mon 15 G2
Grimsby, Great Lincs 45 G1
Grimsetter Orkney 89 B6
Gringley-on-the-Hill Notts 44 C2
Gronant Flint 40 G3
Groombridge Sussex 12 B3
Gruinard B. Ross 85 A7
Guernsey, I. Channel Is. 3 F5
Guildford Surrey 19 E6
Guisborough Yorks 55 E3
Guiseley Yorks 48 D4
Gullane E. Loth 66 C1
Gunnislake Corn 3 H1
Gunwalloe Corn 2 C6
Guyhirn Cambs 37 H4
Gwalchmai Angl 40 B4
Gwbert on the Sea Card 22 D1
Gweek Corn 2 C5
Gwithian Corn 2 B4
Gwyddgrug Carm 23 F2
Gyffylliog Denb 41 F5
Hackney London 19 G3
Hackthorpe W'land 53 E3
Haddenham Bucks 18 C1
Haddenham Cambs 29 H1
Haddington E. Loth 66 D2
Haddiscoe Norf 29 H5
Hadleigh Essex 20 D3
Hadleigh Suff 31 E4
Hailsham Sussex 12 C5
Hale Ches 42 D3
Hale Lancs 42 A3
Halesowen Worcs 35 F5
Halesworth Suff 31 G1
Halfway Brecon 24 D4
Halifax Yorks 48 D5
Halkirk Caith 86 D2
Hallsands Devon 5 E6
Halstead Essex 30 C5
Haltemprice Yorks 51 E5
Haltwhistle N'land 60 C5
Halwell Devon 4 D5
Ham Street Kent 13 F4
Hamble Hants 10 B4
Hambleden Bucks 18 C3
Hambledon Hants 10 D3
Hambledon Surrey 11 F2
Hambleton Hills Yorks 54 D5
Hamilton Lanark 64 D3
Hammersmith London 19 F4
Hampshire, co. 10 B2
Hampstead London 19 F3
Hampton London 19 F4
Hampton Court London 19 F4
Hampton-in-Arden Warks 35 G6
Hanbury Worcs 26 D2
Handcross Sussex 11 H2
Handsworth Yorks 43 H3
Hanley Staffs 42 D6
Hanworth London 19 E4
Happisburgh Norf 39 G2
Harbury Warks 27 G2
Harby Leics 36 C2
Harewood Yorks 49 E4
Haringey London 19 G3
Harlech Mer 32 D2
Harleston Norf 39 F6
Harlow Essex 20 B1
Harpenden Herts 18 E1
Harrington Cumb 52 A3
Harris I'ness 88 A3
Harrogate Yorks 49 E3
Harrow London 19 F3
Harrow-on-the-Hill London 19 F3
Harston Cambs 29 H3
Hartburn N'land 61 F3
Hartfield Sussex 12 B3
Harthill Ches 42 B5
Harthill Lanark 65 F2
Hartington Derby 43 F5
Hartland Devon 6 B3
Hartlepool Durham 54 D2
Harwell Berks 18 A3
Harwich Essex 31 F5
Haslemere Surrey 11 E2
Haslingden Lancs 47 H5
Hastings Sussex 12 D5
Haswell Durham 54 C1
Hatfield Herts 19 F1
Hatfield Yorks 44 B1
Hatfield Broad Oak Essex 30 A6
Hatfield Peverel Essex 30 C6
Hatherleigh Devon 6 D4
Hathern Leics 36 B2
Hathersage Derby 43 G3
Hatton A'deen 83 H3
Havant Hants 10 D4
Haverfordwest Pemb 22 C4
Haverhill Suff 30 B3
Havering London 20 B3
Haverton Hill Durham 54 D3
Hawarden Flint 41 H4
Hawes Water W'land 53 E3
Hawick Rox 60 B1
Hawkshead Lancs 52 D5
Hawkstone Park Shrops 34 C2
Haworth Yorks 48 C4
Haxey Lincs 44 C2
Hay-on-Wye Brecon 25 G4
Haydock Lancs 42 B2
Haydon Bridge N'land 60 D5
Hayes London 19 E3
Hayfield Derby 43 E3
Hayle Corn 2 B4
Hayling I. Hants 10 D4
Hayton Yorks 50 C4
Haywards Heath Sussex 12 A4
Hazel Grove Ches 43 E3
Headington Oxon 28 A6
Headless Cross Worcs 27 E2
Heanor Derby 43 H6
Heathfield Sussex 12 C4
Heaton Park Lancs 42 D1
Hebburn Durham 61 G5
Hebden Bridge Yorks 48 C5
Heckington Lincs 37 F1
Heckmondwike Yorks 48 D5
Heddon-on-the-Wall N'land 61 F5
Hednesford Staffs 35 F3
Hedon Yorks 51 F5
Helensburgh Dunb 64 A1
Helmdon Northants 28 B3
Helmsdale Suth 87 D5
Helmsley Yorks 55 E6
Helston Corn 2 C5
Helvellyn, mt. Cumb 52 D3
Hemel Hempstead Herts 18 E1
Hemswell Lincs 44 D2
Hemsworth Yorks 49 F6
Hendon London 19 F3
Hendy Glam 23 G5
Henfield Sussex 11 H3
Henley-in-Arden Warks 27 F1
Henley-on-Thames Oxon 18 C3
Henstridge Som 9 E3
Hereford Herefs 26 A3
Herefordshire, co. 25 H3
Heriot M'loth 66 B3
Herne Bay Kent 13 G1
Herriard Hants 18 B6
Herstmonceux Sussex 12 C5
Hertford Herts 19 G1
Hertfordshire, co. 29 E6
Hesketh Bank Lancs 47 E5
Hethersett Norf 39 F4
Hetton-le-Hole Durham 61 H6
Hever Castle Kent 12 B2
Hexham N'land 61 E5
Heyford, Upr. & Lr. Oxon 28 A5
Heysham Lancs 47 E2
Heytesbury Wilts 16 D6
Heywood Lancs 42 D1
High Bentham Yorks 47 G2
High Force, waterfall Yorks 53 G2
High Halden Kent 13 E3
High Ongar Essex 20 C2
High Wycombe Bucks 18 D2
Higham Derby 43 H5
Higham Ferrers Northants 29 E1
Highbridge Som 15 G6
Highgate London 19 F3
Highworth Wilts 17 F2
Hilderstone Staffs 35 F1
Hill of Fearn Ross 87 B8
Hillingdon London 19 E3
Hillington Lanark 64 C3
Hillington Norf 38 C2
Hillside Kinc 77 F5
Hinckley Leics 36 A5
Hinderwell Yorks 55 F3
Hindhead Surrey 10 E2
Hindley Lancs 42 B1
Hindon Wilts 9 F1
Hingham Norf 39 E4
Hirwaun Glam 15 E1
Hitchin Herts 29 F5
Hobbs Pt. Pemb 22 C5
Hobkirk Rox 60 B1
Hockering Norf 39 E3
Hockley Heath Warks 27 F1
Hoddesdon Herts 20 A1
Hodnet Shrops 34 C2
Hogs Back Surrey 11 F1
Holbeach Lincs 37 H2
Holland, div. Lincs 37 G2
Hollington Derby 43 G6
Holmbury St. Mary Surrey 11 G1
Holme upon Spalding Moor Yorks 50 C4
Holmes Chapel Ches 42 D4
Holmesfield Derby 43 G3
Holmfirth Yorks 43 F1
Holmwood Surrey 19 F6
Holsworthy Devon 6 C4
Holt Denb 42 A5
Holt Norf 39 E1
Holy I. N'land 67 G4
Holyhead Angl 40 A3
Holywell Flint 41 G4
Honington Suff 38 D6
Honiton Devon 5 G1
Hope under Dinmore Herefs 26 A2
Horbury Yorks 49 E6
Horeb Card 24 A4
Horley Surrey 11 H1
Horncastle Lincs 45 F4
Hornchurch London 20 B3
Horndean Hants 10 D3
Hornsea Yorks 51 F3
Hornsey London 19 G3
Horsebridge Hants 10 B2
Horsebridge Sussex 12 C5
Horsforth Yorks 49 E4
Horsham Sussex 11 G2
Horsham St. Faith Norf 39 F3
Horwich Lancs 42 C1
Houghton Hunts 29 G1
Houghton-le-Spring Durham 61 H6
Hounslow London 19 E4
Housesteads N'land 60 D4
Hove Sussex 11 H4
Howden Yorks 49 H5
Howwood Renf 64 B3
Hoy, I. Orkney 89 A7
Hoylake Ches 41 G3
Hoyland Nether Yorks 43 H1
Hucknall Notts 44 A6
Huddersfield Yorks 48 D6
Huggate Yorks 50 D3
Hugh Town Corn 2 A1
Hull, Kingston upon Yorks 51 E5
Hullavington Wilts 16 D3
Hungerford Berks 17 G4
Hunmanby Yorks 51 E1
Hunstanton Norf 38 B1
Huntingdon Hunts 29 F1
Huntingdon and Peterborough, co. 37 F6
Huntly A'deen 82 D3
Hurlford Ayr 64 C5
Hurn Hants 9 H4
Hursley Hants 10 B2
Hurst Green Sussex 12 D4
Hurstpierpoint Sussex 11 H3
Husbands Bosworth Leics 36 C5
Hutton-le-Hole Yorks 55 E5
Huyton Lancs 42 A3
Hyde Ches 43 E2
Hythe Hants 10 B4
Hythe Kent 13 G3
Ibsley Hants 9 H3
Ickenham London 19 E3
Idle Yorks 48 D4
Ilchester Som 8 C2
Ilford London 19 H3
Ilfracombe Devon 6 D1
Ilkeston Derby 36 B1
Ilkley Yorks 48 D3
Ilminster Som 8 B3
Immingham Lincs 51 F6
Immingham Dock Lincs 51 F6
Ince-in-Makerfield Lancs 42 B1
Inchcolm Fife 73 E6
Inchkeith Fife 73 F6
Inchnadamph Suth 85 C5
Ingatestone Essex 20 C2
Ingleby Cross Yorks 54 D5
Ingliston M'loth 65 G2
Ingleton Yorks 47 G1
Ingoldmells Lincs 45 H4
Innellan Argyll 63 G1
Innerleithen Peebl 66 B5
Insch A'deen 83 E4
Inverallochy A'deen 83 H1
Inveran Suth 85 F6
Inveraray Argyll 70 C4
Inverbervie Kinc 77 G4
Inveresk M'loth 66 B2
Inverewe Ross 78 F2
Inverfarigaig I'ness 81 E5
Invergarry I'ness 74 D2
Invergordon Ross 81 F1
Inverinate Ross 80 A5
Inverkeilor Angus 77 G5
Inverkeithing Fife 73 E6
Inverkirkaig Suth 85 B5
Invermay, Birks of, waterfall Perth 72 D3
Invermoriston I'ness 80 D5
Inverness I'ness 81 F3
Inverness-shire, co. 74 B2
Invershiel Ross 80 A5
Invershin Suth 85 F6
Inverurie A'deen 83 F4
Iona, I. Argyll 69 B6
Ipstones Staffs 43 E6
Ipswich Suff 31 F4
Irlam Lancs 42 C2
Ironbridge Shrops 34 D4
Irthington Cumb 60 B5
Irthlingborough Northants 28 D1
Irvine Ayr 64 B5
Islay, I. Argyll 62 A2
Isle of Ely, div. Cambs 37 H5
Isle of Man 46 A4
Isle of Wight Hants 10 B6
Isle Ornsay Skye 79 E7
Islington London 19 G3
Itchen Hants 10 B4
Iver Bucks 19 E3
Ivybridge Devon 4 C5
Ixworth Suff 30 D1
Jameston Pemb 22 C5
Jamestown Dunb 64 B1
Janetstown Caith 86 D2
Janetstown Caith 86 E4
Jarrow Durham 61 G5
Jedburgh Rox 66 D6
Jersey, I. Channel Is. 3 G6
Jodrell Bank Ches 42 D4
John o' Groat's Caith 86 F1
Johnshaven Kinc 77 G4
Johnstone Renf 64 B3
Jura, I. Argyll 62 C1
Jurby I. of Man 46 B4
Katrine, Loch Perth 71 E4
Kearsley Lancs 42 C1
Keighley Yorks 48 C4
Keiss Caith 86 F2
Keith Banff 82 D2
Kelling Pines Norf 39 E1
Kelsall Ches 42 B4
Kelso Rox 67 E5
Kelty Fife 73 E5
Kelvedon Essex 30 D6
Kemble Glos 17 E2
Kempsey Worcs 26 D3
Kempston Beds 29 E3
Kempton Park Surrey 19 E4
Kendal W'land 53 E5
Kenilworth Warks 27 G1
Kenley Surrey 12 A1
Kenmore Perth 75 H6
Kenninghall Norf 39 E6
Kennoway Fife 73 F4
Kensington and Chelsea London 19 F3
Kent, co. 12 D2
Kentford Suff 30 C2
Kenton Devon 5 E2
Kerrera, I. Argyll 70 A2
Kessingland Suff 39 H6
Kessock, N. Ross 81 F3
Kessock, S. I'ness 81 F3
Kesteven, div. Lincs 36 D1
Keswick Cumb 52 C3
Kettering Northants 36 D6
Kettlewell Yorks 48 C1
Kew Gardens London 19 F4
Keynsham Som 16 B5
Kidderminster Worcs 35 E6
Kidlington Oxon 18 A1
Kidsgrove Staffs 42 D5
Kidwelly Carm 14 A1
Kilbarchan Renf 64 B3
Kilbirnie Ayr 64 B3
Kilchoan Argyll 68 C3
Kilconquhar Fife 73 G4
Kilcreggan Dunb 70 D6
Kildrummy A'deen 82 D5

Midtown Brae *Ross* **78 F2**
Milborne *Dorset* **9 E4**
Milborne Port *Som* **9 E3**
Mildenhall *Suff* **30 C1**
Milford *Surrey* **11 F1**
Milford Haven *Pemb* **22 B5**
Milford-on-Sea *Hants* **10 A5**
Millom *Cumb* **46 C1**
Millport *Bute* **63 H2**
Milnathort *Kinross* **73 E4**
Milngavie *Dunb* **64 C2**
Milnrow *Lancs* **43 E1**
Milnthorpe *W'land* **47 F1**
Milton *Kent* **13 E1**
Milton Keynes *Bucks* **28 D4**
Milverton *Som* **8 A2**
Minchinhampton *Glos* **16 D2**
Minehead *Som* **7 G1**
Mingulay, I. *I'ness* **88 D4**
Mintlaw *A'deen* **83 H2**
Mirfield *Yorks* **48 D6**
Misterton *Notts* **44 C2**
Mitcheldean *Glos* **26 B5**
Modbury *Devon* **4 C5**
Moffat *Dumf* **59 F1**
Mold *Flint* **41 H5**
Moness Falls *Perth* **75 H6**
Moniaive *Dumf* **58 D3**
Monifieth *Angus* **73 G2**
Monkhopton *Shrops* **34 C5**
Monkton *Ayr* **64 B5**
Monmouth *Mon* **16 A1**
Monmouthshire, co. **15 G1**
Montgomery *Mont* **33 H4**
Montgomeryshire, co. **33 F4**
Montrose *Angus* **77 G5**
Monymusk *A'deen* **83 E5**
Moorfoot Hills **66 B3**
Morar *I'ness* **68 E1**
Moray, co. **82 A2**
Morden *London* **19 F4**
More, Loch *Suth* **84 D4**
Morebattle *Rox* **67 E6**
Morecambe *Lancs* **47 E2**
Moretonhampstead *Devon* **4 D2**
Moreton-in-Marsh *Glos* **27 F4**
Morley *Yorks* **49 E5**
Morlich, Loch *I'ness* **81 H6**
Morpeth *N'land* **61 F3**
Morriston *Glam* **14 C2**
Mortehoe *Devon* **6 D1**
Mortimer's Cross *Herefs* **25 H2**
Morvah *Corn* **2 A5**
Morven, mt. *A'deen* **76 D1**
Morven, mt. *Caith* **86 C4**
Morvern *Argyll* **68 E3**
Morville *Shrops* **34 D5**
Mossley *Lancs* **43 E1**
Mostyn *Flint* **41 G3**
Motherwell *Lanark* **65 E3**
Mottram *Ches* **43 E2**
Mountain Ash *Glam* **15 F2**
Mountsorrel *Leics* **36 B3**
Mousehole *Corn* **2 A5**
Mouswald *Dumf* **59 F4**
Moy *I'ness* **75 E3**
Moy *I'ness* **81 G4**
Much Birch *Herefs* **26 A4**
Much Hadham *Herts* **29 H5**
Much Wenlock *Shrops* **34 C4**
Muchalls *Kinc* **77 H2**
Mucklestone *Staffs* **34 D1**
Muir-of-Ord *Ross* **81 E3**
Muirdrum *Angus* **71 H1**
Muirkirk *Ayr* **56 F2**
Mull, I. *Argyll* **69 D5**
Mull of Galloway *Wig* **57 B8**
Mullion *Corn* **2 C6**
Mumbles *Glam* **14 C3**
Mundesley *Norf* **39 G2**
Mundford *Norf* **38 C5**
Munlochy *Ross* **81 F2**
Murthly *Perth* **72 D1**
Musselburgh *M'loth* **66 B2**
Muthill *Perth* **72 C3**
Mybster *Caith* **86 E2**
Mynyddislwyn *Mon* **15 G3**
Mytholmroyd *Yorks* **48 C5**
Nailsworth *Glos* **16 D2**
Nairn *Nairn* **81 H2**
Nairn, co. **81 G3**
Nant-y-glo *Mon* **15 G1**
Nantgaredig *Carm* **23 F3**
Nantwich *Ches* **42 C6**
Narberth *Pemb* **22 D4**
Naunton *Glos* **27 F5**
Naver, Loch *Suth* **84 F4**
Nayland *Suff* **30 D4**
Neath *Glam* **14 D2**
Needham Market *Suff* **31 E3**
Needles, The *I. of Wight* **10 A6**
Nefyn *Caern* **32 B1**
Nelson *Lancs* **47 H4**
Ness, Loch *I'ness* **81 E5**
Neston *Ches* **41 H4**
Nether Stowey *Som* **8 A1**
Netherton *Devon* **5 E3**
Nethybridge *I'ness* **82 A5**
Netley *Hants* **10 B4**
Nettlebed *Oxon* **18 B3**
New Abbey *Kirkcud* **59 E5**
New Aberdour *A'deen* **83 G1**
New Alresford *Hants* **10 C2**
New Barnet *London* **19 F2**
New Brighton *Ches* **41 H2**
New Buckenham *Norf* **39 E5**
New Coylton *Ayr* **64B 6**
New Cumnock *Ayr* **56 F3**
New Dailly *Ayr* **56 C4**
New Deer *A'deen* **83 G2**
New Forest *Hants* **10 A4**
New Galloway *Kirkcud* **58 C4**
New Holland *Lincs* **51 E5**
New Hunstanton *Norf* **38 B1**
New Mills *Derby* **43 E3**
New Pitsligo *A'deen* **83 G2**
New Quay *Card* **24 A2**
New Radnor *Radn* **25 G2**
New Romney *Kent* **13 F4**
New Scone *Perth* **73 E2**
Newark-on-Trent *Notts* **44 C5**
Newbiggin-by-the-Sea *N'land* **61 G3**
Newborough *Angl* **40 B5**
Newbridge *Corn* **3 H2**
Newbridge *Mon* **15 G2**
Newbridge-on-Wye *Radn* **25 E2**
Newbrough *N'land* **60 D4**
Newburgh *A'deen* **83 H4**
Newburgh *Fife* **73 F3**
Newburn *N'land* **61 F5**
Newbury *Berks* **17 H5**
Newby Bridge *Lancs* **52 D6**
Newcastle Emlyn *Carm* **23 E2**
Newcastleton *Rox* **60 B3**
Newcastle-under-Lyme *Staffs* **42 D6**
Newcastle upon Tyne *N'land* **61 G5**
Newent *Glos* **26 C5**
Newham *London* **19 G3**
Newhaven *Sussex* **12 B6**
Newhouse *Lanark* **65 E3**
Newlands Corner *Surrey* **19 E6**
Newlyn *Corn* **2 A5**
Newlyn East *Corn* **2 D3**
Newmachar *A'deen* **83 G5**
Newmarket *Suff* **30 B2**
Newmilns *Ayr* **64 C5**
Newnham *Glos* **26 C6**
Newport *Essex* **30 A4**
Newport *I. of Wight* **10 C5**
Newport *Mon* **15 G3**
Newport *Pemb* **22 C2**
Newport *Shrops* **34 D3**
Newport-on-Tay *Fife* **73 G2**
Newport Pagnell *Bucks* **28 D3**
Newquay *Corn* **2 D2**
Newton *Dumf* **59 F2**
Newton *Notts* **44 B6**
Newton Abbot *Devon* **5 E3**
Newton Aycliffe *Durham* **54 C3**
Newton Ferrers *Devon* **4 C5**
Newton Heath *Lancs* **42 D2**
Newton-le-Willows *Lancs* **42 B2**
Newton-on-the-Moor *N'land* **61 F1**
Newton Poppleford *Devon* **5 F2**
Newton Stewart *Wig* **57 D6**
Newtongrange *M'loth* **66 B2**
Newtonmore *I'ness* **75 G2**
Newtown *Mont* **33 H5**
Newtown St. Boswells *Rox* **66 D5**
Newtyle *Angus* **73 F1**
Neyland *Pemb* **22 C5**
Nigg *Ross* **87 B8**
Norfolk, co. **38 C3**
Norham *N'land* **67 F4**
Normanton *Yorks* **49 F5**
Normanton-on-Trent *Notts* **44 C4**
North Berwick *E. Loth* **66 C1**
North Chapel *Sussex* **11 F2**
North Downs *Kent/Surrey* **12 D1**
North Foreland *Kent* **13 H1**
North Luffenham *Rutl* **37 E4**
North Molton *Devon* **7 E2**
North Riding, div. *Yorks* **54 B5**
North Shields *N'land* **61 H4**
North Tawton *Devon* **7 E5**
North Uist, I. *I'ness* **88 D1**
North Walsham *Norf* **39 G2**
North Weald Bassett *Essex* **20 B2**
Northallerton *Yorks* **54 C4**
Northam *Devon* **6 C3**
Northampton *Northants* **28 C2**
Northamptonshire, co. **28 B1**
Northfield *Warks* **35 F6**
Northfleet *Kent* **20 C4**
Northleach *Glos* **17 F1**
Northolt *London* **19 E3**
Northop *Flint* **41 H4**
Northumberland, co. **60 D3**
Northwich *Ches* **42 C4**
Northwood *London* **19 E3**
Norton *Durham* **54 D3**
Norton *Yorks* **50 C1**
Norton Radstock *Som* **16 C5**
Norwich *Norf* **39 F4**
Nottingham *Notts* **36 B1**
Nottinghamshire, co. **44 A5**
Nuneaton *Warks* **36 A5**
Oadby *Leics* **36 C4**
Oakengates *Shrops* **34 D3**
Oakham *Rutl* **36 D3**
Oakhill *Som* **16 B6**
Oakington *Cambs* **29 H2**
Oakley *Bucks* **18 B1**
Oakworth *Yorks* **48 C4**
Oban *Argyll* **70 B2**
Ochil Hills **72 C4**
Ochiltree *Ayr* **64 C6**
Ockley *Surrey* **11 G1**
Odiham *Hants* **18 C6**
Ogmore *Glam* **14 D4**
Oich, Loch *I'ness* **74 D2**
Okehampton *Devon* **4 C2**
Old Brampton *Derby* **43 H4**
Old Deer *A'deen* **83 G2**
Old Fletton *Hunts* **37 G4**
Old Kilpatrick *Dunb* **64 C2**
Old Meldrum *A'deen* **83 F4**
Old Sarum *Wilts* **9 H1**
Old Shoreham *Sussex* **11 H4**
Old Warden *Beds* **29 F3**
Oldbury *Worcs* **35 F5**
Oldham *Lancs* **43 E1**
Ollerton *Notts* **44 B4**
Olney *Bucks* **28 D3**
Ombersley *Worcs* **26 D2**
Onchan *Isle of Man* **46 B5**
Onich *I'ness* **74 B5**
Orford *Suff* **31 G3**
Orkney, Is. & co. **89**
Ormiston *E. Loth* **66 B2**
Ormskirk *Lancs* **42 A1**
Oronsay, I. *Argyll* **69 C8**
Orpington *London* **19 H5**
Orrell *Lancs* **42 B1**
Orrell Post *Lancs* **42 B1**
Orsett *Essex* **20 C3**
Orton *W'land* **53 F4**
Osbaldeston *Lancs* **47 G5**
Osborne House *I. of Wight* **10 C5**
Osbournby *Lincs* **37 F1**
Ossett *Yorks* **49 E5**
Oswaldtwistle *Lancs* **47 G5**
Oswestry *Shrops* **34 A2**
Otford *Kent* **12 B1**
Othery *Som* **8 B2**
Otley *Yorks* **49 E4**
Otter Ferry *Argyll* **70 B6**
Otterburn *N'land* **60 D2**
Ottershaw *Surrey* **19 E5**
Otterton *Devon* **5 F2**
Ottery St. Mary *Devon* **5 F2**
Ottringham *Yorks* **51 G5**
Oulton Park *Ches* **42 B6**
Oundle *Northants* **37 E5**
Outwell *Cambs/Norf* **38 A4**
Over *Ches* **42 C4**
Over Whitacre *Warks* **35 H5**
Overscaig *Suth* **85 D5**
Overton *Flint* **34 B1**
Ower *Hants* **10 A3**
Oxford *Oxon* **18 A1**
Oxfordshire, co. **27 G5**
Oxshott *Surrey* **19 F5**
Oykel Bridge *Suth* **85 D6**
Padiham *Lancs* **47 H4**
Padstow *Corn* **2 D1**
Paignton *Devon* **5 E4**
Painswick *Glos* **16 D1**
Paisley *Renf* **64 C3**
Pakefield *Suff* **39 H5**
Pangbourne *Berks* **18 B4**
Pannal *Yorks* **49 E3**
Paps of Jura, mt. *Jura* **62 C1**
Par *Corn* **3 F3**
Parkeston *Essex* **31 F5**
Parkgate *Dumf* **59 E3**
Pateley Bridge *Yorks* **48 D2**
Pathhead *Fife* **73 F5**
Pathhead *M'loth* **66 B2**
Patna *Ayr* **56 D3**
Patrington *Yorks* **51 G5**
Patterdale *W'land* **52 D3**
Paul *Corn* **2 A5**
Peacehaven *Sussex* **12 A6**
Peak, The, mt. *Derby* **43 F3**
Peaslake *Surrey* **11 G1**
Peebles *Peebl* **66 A4**
Peeblesshire, co. **66 A6**
Peel *Isle of Man* **46 A5**
Pembrey *Glam* **14 A2**
Pembridge *Herefs* **25 H2**
Pembroke *Pemb* **22 C5**
Pembroke Dock *Pemb* **22 C5**
Pembrokeshire, co. **22 B3**
Pen-y-groes *Caern* **40 B6**
Penarth *Glam* **15 G4**
Pendennis Pt. *Corn* **2 D5**
Pendlebury *Lancs* **42 D1**
Penicuik *M'loth* **65 H3**
Penistone *Yorks* **43 G1**
Penkridge *Staffs* **35 F3**
Penmaen-mawr *Caern* **40 D4**
Penn *Bucks* **18 D2**
Pennan *A'deen* **83 F1**
Penrhyndeudraeth *Mer* **32 D1**
Penrith *Cumb* **53 E2**
Penruddock *Cumb* **52 D2**
Penryn *Corn* **2 D5**
Pensarn *Denb* **41 F3**
Penshurst *Kent* **12 B3**
Pentland Firth **89 A7**
Pentland Hills **65 G3**
Pentraeth *Angl* **40 C4**
Pentrefoelas *Denb* **41 E6**
Penzance *Corn* **2 A5**
Perranporth *Corn* **2 C3**
Pershore *Worcs* **26 D3**
Perth *Perth* **72 D2**
Perthshire, co. **72 A1**
Peterborough *Hunts* **37 G4**
Peterculter *A'deen* **77 G1**
Peterhead *A'deen* **83 H2**
Peterlee *Durham* **54 D1**
Petersfield *Hants* **10 D3**
Petworth *Sussex* **11 F3**
Pewsey *Wilts* **17 F5**
Philleigh *Corn* **2 D4**
Pickering *Yorks* **55 F6**
Pickering, Vale of *Yorks* **50 C2**
Piercebridge *Durham* **54 B3**
Pill *Som* **16 A4**
Pinner *London* **19 E3**
Pinwherry *Ayr* **56 C4**
Pistyll Rhaiadr, waterfall *Denb, Mont* **33 G2**
Pitchcombe *Glos* **16 D1**
Pitlochry *Perth* **76 A5**
Pittenweem *Fife* **73 H4**
Plockton *Ross* **79 F5**
Pluckley *Kent* **13 E3**
Plumpton *Sussex* **12 A5**
Plymouth *Devon* **4 B5**
Plympton *Devon* **4 C5**
Plynlimon Fawr, mts. *Card* **33 E5**
Pocklington *Yorks* **50 C3**
Polegate *Sussex* **12 C6**
Polesden Lacey *Surrey* **19 E6**
Pollokshaws *Lanark* **64 C3**
Polmont *Stirl* **65 F1**
Polperro *Corn* **3 G3**
Polruan *Corn* **3 F3**
Ponders End *London* **19 G2**
Pont-erwyd *Card* **33 E6**
Pont-y-Berem *Carm* **23 F4**
Pontardawe *Glam* **23 H5**
Pontarddulais *Glam* **23 G5**
Pontefract *Yorks* **49 F5**
Ponteland *N'land* **61 F4**
Pontrhydfendigaid *Card* **24 C2**
Pontrilas *Herefs* **25 H5**
Pontypool *Mon* **15 G2**
Pontypridd *Glam* **15 F3**
Poole *Dorset* **9 G5**
Poolewe *Ross* **78 F2**
Porlock *Som* **7 F1**
Port Appin *Argyll* **74 B6**
Port Askaig *Islay* **62 B1**
Port Carlisle *Cumb* **59 G5**
Port Charlotte *Islay* **62 A2**
Port Ellen *Islay* **62 B3**
Port Erin *Isle of Man* **46 A6**
Port Erroll *A'deen* **83 H3**
Port Eynon *Glam* **14 B3**
Port Glasgow *Renf* **64 B2**
Port of Menteith *Perth* **72 A4**
Port of Ness *Lewis* **88 C1**
Port St. Mary *Isle of Man* **46 A6**
Port Seton *E. Loth* **66 B1**
Port Talbot *Glam* **14 D3**
Port William *Wig* **57 D7**
Portencross *Ayr* **64 A4**
Portessie *Banff* **82 D1**
Portgordon *Moray* **82 C1**
Porthcawl *Glam* **14 D4**
Porthleven *Corn* **2 C5**
Portinscale *Cumb* **52 C3**
Portishead *Som* **16 A4**
Portknockie *Banff* **82 D1**
Portland *Dorset* **9 E6**
Portlethen *Kinc* **77 H2**
Portmadoc *Caern* **32 D1**
Portmahomack *Ross* **87 C7**
Portnacroish *Argyll* **74 B6**
Portnahaven *Islay* **62 A3**
Portpatrick *Wig* **57 A7**
Portreath *Corn* **2 C4**
Portree *Skye* **79 C5**
Portsea *Hants* **10 D4**
Portskewett *Mon* **16 A3**
Portslade-by-sea *Sussex* **11 H4**
Portsmouth *Hants* **10 D4**
Portsonachan *Argyll* **70 C3**
Portsoy *Banff* **83 E1**
Postbridge *Devon* **4 C3**
Potters Bar *Herts* **19 F2**
Potton *Beds* **29 F3**
Poulton-le-Fylde *Lancs* **47 E4**
Praze-an-Beeble *Corn* **2 C5**
Preesall *Lancs* **47 E3**
Prendergast *Pemb* **22 C4**
Prescot *Lancs* **42 A2**
Prestatyn *Flint* **41 G3**
Presteigne *Radn* **25 G2**
Preston *Lancs* **47 F5**
Preston Candover *Hants* **10 C1**
Prestonpans *E. Loth* **66 B2**
Prestwich *Lancs* **42 D1**
Prestwick *Ayr* **64 B6**
Princes Risborough *Bucks* **18 C2**
Princetown *Devon* **4 C3**
Probus *Corn* **2 D3**
Prudhoe *N'land* **61 F5**
Puckeridge *Herts* **29 G5**
Puddletown *Dorset* **9 E5**
Pudsey *Yorks* **49 E5**
Pulborough *Sussex* **11 F3**
Pumsaint *Carm* **24 C4**
Purbeck, I. of *Dorset* **9 F6**
Purfleet *Essex* **20 B4**
Purley *London* **19 G5**
Purston Jaglin *Yorks* **49 F6**
Putford E. and W. *Devon* **6 C4**
Putsham *Som* **15 F6**
Pwllheli *Caern* **32 B2**
Quantock Hills *Som* **8 A1**
Queenborough *Kent* **21 E4**
Queensbury *Yorks* **48 D5**
Queensferry, N. *Fife* **73 E6**
Queensferry, S. *W. Loth* **73 E6**
Quiraing, mt. *Skye* **78 C3**
Quoich, Loch *I'ness* **74 B2**
Quoich Bridge *I'ness* **74 B2**
Raasay, I. *I'ness* **79 D5**
Radcliffe *Lancs* **42 D1**
Radcliffe-on-Trent *Notts* **36 C1**
Radlett *Herts* **19 F2**
Radnor Forest *Radn* **25 F2**
Radnorshire, co. **25 E2**
Radstock *Som* **16 C5**
Raglan *Mon* **15 H1**
Rainford *Lancs* **42 B2**
Rainham *London* **20 B3**
Ram *Carm* **24 B3**
Ramasaig *Skye* **79 A5**
Rampside *Lancs* **46 D2**
Ramsbottom *Lancs* **47 H6**
Ramsey *Hunts* **37 G5**
Ramsey *Isle of Man* **46 C4**
Ramsey I. *Pemb* **22 A3**
Ramsgate *Kent* **13 H1**
Rannoch, Loch *Perth* **75 F5**
Rannoch, Moor of *Argyll-Perth* **75 E6**
Ratho *M'loth* **65 G2**
Ratlinghope *Shrops* **34 B4**
Rattlesden *Suff* **30 D2**
Rattray *Perth* **73 E1**
Raunds *Northants* **29 E1**
Ravenglass *Cumb* **52 B5**
Ravenscar *Yorks* **55 G4**
Ravensthorpe *Yorks* **49 E6**
Rawdon *Yorks* **49 E4**
Rawmarsh *Yorks* **43 H2**
Rawtenstall *Lancs* **47 H5**
Rayleigh *Essex* **20 D3**
Raynham *Norf* **38 D2**
Reading *Berks* **18 C4**
Reay *Caith* **86 C2**
Redbourn *Herts* **19 E1**
Redbridge *London* **19 G3**
Redcar *Yorks* **55 E3**
Redditch *Worcs* **27 E1**
Redhill *Surrey* **19 G6**
Redruth *Corn* **2 C4**
Redwick *Glos* **16 B3**
Reedham *Norf* **39 H4**
Reekie Linn, waterfall *Angus* **76 C5**
Reepham *Norf* **39 E3**
Reeth *Yorks* **54 A5**
Regent's Park *London* **19 F3**
Reigate *Surrey* **19 F6**
Reighton *Yorks* **51 F1**
Rempstone *Notts* **36 B2**
Renfrew *Renf* **64 C2**
Renfrewshire, co. **64 B3**
Renton *Dunb* **64 B1**
Rest and be Thankful *Argyll* **70 D4**
Reston *Berwick* **67 F3**
Rhayader *Radn* **25 E2**
Rhayadr Mawr = Aber Falls
Rhayadr-y-Wennol = Swallow Falls
Rhiconich *Suth* **84 C3**
Rhondda *Glam* **15 E2**
Rhoose *Glam* **15 F4**
Rhos *Carm* **23 E2**
Rhosili *Glam* **14 A3**
Rhosllanerchrugog *Denb* **41 H6**
Rhosneigr *Angl* **40 A4**
Rhu *Dunb* **64 A1**
Rhuddlan *Flint* **41 F4**
Rhyd Owen *Card* **24 A4**
Rhydtalog *Flint* **41 H5**
Rhyl *Flint* **41 F3**
Rhymney *Mon* **15 F1**
Riccall *Yorks* **50 B4**
Riccarton *Ayr* **64 B5**
Richards Castle *Shrops* **26 A1**
Richmond upon Thames *London* **19 F4**
Richmond *Yorks* **54 B4**
Rickinghall *Suff* **31 E1**

Rickmansworth *Herts* **19 E2**
Riding Mill *N'land* **61 E5**
Ridsdale *N'land* **61 E3**
Rievaulx *Yorks* **55 E6**
Ringford *Kirkcud* **58 C5**
Ringway *Ches* **42 D3**
Ringwood *Hants* **9 H4**
Rinns of Kells *Kirkcud* **58 B3**
Ripley *Derby* **43 H5**
Ripley *Surrey* **19 E5**
Ripley *Yorks* **49 E2**
Ripon *Yorks* **49 E1**
Ripponden *Yorks* **48 C6**
Risca *Mon* **15 G3**
Rishton *Lancs* **47 G5**
Rivington *Lancs* **47 G6**
Robertsbridge *Sussex* **12 D4**
Robin Hood's Bay *Yorks* **55 G4**
Roborough *Devon* **4 B4**
Rochdale *Lancs* **42 D1**
Roche *Corn* **3 E2**
Rochester *Kent* **20 D5**
Rochford *Essex* **20 E3**
Rockcliffe *Cumb* **59 H5**
Rode *Som* **16 C5**
Rodel *Harris* **88 A4**
Romford *London* **19 H3**
Romiley *Ches* **42 E2**
Romney Marsh *Kent* **13 F4**
Romsey *Hants* **10 A3**
Rona, S., I. *I'ness* **78 D3**
Ronaldsway *Isle of Man* **46 B6**
Rosehearty *A'deen* **83 G1**
Rosemarkie *Ross* **81 G2**
Roslin *M'loth* **66 A2**
Ross & Cromarty ,co. **80 A1**
Ross-on-Wye *Herefs* **26 B5**
Rosyth *Fife* **73 E6**
Rothbury *N'land* **61 F2**
Rotherfield *Sussex* **12 B4**
Rotherham *Yorks* **43 H2**
Rothes-on-Spey *Moray* **82 B2**
Rothesay *Bute* **63 G2**
Rothwell *Northants* **36 D6**
Rothwell *Yorks* **49 E5**
Rouken Glen *Renf* **64 C3**
Rousay, I *Orkney* **89 B6**
Rowardennan *Stirl* **71 E5**
Rowley Regis *Staffs* **35 F5**
Roxburgh *Rox* **66 D5**
Roxburghshire, co. **66 C6**
Roy Bridge *I'ness* **74 D3**
Royal Leamington Spa = Leamington Spa, Royal
Royal Tunbridge Wells = Tunbridge Wells, Royal
Roydon *Essex* **20 B1**
Royston *Herts* **29 G4**
Royston *Yorks* **43 H1**
Royton *Lancs* **42 D1**
Ruabon *Denb* **34 A1**
Ruddington *Notts* **36 B2**
Rufforth *Yorks* **50 A3**
Rufus's Stone *Hants* **10 A3**
Rugby *Warks* **27 H1**
Rugeley *Staffs* **35 F3**
Ruislip *London* **19 E3**
Rum, I. *I'ness* **68 B1**
Rumbling Bridge *Kinross* **72 D4**
Runcorn *Ches* **42 B3**
Rushden *Northants* **28 D1**
Rushyford *Durham* **54 C2**
Rutherglen *Lanark* **64 D3**
Ruthin *Denb* **41 G5**
Rutland, co. **36 D4**
Ryde *I. of Wight* **10 C5**
Rye *Sussex* **13 E5**
Ryhope *Durham* **61 H6**
Ryton *Durham* **61 F5**
Saddleback (Blencathra), mt. *Cumb* **52 C2**
Saddleworth *Yorks* **43 E1**
Saffron Walden *Essex* **30 A4**
St. Abb's Hd. *Berwick* **67 F2**
St. Agnes *Corn* **2 C3**
St. Albans *Herts* **19 F1**
St. Andrews *Fife* **73 G3**
St. Arvans *Mon* **16 A2**
St. Asaph *Flint* **41 F4**
St. Austell *Corn* **3 E3**
St. Bees *Cumb* **52 A4**
St. Blazey *Corn* **3 F3**
St. Boswells *Rox* **66 D5**
St. Briavels *Glos* **16 B1**
St. Bride's B. *Pemb* **22 A4**
St. Buryan *Corn* **2 A5**
St. Catherines *Argyll* **70 C4**
St. Catherines Pt. *I. of Wight* **10 B6**
St. Clears *Carm* **23 E4**
St. Columb Major *Corn* **3 E2**
St. Cyrus *Kinc* **77 G4**
St. David's *Pemb* **22 A3**
St. Day *Corn* **2 C4**
St. Dennis *Corn* **3 E3**
St. Dogmaels *Pemb* **22 D2**
St. Eval *Corn* **2 D2**
St. Fillans *Perth* **72 B2**
St. Helens *I. of Wight* **10 C5**
St. Helens *Lancs* **42 B2**
St. Ives *Corn* **2 B4**
St. Ives *Hunts* **29 G1**
St. Johns *Isle of Man* **46 B5**
St. John's Chapel *Durham* **53 G1**
St. Just *Corn* **2 A5**
St. Keverne *Corn* **2 D6**
St. Leonards *Sussex* **12 D5**
St. Margaret's-at-Cliffe *Kent* **13 H3**
St. Mary's *Corn* **2 A1**
St. Mary's Loch *Selk* **66 A6**
St. Mawes *Corn* **2 D5**
St. Mawgan *Corn* **2 D2**
St. Merryn *Corn* **2 D1**
St. Michaels-on-Wyre *Lancs* **47 E4**
St. Monance *Fife* **73 H4**
St. Neots *Hunts* **29 F2**
St. Osyth *Essex* **31 E6**
St. Peter Port *Channel Is.* **3 G5**
St. Peter's *Kent* **13 H1**
Salcombe *Devon* **4 D6**
Sale *Ches* **42 D2**
Salen *Argyll* **68 E3**
Salen *Mull* **68 D4**
Salford *Lancs* **42 D2**
Salisbury *Wilts* **9 H2**
Salisbury Plain *Wilts* **17 E6**
Saltaire *Yorks* **48 D4**
Saltash *Corn* **3 H2**
Saltburn-by-the Sea *Yorks* **55 E3**
Saltcoats *Ayr* **64 A5**
Saltoun, E. & W. *E. Loth* **66 C2**
Sampford Peverell *Devon* **7 G4**
Sandal Magna *Yorks* **49 E6**
Sandbach *Ches* **42 D5**
Sandbank *Argyll* **70 D6**
Sandbanks *Dorset* **9 G5**
Sandford on Thames *Oxon* **18 A2**
Sandgate *Kent* **13 G3**
Sandhaven *A'deen* **83 G1**
Sandhurst *Berks* **18 C5**
Sandown *I. of Wight* **10 C6**
Sandown *Surrey* **19 E5**
Sandringham *Norf* **38 B2**
Sandwich *Kent* **13 H2**
Sandy *Beds* **29 F3**
Sanquhar *Dumf* **58 D1**
Satterthwaite *W'land* **52 C5**
Saundersfoot *Pemb* **22 D5**
Sawbridgeworth *Herts* **30 A6**
Sawtry *Hunts* **37 F6**
Saxilby *Lincs* **44 D4**
Saxmundham *Suff* **31 G2**
Saxthorpe *Norf* **39 E2**
Scafell Pikes, mt. *Cumb* **52 C4**
Scalby *Yorks* **55 H5**
Scale Force, waterfall *Cumb* **52 B3**
Scaleber Force, waterfall *Yorks* **47 H2**
Scalloway *Shet* **89 E7**
Scalpay, I. *I'ness* **79 D5**
Scampton *Lincs* **44 D3**
Scapa Flow *Orkney* **89 B7**
Scarba, I. *Argyll* **69 E7**
Scarborough *Yorks* **55 H6**
Scarinish *Argyll* **69 A5**
Schiehallion, mt. *Perth* **75 G5**
Scilly, Isles of *Corn* **2 A1**
Scole *Norf* **39 F6**
Scotch Corner *Yorks* **54 B4**
Scotforth *Lancs* **47 F2**
Scourie *Suth* **84 B3**
Scrabster *Caith* **86 D1**
Sculthorpe *Norf* **38 D2**
Scunthorpe *Lincs* **44 D1**
Scwd Henrhyd *Brecon* **14 D1**
Sea Houses *N'land* **67 H5**
Seaford *Sussex* **12 B6**
Seaforth, Loch *Lewis* **88 B3**
Seaham *Durham* **61 H6**
Seamer *Yorks* **55 H6**
Seascale *Cumb* **52 A5**
Seaton *Devon* **5 G2**
Seaton Delaval *N'land* **61 G4**
Seaton Sluice *N'land* **61 H4**
Seaton Valley *N'land* **61 G4**
Sedbergh *Yorks* **53 F5**
Sedgefield *Durham* **54 C2**
Sedgley *Staffs* **35 E5**
Seil, I. *Argyll* **70 A3**
Selborne *Hants* **10 D2**
Selby *Yorks* **49 G5**
Selkirk *Selk* **66 C5**
Selkirkshire, co. **66 A6**
Selsey *Sussex* **11 E5**
Sennybridge *Brecon* **25 E5**
Settle *Yorks* **47 H2**
Sevenoaks *Kent* **12 B2**
Severn, R. *Glos, etc* **16 A3**
Severn Beach *Glos* **16 A3**
Shaftesbury *Dorset* **9 F2**
Shalford *Surrey* **19 E6**
Shanklin *I. of Wight* **10 C6**
Shap *W'land* **53 E3**
Shapinsay, I. *Orkney* **89 B6**
Sharnbrook *Beds* **29 E2**
Sharpness *Glos* **16 B2**
Shaw *Lancs* **43 E1**
Shawbury *Shrops* **34 C2**
Sheerness *Kent* **21 E4**
Sheffield *Yorks* **43 H3**
Shefford *Beds* **29 F4**
Shell Bay *Dorset* **9 G5**
Shelve *Shrops* **34 A4**
Shenfield *Essex* **20 C2**
Shenley *Herts* **19 F2**
Shepperton *Surrey* **19 E5**
Sheppey, I. *Kent* **21 E4**
Shepshed *Leics* **36 B3**
Shepton Mallet *Som* **16 B6**
Sherborne *Dorset* **8 D3**
Sherburn-in-Elmet *Yorks* **49 G5**
Shere *Surrey* **19 E6**
Sheriff Hutton *Yorks* **49 H2**
Sheriff Muir *Perth* **72 C4**
Sheringham *Norf* **39 F1**
Sherston *Wilts* **16 D3**
Sherwood Forest **44 B5**
Shetland, Is. **89**
Shiel, Loch *Argyll-I'ness* **68 F2**
Shiel Bridge *I'ness* **68 E2**
Shiel Bridge *Ross* **80 A5**
Shieldaig *Ross* **78 F4**
Shifnal *Shrops* **34 D3**
Shilbottle *N'land* **61 G1**
Shildon *Durham* **54 B2**
Shin, Loch *Suth* **85 E5**
Shipley *Yorks* **48 D4**
Shipston-on-Stour *Warks* **27 G3**
Shipton-under-Wychwood *Oxon* **27 G5**
Shirehampton *Glos* **16 A4**
Shirenewton *Mon* **16 A2**
Shirrell Heath *Hants* **10 C3**
Shoeburyness *Essex* **21 E3**
Shoreham-by-Sea *Sussex* **11 H4**
Shorwell *I. of Wight* **10 B6**
Shotley Bridge *Durham* **61 F6**
Shottermill *Surrey* **11 E2**
Shotts *Lanark* **65 F3**
Shrewsbury *Shrops* **34 C3**
Shropshire (Salop), co. **34 B4**
Sidlaw Hills *Perth-Angus* **73 E2**
Sidmouth *Devon* **5 G2**
Sigglesthorne *Yorks* **51 F4**
Silchester *Hants* **18 B5**
Silloth *Cumb* **59 F6**
Silsden *Yorks* **48 C4**
Silsoe *Beds* **29 E4**
Silverstone *Northants* **28 B3**
Singleton *Sussex* **11 E4**
Sissinghurst *Kent* **12 D3**
Sittingbourne *Kent* **13 E1**
Sizewell *Suff* **31 H2**
Skateraw *Kinc* **77 H2**
Skegness *Lincs* **45 H5**
Skelmanthorpe *Yorks* **43 G1**
Skelmersdale *Lancs* **42 A1**
Skelton *Cumb* **52 D2**
Skelton *Yorks* **55 E3**
Skelwith Force, waterfall *Lancs* **52 D4**
Skewen *Glam* **14 C2**
Skiddaw, mt. *Cumb* **52 C2**
Skipton *Yorks* **48 C3**
Skipwith *Yorks* **49 H4**
Skirling *Peebl* **65 G4**
Skye, I. *I'ness* **79 C5**
Slaidburn *Yorks* **47 G3**
Slaithwaite *Yorks* **48 D6**
Slaley *N'land* **61 E5**
Slamannan *Stirl* **65 E2**
Sleaford *Lincs* **36 F1**
Sleat, Sound of *I'ness* **79 E7**
Sligachan Hotel *Skye* **79 C6**
Slimbridge *Glos* **26 C6**
Slingsby *Yorks* **50 C1**
Slioch, mt. *Ross* **80 A1**
Slough *Bucks* **18 D3**
Sma' Glen *Perth* **72 C2**
Smailholm *Rox* **66 D5**
Smethwick *Worcs* **35 F5**
Smoo Cave *Suth* **84 D2**
Snaefell, mt. *Isle of Man* **46 B4**
Snaith *Yorks* **49 H5**
Snape *Suff* **31 G2**
Snetterton *Norf* **38 D5**
Snitterfield *Warks* **27 F2**
Snizort, Loch *Skye* **78 B3**
Snowdon, mt. *Caern* **40 C6**
Soay, I. *I'ness* **79 C7**
Soham *Cambs* **30 B1**
Solent, The **10 C5**
Solihull *Warks* **35 G6**
Solva *Pemb* **22 A3**
Somercotes *Derby* **43 H5**
Somerset, co. **8 A1**
Somersham *Hunts* **29 B1**
Somerton *Som* **8 C2**
Sonning *Berks* **18 C4**
Soutergate *Lancs* **46 D1**
South Bank *Yorks* **54 D3**
South Brent *Devon* **4 D4**
South Cave *Yorks* **50 D5**
South Cerney *Glos* **17 E2**
South Downs *Sussex* **11 E3**
South Foreland *Kent* **13 H3**
South Kirkby *Yorks* **49 F6**
South Molton *Devon* **7 E3**
South Ockendon *Essex* **20 C3**
South Petherton *Som* **8 C3**
South Ronaldsay, I. *Orkney* **89 B7**
South Shields *Durham* **61 H4**
South Uist, I. *I'ness* **88 E3**
South Willingham *Lincs* **45 F3**
Southam *Warks* **27 H2**
Southampton *Hants* **10 B3**
Southampton Water *Hants* **10 B4**
Southborough *Kent* **12 C3**
Southend *Argyll* **62 D6**
Southend-on-Sea *Essex* **21 E3**
Southery *Norf* **38 B5**
Southminster *Essex* **21 E2**
Southport *Lancs* **46 D6**
Southrop *Glos* **27 F6**
Southsea *Hants* **10 D5**
Southwark *London* **19 G4**
Southwell *Notts* **44 B5**
Southwick *Sussex* **11 H4**
Southwold *Suff* **31 H1**
Soutra Hill *M'loth* **66 C3**
Sowerby Bridge *Yorks* **48 C5**
Spalding *Lincs* **37 G2**
Sparkford *Som* **8 D2**
Spean Bridge *I'ness* **74 D3**
Speeton *Yorks* **51 F1**
Speke *Lancs* **42 A3**
Spenborough *Yorks* **48 D5**
Spencers Wood *Berks* **18 C5**
Spennymoor *Durham* **54 B2**
Spey, R. **81 H5**
Spey Bay *Moray* **82 C1**
Spilsby *Lincs* **45 G4**
Spithead **10 C5**
Spittal of Glenshee *Perth* **76 B4**
Spofforth *Yorks* **49 F3**
Springfield *Fife* **73 F3**
Sproatley *Yorks* **51 F5**
Sprouston *Rox* **67 E5**
Squires Gate *Lancs* **46 D5**
Stadhampton *Oxon* **18 B2**
Staffa, I. *Argyll* **69 B5**
Staffin *Skye* **78 C3**
Stafford *Staffs* **35 F2**
Staffordshire, co. **35 E2**
Stagshaw Bank *N'land* **61 E4**
Staindrop *Durham* **54 A3**
Staines *Surrey* **19 E4**
Stainforth *Yorks* **49 H6**
Staithes *Yorks* **55 F3**
Stalbridge *Dorset* **9 E3**
Stalham *Norf* **39 G2**
Stalybridge *Ches* **43 E2**
Stamford *Lincs* **37 E4**
Stamfordham *N'land* **61 F4**
Standish *Lancs* **42 B1**
Standlake *Oxon* **17 G2**
Stanford-in-the-Vale *Berks* **17 G2**
Stanford-le-Hope *Essex* **20 C3**
Stanhope *Durham* **53 H1**
Stanley *Durham* **61 G6**
Stanley *Perth* **73 E2**
Stanley *Yorks* **49 E5**
Stanley Force, waterfall *Cumb* **52 B5**
Stannington *N'land* **61 G4**
Stansted *Essex* **29 H5**
Stanton *Suff* **30 D1**
Stanton Harcourt *Oxon* **17 H1**
Stanwix *Cumb* **60 A5**
Stapleford *Cambs* **29 H3**
Stapleford *Notts* **36 B1**
Stapleford *Wilts* **9 G1**
Stapleford Abbotts *Essex* **20 B2**
Starbeck *Yorks* **49 E3**
Start Pt. *Devon* **5 E6**
Staunton *Glos* **26 C4**
Staunton *Glos* **26 B6**
Staunton-on-Wye *Herefs* **25 H3**
Staveley *Derby* **43 H4**
Staveley *W'land* **52 D6**
Staverton *Glos* **26 D5**
Steall Fall *I'ness* **74 C4**
Steeple Aston *Oxon* **27 H5**
Stevenage *Herts* **29 F5**
Stevenston *Ayr* **64 A4**
Stewarton *Ayr* **64 B4**
Steyning *Sussex* **11 G4**
Stibb Cross *Devon* **6 C4**
Stickford *Lincs* **45 G5**
Stickney *Lincs* **45 G5**
Stilton *Hunts* **37 F5**
Stirling *Stirl* **72 B5**
Stirlingshire, co. **72 A5**
Stithians *Corn* **2 C4**
Stock *Essex* **20 D2**
Stockbridge *Hants* **10 B2**
Stockport *Ches* **42 D2**
Stocksbridge *Yorks* **43 G2**
Stockton Heath *Ches* **42 B3**
Stockton-on-Tees *Durham* **54 D3**
Stockwith *Lincs* **44 C2**
Stoke Canon *Devon* **7 G5**
Stoke Ferry *Norf* **38 B4**
Stoke Fleming *Devon* **5 E5**
Stoke-on-Trent *Staffs* **42 D6**
Stoke Poges *Bucks* **18 D3**
Stokenchurch *Bucks* **18 C2**
Stokesley *Yorks* **54 D4**
Stone *Staffs* **35 E1**
Stonefield *Lanark* **64 D3**
Stonehaven *Kinc* **77 H3**
Stonehenge *Wilts* **9 H1**
Stonehouse *Glos* **16 C1**
Stonehouse *Lanark* **65 E4**
Stoneykirk *Wig* **57 B7**
Stony Stratford *Bucks* **28 C4**
Stornoway *Lewis* **88 C2**
Storrington *Sussex* **11 G4**
Stourbridge *Worcs* **35 E5**
Stourport *Worcs* **26 C1**
Stow *M'loth* **66 C4**
Stow-on-the-Wold *Glos* **27 F5**
Stowmarket *Suff* **31 E2**
Strachan *Kinc* **77 F2**
Strachur *Argyll* **70 C4**
Stradbroke *Suff* **31 F1**
Stradishall *Suff* **30 C3**
Stradsett *Norf* **38 B4**
Straiton *Ayr* **56 D3**
Stranraer *Wig* **57 A6**
Stratford *London* **19 G3**
Stratford St. Mary *Essex* **31 E4**
Stratford-upon-Avon *Warks* **27 F2**
Strath Glass *I'ness* **80 D4**
Strath Halladale *Suth* **86 B3**
Strathaven *Lanark* **64 D4**
Strathblane *Stirl* **72 A6**
Strathdon *A'deen* **82 C5**
Strathkanaird *Ross* **85 B6**
Strathmiglo *Fife* **73 E3**
Strathmore *Perth-Angus* **72 D2**
Strathpeffer *Ross* **81 E2**
Strathy *Suth* **86 B2**
Strathyre *Perth* **72 A3**
Stratton *Corn* **6 B4**
Streatley *Berks* **18 B3**
Street *Som* **8 C1**
Strensall *Yorks* **49 G2**
Strete *Devon* **5 E5**
Stretford *Lancs* **42 D2**
Stretham *Cambs* **30 A1**
Stretton *Ches* **42 C3**
Strichen *A'deen* **83 G2**
Strid, The, waterfall *Yorks* **48 D3**
Striven, Loch *Argyll* **63 G1**
Stroma, I. *Caith* **86 F1**
Stromeferry *Ross* **80 A4**
Stromness *Orkney* **89 A6**
Stronachlachar *Stirl* **71 E4**
Stronsay, I. *Orkney* **89 C6**
Strontian *Argyll* **74 A5**
Strood *Kent* **20 D4**
Stroud *Glos* **16 D1**
Struy *I'ness* **80 D3**
Studland *Dorset* **9 G5**
Studley *Warks* **27 E2**
Sturminster Newton *Dorset* **9 E3**
Sudbury *Suff* **30 D4**
Suffolk, co. **30 C2**
Suilven, mt. *Suth* **85 B5**
Sumburgh & Hd. *Shet* **89 E8**
Summercourt *Corn* **2 D3**
Sunbury *Surrey* **19 E4**
Sunderland *Durham* **61 H5**
Sunningdale *Berks* **18 D4**
Surbiton *London* **19 F5**
Surrey, co. **19 E6**
Sussex, co. **11 G3**
Sutherland, co. **84 C4**
Sutterton *Lincs* **37 G1**
Sutton *Cambs* **37 H6**
Sutton *London* **19 F5**
Sutton Coldfield *Warks* **35 G4**
Sutton-in-Ashfield *Notts* **44 A5**
Sutton-on-Sea *Lincs* **45 H3**
Sutton Scotney *Hants* **10 B1**
Sutton-upon-Trent *Notts* **44 C4**
Swadlincote *Derby* **35 H3**
Swaffham *Norf* **38 C4**
Swainswick *Som* **16 C4**
Swallow Falls *Caern* **40 D5**
Swanage *Dorset* **9 G6**
Swanscombe *Kent* **20 C4**
Swansea *Glam* **14 C2**
Swanton Morley *Norf* **39 E3**
Sway *Hants* **10 A5**
Swinbrook *Oxon* **27 G6**
Swinderby *Lincs* **44 C5**
Swindon *Wilts* **17 F3**
Swineshead *Lincs* **37 G1**
Swinton *Berwick* **67 E4**
Swinton *Lancs* **42 C1**
Swinton *Yorks* **43 H2**
Syerston *Notts* **44 C6**
Symington *Ayr* **64 B5**
Symington *Lanark* **65 F5**
Sywell *Northants* **28 D1**
Tadcaster *Yorks* **49 G4**
Tadley *Hants* **18 B5**
Tain *Ross* **87 B7**
Tal-sarnau *Mer* **32 D1**

Tal-y-cafn *Denbigh* **41 E4**
Talgarth *Brecon* **25 F4**
Talybont *Card* **32 D5**
Tamworth *Staffs* **35 G4**
Tangmere *Sussex* **11 E4**
Tarbat Ness *Ross* **87 C7**
Tarbert *Argyll* **63 E1**
Tarbert *Harris* **88 B3**
Tarbet *Dunb* **71 E4**
Tarbolton *Ayr* **64 B6**
Tarland *A'deen* **82 D6**
Tarporley *Ches* **42 B5**
Tattershall *Lincs* **45 F5**
Tatton Park *Ches* **42 C3**
Taunton *Som* **8 A2**
Taunton Deane, Vale of *Som* **8 A2**
Tavistock *Devon* **4 B3**
Tay, Loch *Perth* **72 A2**
Tay, R. *Perth* **73 E3**
Taynuilt *Argyll* **70 B2**
Tayport *Fife* **73 G2**
Tebay *W'land* **53 F4**
Tedburn St. Mary *Devon* **4 D2**
Teddington *London* **19 F4**
Teesside *Yorks* **54 D3**
Teignmouth *Devon* **5 E3**
Telford *Shrops* **34 D3**
Tenbury Wells *Worcs* **26 B1**
Tenby *Pemb* **22 D5**
Tendring *Essex* **31 E5**
Tenterden *Kent* **13 E3**
Tern Hill *Shrops* **34 C2**
Tetbury *Glos* **16 D2**
Tetsworth *Oxon* **18 B2**
Tettenhall *Staffs* **35 E4**
Teversham *Cambs* **30 A2**
Tewkesbury *Glos* **26 D4**
Thame *Oxon* **18 C1**
Thames Ditton *Surrey* **19 F5**
Thamesmead *London* **20 B4**
Thanet, I. of *Kent* **13 H1**
Thaxted *Essex* **30 B4**
Theale *Berks* **18 B4**
Thetford *Norf* **38 D6**
Theydon Bois *Essex* **20 B2**
Thirsk *Yorks* **49 F1**
Thirston *N'land* **61 F2**
Thornaby-on-Tees *Yorks* **54 D3**
Thornbury *Glos* **16 B3**
Thorne *Yorks* **50 C6**
Thorney *Hunts* **37 G4**
Thorney I. *Sussex* **10 D4**
Thornhill *Dumf* **58 D2**
Thornhill *Perth* **71 G4**
Thornhill *Yorks* **49 E6**
Thornton Cleveleys *Lancs* **46 D4**
Thornton Force, waterfall *Yorks* **47 G1**
Thorpe-le-Soken *Essex* **31 F5**
Thorpe-on-the-Hill *Lincs* **44 D4**
Thorpeness *Suff* **31 H2**
Thrapston *Northants* **37 E6**
Threlkeld *Cumb* **52 C3**
Threshfield *Yorks* **48 C2**
Thruxton *Hants* **10 A1**
Thurlow *Suff* **30 B3**
Thursby *Cumb* **59 H6**
Thurso *Caith* **86 D1**
Tibberton *Shrops* **34 D3**
Ticehurst *Sussex* **12 C4**
Tickhill *Yorks* **44 B2**
Tideswell *Derby* **43 F4**
Tighnabruaich *Argyll* **63 F1**
Tilbury *Essex* **20 C4**
Tillicoultry *Clack* **72 C5**
Tilshead *Wilts* **17 E6**
Tintagel *Corn* **6 A6**
Tintern Abbey *Mon* **16 A2**
Tipton *Staffs* **35 F5**
Tiptree *Essex* **30 D6**
Tiree, I. *Argyll* **69 A7**
Tisbury *Wilts* **9 F2**
Titchfield *Hants* **10 C4**
Tiverton *Devon* **7 G4**
Tobermory *Argyll* **68 C3**
Todmorden *Yorks* **48 C5**
Tollerton *Notts* **36 C1**
Tollesbury *Essex* **21 E1**
Tolleshunt D'Arcy *Essex* **21 E1**
Tomatin *I'ness* **81 G4**
Tomdoun *I'ness* **74 C2**
Tomintoul *Banff* **82 B5**
Tonbridge *Kent* **12 C2**
Tongue *Suth* **84 F2**
Topcliffe *Yorks* **49 F1**
Topsham *Devon* **5 F2**
Torbay *Devon* **5 E4**
Torcross *Devon* **5 E6**
Torpoint *Corn* **3 H3**
Torquay *Devon* **5 E4**
Torrance *Stirl* **64 D2**
Torridon *Ross* **80 A2**
Torver *W'land* **52 C5**
Totland *I. of Wight* **10 A5**
Totley *Yorks* **43 G3**
Totnes *Devon* **5 E4**
Tottenham *London* **19 G3**
Tottington *Lancs* **42 D1**
Totton *Hants* **10 B3**
Tow Law *Durham* **54 A1**
Towcester *Northants* **28 C3**
Tower Hamlets *London* **19 G3**
Towyn *Mer* **32 D4**
Tranent *E. Loth* **66 B2**
Traquair *Peebl* **66 B5**
Trawden *Lancs* **48 B4**
Tredegar *Mon* **15 F1**
Treforest *Glam* **15 F3**
Tregaron *Cardigan* **24 C2**
Tregony *Corn* **3 E4**
Treharris *Glam* **15 F2**
Trelleck *Mon* **16 A1**
Treorci *Glam* **15 E2**
Tresco, I. *Corn* **2 A1**
Tresparrett Posts *Corn* **6 A5**
Trimdon *Durham* **54 C2**
Trimley *Suff* **31 F4**
Tring *Herts* **18 D1**
Troon *Ayr* **64 B5**
Trossachs, The *Perth* **71 F4**
Trowbridge *Wilts* **16 D4**
Trumpington *Cambs* **29 H2**
Truro *Corn* **2 D4**
Tugby *Leics* **36 D4**
Tulloch *I'ness* **75 E3**
Tumby *Lincs* **45 F5**
Tummel, Loch *Perth* **75 H5**
Tummel Bridge *Perth* **75 G5**
Tunbridge Wells, Royal *Kent* **12 C3**
Tunstall *Staffs* **42 D5**
Turnberry *Ayr* **56 C3**
Turnditch *Derby* **43 G6**
Turnershill *Sussex* **11 H2**
Turnhouse *M'loth* **65 G2**
Turriff *A'deen* **83 F2**
Turton *Lancs* **47 G6**
Tutbury *Staffs* **35 H2**
Tuxford *Notts* **44 C4**
Tweed, R. **67 F3**
Tweedmouth *N'land* **67 F3**
Tweedsmuir *Peebl* **65 G6**
Twickenham *London* **19 F4**
Two Bridges *Devon* **4 C3**
Twycross *Leics* **36 A4**
Twyford *Berks* **18 C4**
Twyford *Bucks* **28 B5**
Twyford *Hants* **10 B3**
Twynholm *Kirkcud* **58 C6**
Tyldesley *Lancs* **42 C1**
Tyn-y-Groes *Caern* **40 D4**
Tyndrum *Perth* **71 E2**
Tyne, R. *N'land* **61 G5**
Tynemouth *N'land* **61 H4**
Tywyn *Mer* **41 E3**
Uckfield *Sussex* **12 B4**
Uddingston *Lanark* **64 D3**
Uffculme *Devon* **7 H4**
Uig *Lewis* **88 A2**
Uig *Skye* **78 B3**
Ulceby *Lincs* **51 E6**
Ulceby Cross *Lincs* **45 G4**
Uldale *Cumb* **52 C2**
Ullapool *Ross* **85 B7**
Ullswater *Cumb-W'land* **52 D3**
Ulva, I. *Argyll* **68 C4**
Ulverston *Lancs* **46 D1**
Unapool *Suth* **84 C4**
Unst, I. *Shet* **89 F5**
Uny Lelant *Corn* **2 B4**
Upavon *Wilts* **17 F5**
Uphall *W. Loth* **65 G2**
Upham *Hants* **10 C3**
Upholland *Lancs* **42 B1**
Upper Tean *Staffs* **35 F1**
Uppingham *Rutl* **36 D4**
Upton-upon-Severn *Worcs* **26 D4**
Urmston *Lancs* **42 D2**
Urquhart *Moray* **82 C1**
Usk *Mon* **15 H2**
Uttoxeter *Staffs* **35 G1**
Uxbridge *London* **19 E3**
Valley *Angl* **40 A3**
Vatersay, I. *I'ness* **88 D4**
Venachar, Loch *Perth* **71 G4**
Ventnor *I. of Wight* **10 C6**
Virginia Water *Surrey* **18 D4**
Voil, Loch *Perth* **71 F3**
Vyrnwy, L. *Mont* **33 F2**
Waddesdon *Bucks* **28 C5**
Waddington *Lincs* **44 D4**
Wadebridge *Corn* **3 E1**
Wadhurst *Sussex* **12 C4**
Wainfleet *Lincs* **45 H5**
Wakefield *Yorks* **49 E6**
Wakes Colne *Essex* **30 D5**
Walford *Herefs* **25 H1**
Walkden *Lancs* **42 C1**
Walkerburn *Peebl* **66 B5**
Wallasey *Ches* **41 H2**
Wallingford *Berks* **18 B3**
Walls *Shet* **89 D7**
Wallsend *N'land* **61 G4**
Walmer *Kent* **13 H2**
Walney I. *Lancs* **46 C2**
Walsall *Staffs* **35 F4**
Walsall Wood *Staffs* **35 F4**
Walsingham *Norf* **38 D1**
Waltham Abbey *Essex* **19 G2**
Waltham Cross *Herts* **19 G2**
Waltham Forest *London* **19 G3**
Waltham-on-the-Wolds *Leics* **36 D2**
Walthamstow *London* **19 G3**
Walton *Cumb* **60 B5**
Walton-le-dale *Lancs* **47 F5**
Walton-on-Thames *Surrey* **19 E5**
Walton-on-the-Hill *Surrey* **19 F5**
Walton-on-the-Naze *Essex* **31 F6**
Wandsworth *London* **19 F4**
Wangford *Suff* **31 H1**
Wanlockhead *Dumf* **58 D1**
Wanstead *London* **19 G3**
Wantage *Berks* **17 G3**
Warboys *Hunts* **37 G6**
Wardington *Oxon* **27 H3**
Wardle *Lancs* **48 B6**
Ware *Herts* **19 G1**
Wareham *Dorset* **9 F5**
Wargrave *Berks* **18 C4**
Wark *N'land* **60 D4**
Warkworth *N'land* **61 G1**
Warley *Worcs* **35 F5**
Warlingham *Surrey* **12 A1**
Warminster *Wilts* **16 D6**
Warnham *Sussex* **11 G2**
Warrington *Lancs* **42 B3**
Warsop *Notts* **44 B3**
Warton *Lancs* **47 E5**
Warwick *Cumb* **60 A5**
Warwick *Warks* **27 G2**
Warwickshire, co. **27 F1**
Wash, The **38 A1**
Washington *Durham* **61 G5**
Washington *Sussex* **11 G4**
Wast Water *Cumb* **52 B4**
Watchet *Som* **7 H1**
Waterbeach *Cambs* **30 A2**
Waterloo *Hants* **10 D4**
Watford *Herts* **19 E2**
Wath upon Dearne *Yorks* **43 H1**
Watling Street *Northants* **28 C3**
Watlington *Oxon* **18 B2**
Watten *Caith* **86 E2**
Watton *Norf* **38 D4**
Watton-at-Stone *Herts* **29 G5**
Wealdstone *London* **19 F3**
Wednesbury *Staffs* **35 F5**
Wednesfield *Staffs* **35 F4**
Weedon Bec *Northants* **28 B2**
Week St. Mary *Corn* **6 B5**
Weeley *Essex* **31 E5**
Welbeck Abbey *Notts* **44 A4**
Welford *Northants* **36 C6**
Wellburnspout, waterfall *Dumf* **59 G2**
Wellingborough *Northants* **28 D1**
Wellington *Shrops* **34 D3**
Wellington *Som* **8 A2**
Wells *Som* **16 B6**
Wells next the Sea *Norf* **38 D1**
Welshampton *Shrops* **34 B1**
Welshpool *Mont* **33 H4**
Welwyn *Herts* **29 F6**
Welwyn Garden City *Herts* **19 F1**
Wem *Shrops* **34 C2**
Wembley *London* **19 F3**
Wemyss Bay *Renfrew* **63 H1**
Wendover *Bucks* **18 D1**
Wendron *Corn* **2 C5**
Wenlock Edge *Shrops* **34 B5**
Wensleydale *Yorks* **54 A5**
Wenvoe *Glam* **15 F4**
Weobley *Herefs* **25 H3**
West Auckland *Durham* **54 B2**
West Bridgford *Notts* **36 B1**
West Bromwich *Staffs* **35 F5**
West Calder *M'loth* **65 G3**
West Gordon *Berwick* **66 D4**
West Haddon *Northants* **28 B1**
West Ham *London* **20 A3**
West Kilbride *Ayr* **64 A4**
West Kirby *Ches* **41 G3**
West Linton *Peebl* **65 G3**
West Lothian, co. **65 F2**
West Meon *Hants* **10 D3**
West Mersea *Essex* **21 F1**
West Riding, div. *Yorks* **48 D4**
West Thurrock *Essex* **20 C4**
West Wycombe *Bucks* **18 C2**
Westbury *Wilts* **16 D6**
Westbury-upon-Severn *Glos* **26 C6**
Westerham *Kent* **12 B2**
Westgate-on-Sea *Kent* **13 H1**
Westhoughton *Lancs* **42C1**
Westminster *London* **19 F3**
Westmorland, co. **52 D4**
Weston-super-Mare *Som* **15 G5**
Westonbirt *Glos* **16 D3**
Westray, I. *Orkney* **89 B5**
Westruther *Berwick* **66 D3**
Westward Ho! *Devon* **6 C2**
Wetherby *Yorks* **49 F3**
Wetwang *Yorks* **50 D3**
Weybridge *Surrey* **19 E5**
Weyhill *Hants* **10 A1**
Weymouth *Dorset* **9 E6**
Whaley Bridge *Derby* **43 E3**
Whalley *Lancs* **47 G4**
Whalsay, I. *Shet* **89 F7**
Whalton *N'land* **61 F3**
Wharfedale *Yorks* **48 D3**
Wheathampstead *Herts* **19 F1**
Wheatley *Oxon* **18 B1**
Whickham *Durham* **61 G5**
Whiddon Down *Devon* **4 D2**
Whimple *Devon* **5 F1**
Whipsnade *Beds* **29 E6**
Whitburn *Durham* **61 H5**
Whitburn *W. Loth* **65 F2**
Whitby *Yorks* **55 G4**
Whitchurch *Bucks* **28 C5**
Whitchurch *Glam* **15 F3**
Whitchurch *Hants* **10 B1**
Whitchurch *Herefs* **26 B5**
Whitchurch *Shrops* **34 C1**
White Horse, Vale of *Berks* **17 G2**
White Waltham *Berks* **18 D4**
Whitefield *Lancs* **42 D1**
Whitehaven *Cumb* **52 A3**
Whitehills *Banff* **83 E1**
Whitekirk *E. Loth* **66 D1**
Whiteparish *Wilts* **10 A3**
Whithorn *Wig* **57 E8**
Whiting Bay *Arran* **63 G5**
Whitland *Carm* **22 D4**
Whitletts *Ayr* **64 B6**
Whitley *Yorks* **49 E6**
Whitley Bay *N'land* **61 H4**
Whitstable *Kent* **13 F1**
Whittingham *N'land* **60 F1**
Whittington *Shrops* **34 A2**
Whittlesey *Cambs* **37 G4**
Whitton *Radn* **25 G2**
Whitwell *I. of Wight* **10 C6**
Whitworth *Lancs* **48 B6**
Wick *Caith* **86 F3**
Wickford *Essex* **20 D2**
Wickham *Hants* **10 C4**
Wickham Market *Suff* **31 G3**
Wickwar *Glos* **16 C3**
Widdington *Essex* **30 A4**
Widecombe-in-the-Moor *Devon* **4 D3**
Widmerpool *Notts* **36 C2**
Widnes *Lancs* **42 B3**
Wigan *Lancs* **42 B1**
Wigginton *Yorks* **49 G2**
Wight, Isle of *Hants* **10 B6**
Wigmore *Herefs* **25 H1**
Wigston Magna *Leics* **36 C4**
Wigton *Cumb* **52 C1**
Wigtown *Wig* **57 E7**
Wigtownshire, co. **57 B6**
Wilburton *Cambs* **29 H1**
Willenhall *Staffs* **35 F4**
Willersley *Herefs* **25 G3**
Willesden *London* **19 F3**
Willingham *Cambs* **29 H1**
Willington *Derby* **35 H2**
Willington *Durham* **54 B2**
Williton *Som* **7 H1**
Wilmington *Kent* **20 B4**
Wilmslow *Ches* **42 D3**
Wilton *Wilts* **9 G2**
Wiltshire, co. **16 D5**
Wimbledon *London* **19 F4**
Wimborne Minster *Dorset* **9 G4**
Wincanton *Som* **9 E2**
Winchburgh *W. Loth* **65 G2**
Winchcombe *Glos* **27 E4**
Winchelsea *Sussex* **13 E5**
Winchester *Hants* **10 C2**
Windermere *W'land* **52 D5**
Windsor, New *Berks* **18 D4**
Windsor Great Park *Berks* **18 D4**
Windygates *Fife* **73 F4**
Winfrith Heath *Dorset* **9 E5**
Wingham *Kent* **13 G2**
Winnersh *Berks* **18 C4**
Winscales *W'land* **52 A4**
Winsford *Ches* **42 C4**
Winslow *Bucks* **28 C5**
Winstanley *Lancs* **42 B2**
Winster *Derby* **43 G5**
Winterbourne Stoke *Wilts* **9 G1**
Winteringham *Lincs* **50 D5**
Winterton *Lincs* **50 D6**
Winterton *Norf* **39 H3**
Wirksworth *Derby* **43 G5**
Wirral Pen. *Ches* **41 H3**
Wisbech *Cambs* **37 H3**
Wisborough Green *Sussex* **11 F3**
Wishaw *Lanark* **65 E3**
Witchampton *Dorset* **9 G4**
Witham *Essex* **21 E1**
Witheridge *Devon* **7 F4**
Withern *Lincs* **45 H3**
Withernsea *Yorks* **51 G5**
Withington *Glos* **27 E6**
Withington *Herefs* **26 B3**
Withington *Lancs* **42 D2**
Withnell *Lancs* **47 G5**
Witley *Surrey* **11 F1**
Witney *Oxon* **17 G1**
Wittering *Hunts* **37 F4**
Wittering, E. and W. *Sussex* **11 E5**
Witton-le-Wear *Durham* **54 B2**
Wiveliscombe *Som* **7 H2**
Wivenhoe *Essex* **31 E5**
Woburn Park *Beds* **28 D4**
Woburn Sands *Beds/Bucks* **28 D4**
Woking *Surrey* **19 E5**
Wokingham *Berks* **18 C4**
Wolsingham *Durham* **54 A2**
Wolston *Warks* **27 H1**
Wolverhampton *Staffs* **35 E4**
Wolverton *Bucks* **28 C4**
Wolvey *Warks* **36 A5**
Wolviston *Durham* **54 D3**
Wombwell *Yorks* **43 H1**
Womersley *Yorks* **49 G6**
Wonersh *Surrey* **19 E6**
Wood End *Warks* **27 F1**
Woodbridge *Suff* **31 G3**
Woodchester *Glos* **16 D2**
Woodchurch *Kent* **13 E3**
Woodford *London* **20 B3**
Woodford Halse *Northants* **28 B3**
Woodhall Spa *Lincs* **45 F5**
Woodhead *Ches* **43 F2**
Woodstock *Oxon* **27 H5**
Woofferton *Shrops* **26 A1**
Wookey Hole *Som* **16 A6**
Woolacombe *Devon* **6 C1**
Wooler *N'land* **67 F5**
Woolsington *N'land* **61 G4**
Woolston *Hants* **10 B4**
Woolton *Lancs* **42 A3**
Woolwich *London* **19 H4**
Woore *Shrops* **42 C6**
Wootton Bassett *Wilts* **17 E3**
Wootton Glanville *Dorset* **9 E3**
Worcester *Worcs* **26 D2**
Worcestershire, co. **26 C2**
Workington *Cumb* **52 A2**
Worksop *Notts* **44 B3**
Worle *Som* **15 H5**
Worlingham *Suff* **39 H5**
Wormit *Fife* **73 G2**
Worsbrough *Lancs* **43 H1**
Worsley *Lancs* **42 C2**
Worthing *Sussex* **11 G4**
Wotton-under-Edge *Glos* **16 C2**
Wragby *Lincs* **45 E3**
Wragby *Yorks* **49 F6**
Wrath, C. *Suth* **84 C1**
Wrekin, The, mt. *Shrops* **34 C3**
Wrentham *Suff* **31 H1**
Wrexham *Denb* **42 A6**
Wrightington *Lancs* **47 F6**
Writtle *Essex* **20 C1**
Wrotham *Kent* **12 C1**
Wroughton *Wilts* **17 F3**
Wroxham *Norfolk* **39 G3**
Wye *Kent* **13 F2**
Wyke Regis *Dorset* **8 D6**
Wylye *Wilts* **9 G1**
Wymeswold *Leics* **36 B2**
Wymondham *Norf* **39 E4**
Yapton *Sussex* **11 F4**
Yardley *Warks* **35 G5**
Yardley Chase *Northants* **28 D2**
Yarm *Yorks* **54 C3**
Yarmouth *I. of Wight* **10 B5**
Yarrow Church *Selk* **66 B5**
Yatton *Som* **16 A5**
Yeadon *Yorks* **49 E4**
Yealmpton *Devon* **4 C5**
Yell, I. *Shet* **89 E6**
Yelverton *Devon* **4 B4**
Yeovil *Som* **8 D3**
Yiewsley *London* **19 E3**
Yoker *Lanark* **64 C2**
York *Yorks* **49 G3**
Yorkshire, co. **48 D1**
Youlgreave *Derby* **43 G4**
Yoxall *Staffs* **35 G3**
Yoxford *Suff* **31 G2**
Ystalyfera *Glam* **14 D1**
Ystrad Mynach *Glam* **15 F2**
Ystrad Rhondda *Glam* **15 E2**
Ystradgynlais *Brecon* **24 D6**
Zennor *Corn* **2 A4**
Zetland, co. (Shetland) **89**

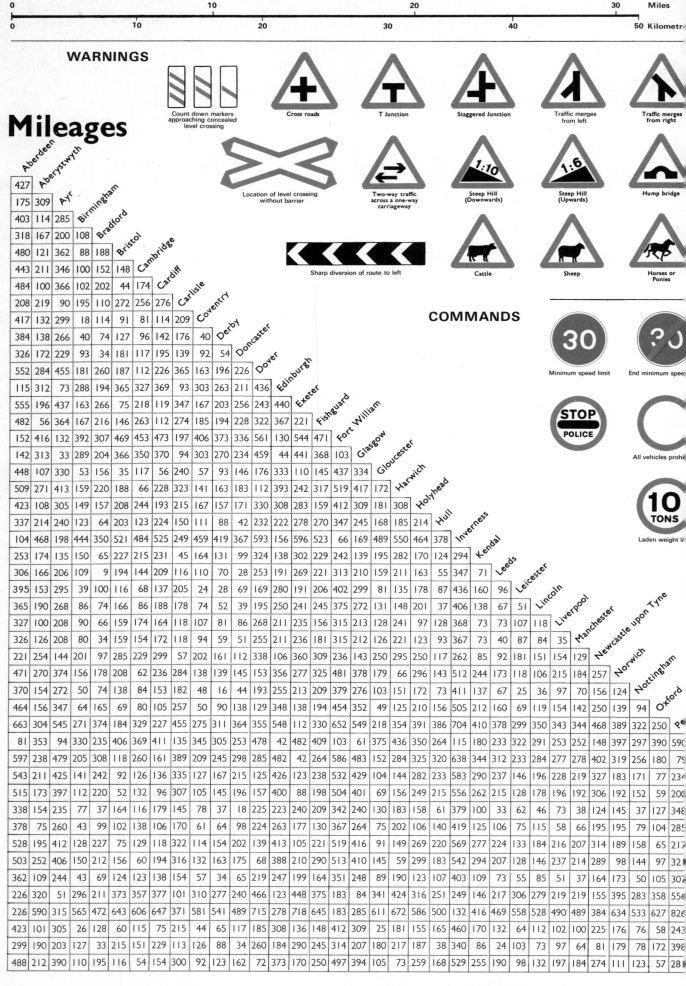

0   10   20   30   Miles

0   10   20   30   40   50 Kilometres

WARNINGS

Count down markers approaching concealed level crossing — Cross roads — T Junction — Staggered Junction — Traffic merges from left — Traffic merges from right

Location of level crossing without barrier — Two-way traffic across a one-way carriageway — Steep Hill (Downwards) 1:10 — Steep Hill (Upwards) 1:6 — Hump bridge

Sharp diversion of route to left — Cattle — Sheep — Horses or Ponies

COMMANDS

30 Minimum speed limit — 30 End minimum speed — STOP POLICE — All vehicles prohibited — 10 TONS Laden weight limit

Mileages

Mileage chart (distances in miles between towns). Diagonal labels, in order:
Aberdeen, Aberystwyth, Ayr, Birmingham, Bradford, Bristol, Cambridge, Cardiff, Carlisle, Coventry, Derby, Doncaster, Dover, Edinburgh, Exeter, Fishguard, Fort William, Glasgow, Gloucester, Harwich, Holyhead, Hull, Inverness, Kendal, Leeds, Leicester, Lincoln, Liverpool, Manchester, Newcastle upon Tyne, Norwich, Nottingham, Oxford, Pe…

```
Aberystwyth          427
Ayr                  175 309
Birmingham           403 114 285
Bradford             318 167 200 108
Bristol              480 121 362  88 188
Cambridge            443 211 346 100 152 148
Cardiff              484 100 366 102 202  44 174
Carlisle             208 219  90 195 110 272 256 276
Coventry             417 132 299  18 114  91  81 114 209
Derby                384 138 266  40  74 127  96 142 176  40
Doncaster            326 172 229  93  34 181 117 195 139  92  54
Dover                552 284 455 181 260 187 112 226 365 163 196 226
Edinburgh            115 312  73 288 194 365 327 369  93 303 263 211 436
Exeter               555 196 437 163 266  75 218 119 347 167 203 256 243 440
Fishguard            482  56 364 167 216 146 263 112 274 185 194 228 322 367 221
Fort William         152 416 132 392 307 469 453 473 197 406 373 336 561 130 544 471
Glasgow              142 313  33 289 204 366 350 370  94 303 270 234 459  44 441 368 103
Gloucester           448 107 330  53 156  35 117  56 240  57  93 146 176 333 110 145 437 334
Harwich              509 271 413 159 220 188  66 228 323 141 163 183 112 393 242 317 519 417 172
Holyhead             423 108 305 149 157 208 244 193 215 167 157 171 330 308 283 159 412 309 181 308
Hull                 337 214 240 123  64 203 123 224 150 111  88  42 232 222 278 270 347 245 168 185 214
Inverness            104 468 198 444 350 521 484 525 249 459 419 367 593 156 596 523  66 169 489 550 464 378
Kendal               253 174 135 150  65 227 215 231  45 164 131  99 324 138 302 229 242 139 195 282 170 124 294
Leeds                306 166 206 109   9 194 144 209 116 110  70  28 253 191 269 221 313 210 159 211 163  55 347  71
Leicester            395 153 295  39 100 116  68 137 205  24  28  69 169 280 191 206 402 299  81 135 178  87 436 160  96
Lincoln              365 190 268  86  74 166  86 188 178  74  52  39 195 250 241 245 375 272 131 148 201  37 406 138  67  51
Liverpool            327 100 208  90  66 159 174 164 118 107  81  86 268 211 235 156 315 213 128 241  97 128 368  73  73 107 118
Manchester           326 126 208  80  34 159 154 172 118  94  59  51 255 211 236 181 315 212 126 221 123  93 367  73  40  87  84  35
Newcastle upon Tyne  221 254 144 201  97 285 229 299  57 202 161 112 338 106 360 309 236 143 250 295 250 117 262  85  92 181 151 154 129
Norwich              471 270 374 156 178 208  62 236 284 138 139 145 153 356 277 325 481 378 179  66 296 143 512 244 173 118 106 215 184 257
Nottingham           370 154 272  50  74 138  84 153 182  48  16  44 193 255 213 209 379 276 103 151 172  73 411 137  67  25  36  97  70 156 124
Oxford               464 156 347  64 165  69  80 105 257  50  90 138 129 348 138 194 454 352  49 125 210 156 505 212 160  69 119 154 142 250 139  94
Pe…                  663 304 545 271 374 184 329 227 455 275 311 364 355 548 112 330 652 549 218 354 391 386 704 410 378 299 350 343 344 468 389 322 250
                      81 353  94 330 235 406 369 411 135 345 305 253 478  42 482 409 103  61 375 436 350 264 115 180 233 322 291 253 252 148 397 297 390 590
                     597 238 479 205 308 118 260 161 389 209 245 298 285 482  42 264 586 483 152 284 325 320 638 344 312 233 284 277 278 402 319 256 180  79…
                     543 211 425 141 242  92 126 136 335 127 167 215 125 426 123 238 532 429 104 144 282 233 583 290 237 146 196 228 219 327 183 171  77 234…
                     515 173 397 112 220  52 132  96 307 105 145 196 157 400  88 198 504 401  69 156 249 215 556 262 215 128 178 196 192 306 192 152  59 200…
                     338 154 235  77  37 164 116 179 145  78  37  18 225 223 240 209 342 240 130 183 158  61 379 100  33  62  46  73  38 124 145  37 127 348
                     378  75 260  43  99 102 138 106 170  61  64  98 224 263 177 130 367 264  75 202 106 140 419 125 106  75 115  58  66 195 195  79 104 285
                     528 195 412 128 227  75 129 118 322 114 154 202 139 413 105 221 519 416  91 149 269 220 569 277 224 133 184 216 207 314 189 158  65 217
                     503 252 406 150 212 156  60 194 316 132 163 175  68 388 210 290 513 410 145  59 299 183 542 294 207 128 146 237 214 289  98 144  97  32…
                     362 109 244  43  69 124 123 138 154  57  34  65 219 247 199 164 351 248  89 190 123 107 403 109  73  55  51  37 164 173  50 105 307
                     226 320  51 296 211 373 357 377 101 310 277 240 466 123 448 375 183  84 341 424 316 251 249 146 217 306 279 219 219 155 395 283 358 55…
                     226 590 315 565 472 643 606 647 371 581 541 489 715 278 718 645 183 285 611 672 586 500 132 416 469 558 528 490 489 384 634 533 627 82…
                     423 101 305  26 128  60 115  75 215  44  65 117 185 308 136 148 412 309  25 181 155 165 460 170 132  64 112 102 100 225 176  76  58 243
                     299 190 203 127  33 215 151 229 113 126  88  34 260 184 290 245 314 207 180 217 187  38 340  86  24 103  73  97  64  81 179  78 172 398
                     488 212 390 110 195 116  54 154 300  92 123 162  72 373 170 250 497 394 105  73 259 168 529 255 190  98 132 197 184 274 111 123  57 28…
```

Distances assume the use of ferries where appropriate